THE *Best* OF AMERICA

TORMONT

PHOTOGRAPHY:
Éditions Multi-Concept, Inc.
Michel Paquet, Photographer

EDITOR:
Robyn Bryant

GRAPHIC DESIGN:
Robert Doutre
Claude Bernard

COVER DESIGN:
Zapp

Copyright © 1996 Tormont Publications Inc.
338 St. Antoine St. East
Montreal, Canada H2Y 1A3
Tel: (514) 954-1441
Fax: (514) 954-5086

ISBN 2-89429-945-1

Printed in Canada

CONTENTS

APPETIZERS

~

A well-chosen starter whets the appetite
and sets the tone for the meal to follow.
A meal made up entirely of appetizers, selected
to provide balanced nutrition, can be an elegant
and exciting dining adventure. But appetizers
need not be reserved only for special occasions!

All the appetizers in this chapter
are easy to make, and some can be prepared
in advance. And while some are fairly elaborate,
and definitely for special occasions, many can
be created in minutes using a few simple
ingredients.

Start serving appetizers more often,
and you will discover that the simplest ones
are often the most appreciated. Everybody loves
dips, for example. And a few spears of fresh
asparagus with a tasty dressing can make
a real impact when served at the start of a meal;
serve the same few spears beside your steak
and potatoes and they won't make nearly
the same impression.

Likewise, a colorful salad
served before the main course stimulates
the taste buds; eaten after the main course,
salad may feel like a nutritional obligation!

So the next time you make meatloaf
or warm up some leftovers, start off
with a simple appetizer. It can turn even
an everyday meal into a special event!

~

CHILLED SALMON TERRINES

4 SERVINGS

7 oz	can waterpacked red salmon, drained	200 g
1/4 cup	finely chopped onion	50 mL
2 tbsp	finely chopped fresh parsley	30 mL
1/3 cup	mayonnaise (not salad dressing)	75 mL
1 tbsp	freshly chopped rosemary	15 mL
12 to 16	slices smoked salmon	12 to 16
	vegetable oil	

COOK'S TIP

This elegant-looking appetizer is a snap to make as long as you plan ahead. Vary the flavors by substituting fresh dill for the rosemary, or adding chopped capers.

In a bowl, combine salmon, onion, parsley, mayonnaise, and rosemary. Set aside.

Lightly oil 4 ramekins and line the bottom and sides of each with smoked salmon slices.

Divide canned salmon mixture among ramekins. Cover tightly with plastic wrap and refrigerate 5 to 6 hours.

Unmold each ramekin upside-down onto individual plates. Garnish plates with lettuce, herb-flavored mayonnaise and yellow bell pepper, if desired. Serve salmon terrine with rye crackers or crusty French bread.

1 Combine canned salmon with onion, herbs and mayonnaise.

2 Oil 4 small ramekins and line with smoked salmon.

3 Divide salmon mixture among ramekins, packing firmly.

4 Cover with plastic wrap and refrigerate to chill.

1 SERVING		
339 CALORIES	1 g CARBOHYDRATE	14 g PROTEIN
31 g FAT	0.1 g FIBER	50 mg CHOLESTEROL

SCALLOP MOUSSE WITH SAFFRON SAUCE

4 SERVINGS

2 cups	scallops, fresh or frozen and thawed	500 mL
I	pinch nutmeg	I
I cup	15% cream	250 mL
	freshly ground pepper	

SAFFRON SAUCE

2 tsp	butter or margarine	10 mL
2	dry French shallots, finely chopped	2
¼ cup	dry white vermouth	50 mL
I	pinch saffron	I
I tbsp	commercial white sauce and gravy thickener	15 mL
1¼ cups	low-fat milk	300 mL

Preheat oven to 350°F (180°C). Process scallops, nutmeg and pepper in food processor until smooth. Gradually add cream, with motor running. Do not overmix.

Divide scallop mixture among 4 oiled ramekins and cover each with a circle of lightly greased waxed paper, cut to fit exactly. Arrange ramekins in a baking dish. Add hot water to the baking dish to halfway up the sides of ramekins. Bake 25 to 30 minutes, until firm.

Meanwhile, prepare the sauce. Melt butter over medium heat in a small saucepan. Add shallots and cook 3 minutes. Add vermouth, and cook until reduced by half. Stir in saffron, thickener and milk. Cook over low heat 5 to 6 minutes, until creamy.

To serve, unmold ramekins onto plates decorated with saffron sauce. If you wish, garnish with sweet pepper diamonds.

~

1 SERVING		
258 CALORIES	11g CARBOHYDRATE	22g PROTEIN
14g FAT	0g FIBER	83mg CHOLESTEROL

SAVORY MUSSELS WITH TOMATOES

8 SERVINGS

3 lbs	mussels, cleaned and debearded	1.5 kg
½ cup	dry white wine or dry cider	125 mL
6	tomatoes, peeled, seeded and diced	6
2	garlic cloves, finely chopped	2
2	dry French shallots, finely chopped	2
2 tbsp	chopped fresh parsley	30 mL
2 tbsp	olive oil	30 mL
¼ cup	dry breadcrumbs	50 mL
	basil or oregano	
	pepper	

Place mussels in a large saucepan with the wine or cider.

Cover and bring to a boil. Let mussels steam about 1 minute, until shells open. Remove from heat and let cool in cooking juices. Discard any unopened shells.

In a bowl, combine diced tomatoes, garlic and shallots. Add parsley, olive oil, basil and pepper.

Remove mussels from their shells, reserving half the shells. Place 1 mussel in each half-shell.

Spoon a little tomato mixture over each mussel, and sprinkle with breadcrumbs.

Arrange mussels on individual plates. Serve cold or at room temperature, or place under the broiler for a few seconds to serve hot.

1 SERVING		
109 CALORIES	9g CARBOHYDRATE	8g PROTEIN
5g FAT	0.7g FIBER	15mg CHOLESTEROL

MANGO CRAB CANAPÉS

16 CANAPÉS

1/2 lb	crabmeat or imitation crabmeat, shredded	225 g
4	green onions, finely chopped	4
3 tbsp	mayonnaise	45 mL
10	drops Tabasco sauce	10
4	slices rye bread	4
1	mango, peeled, pitted and sliced	1
	lemon juice	
	pepper	
	leaf lettuce for garnish	

In a bowl, combine crabmeat, green onions, mayonnaise, Tabasco and lemon juice. Season to taste. Set aside.

Cut bread into triangles and garnish with lettuce. Arrange crab mixture on top.

Arrange mango slices over crab mixture.

NUTRITION TIP

Rye bread and pumpernickel are good sources of fiber, but pack more flavor than ordinary wholewheat bread. Use low-calorie style mayonnaise to cut the fat and calories further.

1 SERVING		
67 CALORIES	6g CARBOHYDRATE	4g PROTEIN
3g FAT	0.4g FIBER	8mg CHOLESTEROL

MARINATED SALMON WITH MUSTARD SAUCE

~

4 SERVINGS

I tbsp	coarse salt	15 mL
I tbsp	freshly ground pepper	15 mL
I tbsp	brown sugar	15 mL
I tbsp	coarsely chopped fresh fennel leaf	15 mL
I tbsp	coarsely chopped fresh dill	15 mL
1/2 lb	fresh Atlantic salmon filet (preferably center cut)	225 g
I tbsp	vegetable oil	15 mL
	rye bread, pumpernickel or bagels	

MUSTARD SAUCE

1/3 cup	olive oil	75 mL
I tsp	Dijon mustard	5 mL
I tsp	honey	5 mL
I tbsp	tarragon vinegar or raspberry vinegar	15 mL

In a bowl, combine salt, pepper, sugar, fennel, and dill. Spread ½ of mixture in the bottom of a shallow glass dish.

Rub the salmon lightly with oil and place on herb mixture. Cover with remaining mixture.

Cover salmon with plastic wrap. Place a weight on top. Refrigerate salmon at least 48 hours, turning the filet 2 or 3 times during this period.

To make mustard sauce, combine sauce ingredients, mixing well. Let stand several hours before serving so that flavors combine.

When ready to serve, slice salmon thinly, and arrange on individual plates with mustard sauce and bread of your choice.

~

TO MAKE A SALMON ROSE

I Roll I slice of smoked salmon tightly to make the rose center.

2 Wrap a second slice more loosely around the first slice.

3 Repeat step 2, pulling the edges outwards to make a rose shape.

1 SERVING		
288 CALORIES	7g CARBOHYDRATE	11g PROTEIN
24g FAT	0g FIBER	31mg CHOLESTEROL

SHRIMP AND HAM FILO PARCELS

4 SERVINGS

I	small onion, finely chopped	I
2	green onions, chopped	2
I cup	finely chopped celery	250 mL
1/2 cup	finely chopped carrot	125 mL
I cup	chopped mushrooms	250 mL
I	garlic clove, finely chopped	I
I cup	small shrimp, cooked and peeled	250 mL
1/2 cup	diced cooked ham	125 mL
2 tbsp	chopped fresh parsley	30 mL
I	egg, beaten	I
4	sheets filo pastry	4
	vegetable oil	
	salt and pepper	

COOK'S TIP

Filo pastry produces exotic results, but is surprisingly easy to use. Look for it ready-made in the frozen food section. Thaw in refrigerator before using, and rewrap and freeze unused portion.

Preheat oven to 375°F (190°C). Lightly oil a nonstick skillet and add onions, celery, carrot, mushrooms and garlic. Cook over medium heat 3 to 5 minutes.

Add shrimp, ham and parsley. Let mixture cool. Stir in beaten egg and season to taste.

Baste edges of filo sheets with water and stack them. Spread shrimp mixture along one edge of pastry and roll it up.

Arrange pastry on a baking sheet and bake about 20 minutes. Slice to serve.

I Sauté the vegetables.

2 Add shrimp, ham and parsley. Let cool.

3 Stir in egg and seasonings.

4 Spread mixture on layered filo and roll up.

1 SERVING		
152 CALORIES	15 g CARBOHYDRATE	14 g PROTEIN
4 g FAT	1.5 g FIBER	120 mg CHOLESTEROL

FISHERMAN'S STUFFED POTATO

4 SERVINGS

COOK'S TIP

Serve stuffed potatoes for brunch instead of the usual bacon and eggs. They are delicious either hot or at room temperature.

4	potatoes, baked	4
1/2 cup	low-fat cream cheese	125 mL
1/2 cup	plain yogurt	125 mL
3	drops Tabasco sauce	3
2 tsp	chopped fresh dill or tarragon	10 mL
2 oz	smoked trout or smoked salmon, slivered	60 g
	pepper	
	capers and pimento strips for garnish	

Cut baked potatoes in half lengthwise with a sharp knife. Scoop out potato flesh, being careful not to puncture the skins. Set aside.

Mash potato flesh together with cream cheese, yogurt, Tabasco, dill, smoked fish and pepper.

Use a spoon or a pastry bag to fill potato skins with mashed potato mixture. Arrange potato halves on a baking sheet and reheat about 8 minutes in a 350°F (180°C) oven.

Garnish heated potatoes with capers and pimento strips before serving.

1 SERVING		
284 CALORIES	42g CARBOHYDRATE	11g PROTEIN
8g FAT	3.3g FIBER	26mg CHOLESTEROL

HAM MUFFINS

MAKES 12 MUFFINS

I	egg, beaten	I
³/₄ cup	soft breadcrumbs	175 mL
I¹/₂ lbs	cooked ham, ground	675 g
I	celery stalk, finely chopped	I
I	onion, finely chopped	I
¹/₂ cup	skim milk	125 mL
I tbsp	hot mustard	15 mL
2 tbsp	chopped fresh parsley	30 mL
I tbsp	melted butter	15 mL

Preheat oven to 350°F (180°C).

In a large bowl, combine all ingredients, except melted butter. Mix well.

Brush 12 muffin molds with melted butter.

Spoon ham mixture into molds. Bake in oven about 30 minutes, until golden brown.

Let cool before unmolding.

1 Combine muffin ingredients.

2 Spoon into muffin molds.

3 Bake. Let cool before unmolding.

1 SERVING		
125 CALORIES	7g CARBOHYDRATE	13g PROTEIN
5g FAT	0.2g FIBER	49mg CHOLESTEROL

ELEGANT LAYERED TERRINE

I lb	lean ground beef	450 g
I lb	lean ground pork	450 g
I lb	lean ground veal	450 g
6	bacon slices, chopped	6
2 tbsp	butter or margarine	30 mL
I	onion, chopped	I
I	garlic clove, finely chopped	I
2 cups	chopped fresh spinach	500 mL
I tsp	dried basil	5 mL
I tsp	dried rosemary	5 mL
I tsp	fennel seeds	5 mL
I tsp	freshly ground pepper	5 mL
I	envelope onion soup mix	I
1/4 cup	chopped fresh parsley	50 mL
2	eggs	2
I cup	fresh breadcrumbs	250 mL
3/4 cup	milk	175 mL
10	bacon slices (optional)	10
8	hardboiled eggs	8

Preheat oven to 350°F (180°C). In a large bowl, combine beef, pork, veal and chopped bacon. Set aside.

Melt butter in a large skillet and add onion and garlic. Cook until limp. Stir in spinach, basil, rosemary and fennel. Cook 1 minute, stirring.

Stir spinach into meat mixture. Add pepper, onion soup mix, parsley, 2 eggs, breadcrumbs and milk. Combine well and set aside.

Line 2 loaf pans with bacon slices (optional). Spread 1/4 of meat mixture in bottom of both loaf pans. Arrange 4 hardboiled eggs lengthwise in a row down the center of each pan. Cover eggs with remaining meat mixture, packing down lightly.

Cover each loaf pan with foil, and place pans side by side in a larger baking pan. Fill larger pan with water to halfway up sides of loaf pans. Bake in oven about 1¼ hours.

Remove pans from oven and uncover. Let loaves stand 30 minutes, then pour off any standing fat and liquid. Cover each pan with foil again, place a weight on top of each loaf, and refrigerate overnight before serving. Slice each loaf thinly into about 10 slices to serve.

1 Combine beef, pork, veal and chopped bacon.

2 Add cooked spinach and remaining ingredients to meat mixture.

3 Spread 1/4 of meat mixture in each pan. Place eggs on top.

4 Cover loaf pans with foil and place in larger baking pan.

1 SERVING		
234 CALORIES	6 g CARBOHYDRATE	21 g PROTEIN
14 g FAT	0.5 g FIBER	188 mg CHOLESTEROL

LEEKS VINAIGRETTE

4 SERVINGS

COOK'S TIP

Sprinkle some crumbled crisp bacon or a few strips of ham over the leeks for added flavor and color contrast.

8	leeks, white part only, cleaned	8
1 cup	hot chicken stock	250 mL
1 tbsp	lemon juice	15 mL
2	hardboiled eggs, chopped	2
1 tbsp	chopped fresh parsley	15 mL
1 tbsp	Dijon mustard	15 mL
3 tbsp	wine vinegar	45 mL
½ cup	olive oil	125 mL
	pepper	

Split leeks in half lengthwise. Cook, covered, in chicken stock until tender. Let cool in the cooking liquid, then refrigerate to chill.

Meanwhile, make the vinaigrette: in a bowl, combine chopped eggs, parsley, mustard and vinegar. Add oil in a thin stream, beating vigorously all the time. Season to taste.

Drain leeks well and arrange on a serving dish or individual plates. Top with vinaigrette to serve.

1 SERVING		
392 CALORIES	21g CARBOHYDRATE	5g PROTEIN
32g FAT	2.8g FIBER	137mg CHOLESTEROL

TOASTED ASPARAGUS ROLLS

4 SERVINGS

16	slices wholewheat bread, crusts trimmed	16
1/4 cup	butter or margarine	50 mL
1/4 cup	light cream cheese	50 mL
8	thin slices cooked ham	8
24	asparagus spears, freshly cooked or canned	24
	SAUCE	
2 cups	skim milk	500 mL
1 tbsp	butter or margarine	15 mL
1	pinch nutmeg	1
1 tbsp	dehydrated chicken stock powder	15 mL
2 tbsp	cornstarch dissolved in a little water	30 mL
	salt and pepper	

Stack 2 slices of bread and flatten lightly with a rolling pin. Repeat with remaining slices.

Butter bread stacks on one side only. Spread cream cheese on other side. Arrange a ham slice and 3 asparagus spears on cheese side of each bread stack.

Roll bread around asparagus, and wrap each roll tightly in plastic wrap or waxed paper. Refrigerate 1 hour.

Meanwhile, make the sauce: heat milk and butter together in a saucepan over medium heat. Add nutmeg, pepper and chicken stock powder. Bring to a boil, then stir in dissolved cornstarch to thicken.

Preheat oven to 350°F (180°C). Unwrap asparagus rolls and arrange on a nonstick baking sheet. Bake 12 to 15 minutes, or until bread is golden.

Arrange rolls on individual plates with heated sauce. Serve 2 asparagus rolls per person.

COOK'S TIP

Cheese and asparagus are a classic combination. If you don't mind adding a few extra calories to this recipe, stir a handful or two of grated aged cheddar, Parmesan or other cheese into the sauce.

1 SERVING		
497 CALORIES	56g CARBOHYDRATE	21g PROTEIN
21g FAT	6.4g FIBER	66mg CHOLESTEROL

JULIENNE OF ZUCCHINI
WITH TOMATO COULIS

~

4 SERVINGS

8	small zucchini	8
2 tbsp	vegetable oil	30 mL
1/4 cup	chopped green onion	50 mL
1	red or yellow bell pepper, chopped	1
2	garlic cloves, chopped	2
1 tsp	dried oregano	5 mL
2 tbsp	chopped fresh parsley	30 mL
	salt and pepper	

TOMATO COULIS

1	small onion, chopped	1
1 tbsp	vegetable oil	15 mL
1 tbsp	finely chopped garlic	15 mL
28 oz	can tomatoes, crushed	796 mL
2 tbsp	chopped fresh parsley	30 mL
2 tbsp	chopped fresh basil	30 mL
1	sprig fresh rosemary	1
1	bay leaf	1
	salt and pepper	

Slice zucchini thinly lengthwise into strips. Cut strips thinly lengthwise to make thin strands the size of spaghetti.

Heat oil in a skillet. Add zucchini, green onion, bell pepper and garlic and toss over medium heat several minutes until tender-crisp.

Stir in oregano, parsley and salt and pepper. Set aside.

To make the tomato coulis: in a saucepan, cook onion in oil until limp. Add garlic and tomatoes.

Stir in herbs and season to taste. Let simmer over low heat about 30 minutes. Press tomato mixture through a sieve to remove seeds and solids.

Pour tomato coulis onto plates, and arrange zucchini mixture on top. Garnish with fresh herbs, if desired.

~

1 Cut zucchini into thin strands.

2 Sauté zucchini, green onion, bell pepper and garlic.

3 Add herbs and seasonings.

4 Pour tomato coulis on plates. Top with zucchini mixture.

1 SERVING		
199 CALORIES	19g CARBOHYDRATE	6g PROTEIN
11g FAT	7.1g FIBER	0mg CHOLESTEROL

ASPARAGUS VINAIGRETTE

4 SERVINGS

24	fresh asparagus spears, stalks peeled	24
I	hardboiled egg, chopped	I
I	tomato, peeled and chopped	I

VINAIGRETTE

2 tsp	Dijon mustard	10 mL
2 tbsp	hazelnut oil	30 mL
I tbsp	virgin olive oil	15 mL
¹/₄ cup	balsamic vinegar	50 mL
¹/₄ cup	white grape juice	50 mL
I tbsp	water	15 mL

Drop asparagus into a large pot of boiling salted water and cook 5 to 6 minutes or until tender-crisp. Immediately cool asparagus under cold running water and drain well. Pat dry.

Divide asparagus among 4 plates. Sprinkle chopped egg and tomato on top.

Stir together dressing ingredients. Pour over asparagus spears.

COOK'S TIP

Fresh asparagus will keep 4 to 6 days in the refrigerator. Wrap the stalks in damp paper towels and place in a plastic bag.

1 SERVING		
160 CALORIES	8g CARBOHYDRATE	5g PROTEIN
12g FAT	2.1g FIBER	68mg CHOLESTEROL

CRISPY POTATO SKINS

~

2 SERVINGS

4	potatoes, scrubbed	4
1/2 cup	vegetable oil or margarine	125 mL
	salt and pepper	

Wrap each potato in foil and bake 45 to 60 minutes at 350°F (180°C).

Cut each potato in half lengthwise and scoop out flesh. Set aside potato flesh for another use.

Cut potato skins into strips.

Stir pepper into oil (or melted margarine). Dip potato skins into mixture.

Arrange potato skins on a baking sheet and place under preheated broiler for 5 to 7 minutes, turning potato skins from time to time. Sprinkle with salt and serve very hot.

~

1 Cut baked potatoes in half and scoop out flesh.

2 Cut potato skins into strips.

3 Dip potato strips in oil mixture.

4 Arrange oiled potato skins on baking sheet and broil.

1 SERVING			APPETIZERS
762 CALORIES	54g CARBOHYDRATE	6g PROTEIN	
58g FAT	7.6g FIBER	0mg CHOLESTEROL	**23**

GOUGÈRE

8 SERVINGS

1 cup	low-fat milk	250 mL
1/4 cup	cold butter, diced	50 mL
1/2 tsp	salt	2 mL
1/2 tsp	white pepper	2 mL
1 cup	all-purpose flour	250 mL
4	large eggs	4
3/4 cup	grated **Gruyère** or **Emmenthal cheese**	175 mL
2 tbsp	low-fat milk	30 mL
1/4 cup	grated **Parmesan cheese**	50 mL

Preheat oven to 375°F (190°C). Place 1 cup (250 mL) milk in a saucepan with butter, salt and pepper. Bring to a boil.

Immediately remove saucepan from heat. Add flour all at once, stirring vigorously until well mixed. Return saucepan to medium heat, and cook about 2 minutes, or until mixture forms a ball which sticks slightly to the pan. Remove from heat.

Place dough mixture in food processor. Add eggs one by one, processing well after each addition. Add grated Gruyère cheese and mix again.

Grease a cookie sheet and dust lightly with flour. Trace a circle in the flour about 9 inches (23 cm) in diameter. Drop spoonfuls of batter side by side around the circle.

Brush the top lightly with remaining milk and sprinkle with Parmesan. Bake in preheated oven 35 to 40 minutes, or until golden brown.

~

1 Bring to a boil the milk, butter, salt and pepper.

2 Add flour all at once. Stir well.

3 Place batter in food processor. Add eggs one by one, then grated cheese, processing well after each addition.

4 Drop spoonfuls of batter in a circle onto prepared cookie sheet. Bake until golden brown.

1 SERVING		
222 CALORIES	14g CARBOHYDRATE	10g PROTEIN
14g FAT	0.5g FIBER	170 mg CHOLESTEROL

FENNEL AND PISTACHIO SALAD

4 SERVINGS

COOK'S TIP

Fennel resembles celery, and has a mild licorice flavor. You can use it instead of celery in almost any recipe.

1	fennel bulb, cut in julienne	1
1	red or green apple, cut in julienne	1
3	radicchio leaves, cut in julienne	3
1/4 cup	shelled pistachios, chopped	50 mL
4	leaves Boston lettuce	4
4	sprigs fresh chervil or coriander	4

DRESSING

3 tbsp	red wine vinegar	45 mL
2 tbsp	olive oil	30 mL
1/4 cup	plain low-fat yogurt	50 mL
1 tsp	Dijon mustard	5 mL
1 tbsp	chopped fresh chervil or coriander	15 mL

Combine all dressing ingredients in a small bowl. Set aside.

In a salad bowl, combine fennel, apple, radicchio and pistachios. Add dressing and toss well.

Arrange a Boston lettuce leaf on each of 4 plates. Divide salad mixture among plates. Garnish with chervil or coriander.

~

1 SERVING		
163 CALORIES	13g CARBOHYDRATE	3g PROTEIN
11g FAT	3.3g FIBER	1mg CHOLESTEROL

SALADE COMPOSÉE

4 SERVINGS

8	Boston lettuce leaves	8
1 cup	grated raw carrots	250 mL
1 cup	parboiled, grated beets	250 mL
1 cup	grated celeriac (celery root)	250 mL
1 cup	fresh spinach, shredded	250 mL
1 cup	alfalfa sprouts	250 mL

DRESSING

1/2 cup	plain low-fat yogurt	125 mL
1 tbsp	olive oil	15 mL
2 tbsp	chopped fresh lemon grass	30 mL
1/4 cup	unsweetened orange juice	50 mL

Arrange lettuce leaves on 4 salad plates.
Arrange grated vegetables decoratively
over lettuce.

Combine dressing ingredients well
in a small bowl.

Pour dressing over salad just before
serving.

~

COOK'S TIPS

*Celeriac is a type
of celery grown for its
bulbous root, which
tastes like mild celery
but is not stringy.
Once cut, it should
be kept in acidulated
water until ready
to use (add a little
lemon juice or vinegar
to cold water).*

*Lemon grass, or
citronella, is a lemony
tasting plant that looks
like grass. You can find
it in Oriental grocery
stores, or substitute
1 tsp (5 mL) grated
lemon zest.*

	1 SERVING	
104 CALORIES	13g CARBOHYDRATE	4g PROTEIN
4g FAT	3.4g FIBER	3mg CHOLESTEROL

RUTABAGA AND CARROT SALAD

4 SERVINGS

2 cups	shredded carrots	500 mL
2 cups	shredded rutabaga (Swede turnips) or turnip	500 mL
1 tbsp	finely chopped fresh coriander or dill	15 mL
¹/₂ cup	shredded fresh spinach	125 mL

DRESSING

¹/₄ cup	plain low-fat yogurt	50 mL
2 tbsp	low-fat mayonnaise	30 mL
2 tbsp	liquid honey	30 mL
	freshly ground pepper	

Combine shredded carrots and rutabaga in a bowl with coriander or dill.

Mix together dressing ingredients in a small bowl.

Stir dressing into carrot mixture. Arrange mixture on top of shredded spinach to serve.

~

COOK'S TIP

Rutabagas or Swede turnips are closely related to turnips. Turnips are smaller and round with white flesh, whereas the larger rutabagas have yellow flesh. Grated or shredded raw, both of them have a tangy sweet flavor and are packed with nutrition.

1 SERVING		
94 CALORIES	17g CARBOHYDRATE	2g PROTEIN
2g FAT	2.0g FIBER	3mg CHOLESTEROL

CALIFORNIA SALAD

4 SERVINGS

2	endives, sliced	2
8	radicchio leaves, shredded	8
I cup	alfalfa sprouts	250 mL
1/4 cup	chopped black olives	50 mL
I	red bell pepper, thinly sliced	I

DRESSING

1/2 cup	plain yogurt	125 mL
1/2 cup	buttermilk	125 mL
1/2 tsp	dried oregano	2 mL
I tsp	chopped fresh coriander	5 mL
	salt and pepper	

In a bowl, combine endives, radicchio, sprouts, olives and red pepper.

Combine dressing ingredients in a small bowl.

Just before serving, arrange salad on small plates and top with dressing.

~

NUTRITION TIP

Despite its name, buttermilk contains no butter. In fact, it contains as much fat as 1% milk, and has the same amount of calcium.

1 SERVING		
80 CALORIES	7g CARBOHYDRATE	4g PROTEIN
4g FAT	1.7g FIBER	4mg CHOLESTEROL

BOCCONCINI WITH LEMON GRASS DRESSING

4 SERVINGS

8	bocconcini cheeses, drained	8
¹/₄ cup	olive oil	50 mL
¹/₄ cup	white wine vinegar	50 mL
¹/₄ cup	chopped fresh lemon grass	50 mL
2	oil-packed sundried tomatoes, drained and finely chopped	2
4	leaves Romaine lettuce	4
	salt and freshly ground pepper	

Cut cheeses ¼ inch (5 mm) thick and set aside in a bowl.

In a bowl, combine olive oil, vinegar, lemon grass, tomatoes and seasoning. Pour over cheese slices and let marinate at room temperature at least 2 hours.

Arrange lettuce leaves in center of salad plates, surround with cheese slices, and pour remaining dressing over.

1 Slice the cheeses.

2 Combine oil, vinegar, lemon grass, tomatoes, and seasoning.

3 Marinate cheese slices in dressing.

4 Arrange cheese on salad plates with lettuce and remaining dressing.

1 SERVING		
415 CALORIES	7g CARBOHYDRATE	18g PROTEIN
35g FAT	1.5g FIBER	43mg CHOLESTEROL

COOK'S TIP

*The easiest way to seed
tomatoes is to cut them in
half crosswise, then
squeeze the halves gently
to remove the seeds.*

PEPPERY TABOULI

4 SERVINGS

2 cups	water	500 mL
3 tbsp	liquid chicken stock concentrate	45 mL
2 cups	quick-cooking bulgur	500 mL
2 tbsp	olive oil	30 mL
2 tbsp	chopped fresh mint	30 mL
1/4 cup	chopped parsley	50 mL
I tsp	freshly ground black pepper	5 mL
I	tomato, peeled, seeded and chopped	I
	a few drops hot pepper sauce	

In a large saucepan, bring water to a boil and add liquid chicken stock. Stir in bulgur, cover, and remove from heat. Let stand until grains absorb all the liquid.

Add olive oil, mint, parsley and pepper. Toss well. Stir in diced tomato and hot sauce. Serve chilled or at room temperature, garnished with fresh raw vegetables, if desired.

1 SERVING		
244 CALORIES	37g CARBOHYDRATE	6g PROTEIN
8g FAT	1.0g FIBER	0mg CHOLESTEROL

HERBED CHEESE SPREAD

~

MAKES ABOUT 2 CUPS (500 mL)

8 oz	light cream cheese	225 g
1/2 cup	sour cream	125 mL
3	bacon slices, cooked and crumbled	3
2 tbsp	finely chopped fresh chives	30 mL
2 tbsp	finely chopped fresh dill	30 mL
2 tbsp	finely chopped fresh chervil	30 mL
2 tbsp	finely chopped fresh parsley	30 mL
1 tbsp	lemon juice	15 mL
	freshly ground pepper	

In a bowl, combine cream cheese, sour cream and bacon.

Stir in fresh chopped herbs, lemon juice and pepper.

Mound into a small serving bowl or onto a platter, and surround with crackers of your choice.

~

COOK'S TIP

Feel free to substitute your own choice of fresh herbs. Just make sure the total equals at least 1/2 cup (125 mL). Do not use dried herbs in this recipe – the result will be disappointing.

1 SERVING (2 TBSP/30 ML)		
48 CALORIES	1g CARBOHYDRATE	2g PROTEIN
4g FAT	0.1g FIBER	11mg CHOLESTEROL

SOUPS

~

All too many people these days think of soup
as an emergency food that comes in a can.
But real homemade soup is much more than
just a food that you eat with a spoon.

In one sense, soup is the ultimate comfort food.
But, as you will see from the variety of recipes
in this chapter, it can bring an exotic or a homey
touch to your meal. It can be a stick-to-your-
ribs meal in a bowl, or a delicate starter course.
It can involve extravagant ingredients like
lobster, or be a thrifty way to use up odds
and ends from the refrigerator. It can warm
your bones in the chill of winter, or cool
and soothe you on a hot summer evening.

Soup can also be easy to make. Modern
appliances like the blender and food processor
have eliminated the drudgery of chopping,
mashing and sieving that used to go with
soup-making. And when you need to save time,
good-quality stocks are available at your
supermarket (although you will want to watch
for the salt content in many brands.)

So let the photographs in this chapter
entice you into the pleasures of soup making.
Your family will love you for it!

~

CREAM OF CELERY SOUP

4 SERVINGS

COOK'S TIP

*Some food processors
and blenders should not
be used with hot liquids.
Read the manufacturer's
instructions before
puréeing soup.
You may have to let
the soup cool first.*

1 tbsp	butter or margarine	15 mL
1 cup	chopped celery	250 mL
1	onion, chopped	1
1	potato, peeled and chopped	1
2 cups	chicken stock	500 mL
1½ cups	skim milk	375 mL
¼ cup	sour cream	50 mL
1 tbsp	chopped fresh parsley	15 mL
	salt and pepper	

Melt butter in a saucepan. Add celery
and onion, and cook over medium heat
5 to 7 minutes, or until onion is soft.

Add potato and chicken stock. Simmer
15 to 20 minutes. Stir in milk and season
to taste.

Process mixture in food processor
or blender until smooth. Reheat soup
if necessary. Serve topped with a dollop
of sour cream and sprinkled with parsley.

1 SERVING		
121 CALORIES	14 g CARBOHYDRATE	5 g PROTEIN
5 g FAT	1.4 g FIBER	15 mg CHOLESTEROL

CREAM OF MUSSELS WITH SAFFRON

4 SERVINGS

2	dry French shallots or 1 red onion, chopped	2
2 tsp	butter or margarine	10 mL
2 lbs	fresh mussels	1 kg
1 cup	dry white wine	250 mL
1 cup	fish stock	250 mL
1	pinch saffron	1
1¹/₂ cups	15% cream	375 mL

Melt butter in a large saucepan. Add shallots and cook over medium heat until soft. Stir in mussels and wine, cover, and cook 5 minutes, stirring from time to time.

Remove mussels from saucepan. Remove mussel meat from shells and keep warm. Discard any mussels that did not open.

Add fish stock and saffron to saucepan. Cook, uncovered, about 5 minutes, until slightly reduced.

Stir in cream. Cook over medium heat about 5 minutes, without allowing to boil, until slightly reduced. Stir in reserved mussels and serve hot. Decorate with a few cooked mussels in their shells, if desired.

COOK'S TIPS

This makes an elegant but rich soup course. Serve it with a light main course such as plain grilled meat.

To turn this into a hearty chowder, add 2 cups (500 mL) parboiled diced potatoes with the onions, and replace the cream with milk.

1 SERVING		
246 CALORIES	10g CARBOHYDRATE	11g PROTEIN
18g FAT	0.3g FIBER	73mg CHOLESTEROL

MILANESE CHICKEN AND MUSHROOM SOUP

8 SERVINGS

COOK'S TIP

*This is a rich soup.
Serve it before
a main course
of plain grilled
fish or meat, or with
a hearty salad.*

4 cups	chicken stock	1 liter
1 tsp	butter or margarine	5 mL
1/2 lb	skinless, boneless chicken breast	225 g
1/2 cup	slivered cooked ham	125 mL
1 1/2 cups	sliced fresh mushrooms	375 mL
1/4 cup	commercial white sauce and gravy thickener	50 mL
1 cup	15% cream	250 mL
1/2 cup	tomato paste	125 mL
1/4 cup	grated Parmesan cheese	50 mL

Bring chicken stock to boil in a large saucepan. Reduce heat and let simmer.

Melt butter in a nonstick skillet. Brown chicken breast on all sides; remove and set aside. In the same pan, cook ham and mushrooms 5 minutes, stirring. Remove from heat.

Stir sauce thickener, cream and tomato paste into chicken stock. Whisk together well.

Cut chicken breast into thin strips. Stir chicken, ham and mushrooms into stock. Serve with grated Parmesan.

SOUPS

40

1 SERVING		
295 CALORIES	17g CARBOHYDRATE	23g PROTEIN
15g FAT	2.1g FIBER	81mg CHOLESTEROL

SUNNY CARROT AND LENTIL SOUP

~

4 SERVINGS

2 tbsp	butter or margarine	30 mL
1	onion, finely chopped	1
2 cups	finely chopped carrots	500 mL
1/4 cup	red lentils, sorted and rinsed	50 mL
2 1/2 cups	vegetable stock	625 mL
	juice of 1 orange	
	salt and pepper	

Melt butter in a saucepan. Add onions and cook, stirring, until soft.

Add carrots, lentils, and vegetable stock. Bring mixture to a boil, reduce heat, and let simmer about 15 minutes.

Process mixture in food processor until smooth.

Return soup to saucepan. Stir in orange juice, salt and pepper, and reheat gently until hot. Serve immediately, garnished with a drizzle of yogurt and some fresh herbs, if desired.

~

COOK'S TIP

Red lentils cook quickly. If you substitute brown lentils, you will have to cook the soup a little longer.

1 SERVING		
134 CALORIES	16g CARBOHYDRATE	4g PROTEIN
6g FAT	2.9g FIBER	16mg CHOLESTEROL

CREAM OF ASPARAGUS SOUP

4 SERVINGS

COOK'S TIP

Some food processors and blenders should not be used with hot liquids. Read the manufacturer's instructions before puréeing soup. You may have to let the soup cool first.

1 tbsp	butter or margarine	15 mL
1	red onion, chopped	1
2	celery stalks, chopped	2
1	garlic clove, chopped	1
1	green onion, chopped	1
1 tbsp	all-purpose flour	15 mL
3 cups	skim milk	750 mL
1 tbsp	dry sherry	15 mL
1	bay leaf	1
1 tsp	fresh lemon juice	5 mL
1/2 tsp	ground thyme	2 mL
2 cups	chopped cooked asparagus, drained (reserve a few asparagus tips for garnish)	500 mL
	salt and freshly ground pepper	
	chopped fresh parsley, for garnish	

Melt butter in a large saucepan. Add onion, celery, garlic and green onion. Cook, stirring, until onion is soft.

Sprinkle flour over onion mixture and mix. Gradually stir in milk until mixture is smooth. Add remaining ingredients, cover, and let simmer about 20 minutes.

Remove from heat and process the soup mixture in food processor until smooth and creamy.

Serve hot, garnished with asparagus spears and chopped fresh parsley.

~

1 Cook onion, celery, garlic and green onion until soft.

2 Stir in flour, then add milk gradually.

3 Add remaining ingredients and let simmer.

4 Process until smooth and creamy.

1 SERVING

144 CALORIES	17g CARBOHYDRATE	10g PROTEIN
4g FAT	2.8g FIBER	12mg CHOLESTEROL

CREAMY ONION SOUP

4 SERVINGS

COOK'S TIP

The split peas and carrots add fiber and minerals to this easy version of onion soup. Take the time to brown the onions to a deep golden color to give the richest flavor.

¹/₃ cup	yellow split peas, sorted and rinsed	75 mL
2 cups	water	500 mL
1 cup	chopped onions	250 mL
¹/₃ cup	chopped carrots	75 mL
2 tbsp	butter or margarine	30 mL
1 cup	vegetable or chicken stock	250 mL
1	bay leaf	1
¹/₂ tsp	dried dill	2 mL
¹/₄ tsp	dried thyme	1 mL
¹/₃ cup	skim milk	75 mL
	salt and pepper	
	sour cream for garnish	

Place split peas in a saucepan with the water. Bring to a boil, reduce heat to medium, and let simmer about 30 minutes. Do not drain.

Melt butter in a nonstick skillet and add onions and carrots. Cook over medium heat about 10 minutes or until onions are nicely browned. Stir mixture into peas. (Reserve a few nice slices of onion to garnish soup, if desired.)

Add vegetable stock, bay leaf, dill and thyme. Partially cover and let simmer about 30 minutes.

Season to taste and remove bay leaf. Stir in milk. Process mixture in food processor until smooth.

Reheat to serve, garnished with a dollop of sour cream.

~

1 SERVING		
200 CALORIES	16g CARBOHYDRATE	6g PROTEIN
8g FAT	3.0g FIBER	22mg CHOLESTEROL

CREAM OF CARROT AND ORANGE SOUP

4 SERVINGS

I tbsp	vegetable oil	15 mL
8	carrots, peeled and chopped	8
2	onions, finely chopped	2
4 cups	vegetable stock	I liter
2 tbsp	butter or margarine	30 mL
2 tbsp	all-purpose flour	30 mL
I cup	unsweetened orange juice	250 mL
	grated zest of I orange	
	salt and pepper	
	yogurt or orange slices for garnish	

Heat oil in a saucepan. Add carrots, onions and orange zest. Cook, stirring, until onion is soft. Add vegetable stock. Cover and cook over medium-high heat 15 to 20 minutes.

Melt butter in a small saucepan. Stir in flour and cook a few seconds to remove raw taste of flour. Stir in orange juice, salt and pepper. Cook, stirring, until thickened slightly.

Remove carrots and other solids from stock. Process carrots in food processor until smooth. Return to saucepan with stock. Stir in thickened juice mixture until smooth. Serve hot, garnished with orange slices or yogurt, as desired.

1 SERVING		
214 CALORIES	28g CARBOHYDRATE	3g PROTEIN
10g FAT	5.5g FIBER	16mg CHOLESTEROL

CREAM OF AVOCADO SOUP

4 SERVINGS

1 tbsp	butter or margarine	15 mL
1	onion, sliced	1
2	garlic cloves, chopped	2
2	ripe avocados, peeled and chopped	2
2 tbsp	lemon juice	30 mL
2 tbsp	dry sherry	30 mL
2 cups	chicken stock	500 mL
1 tbsp	cornstarch	15 mL
2 cups	skim milk	500 mL
1/4 cup	light cream	50 mL
	salt and freshly ground pepper	

NUTRITION TIP

Don't avoid avocados just because you are watching your fat and cholesterol intake. Like olive oil, avocados are high in the antioxidant fatty acids that help detoxify bad cholesterol.

Melt butter in a saucepan over medium heat. Add onion, garlic and avocados; cook, stirring, until onion is soft. Add lemon juice, sherry, and chicken stock. Season to taste and simmer 5 minutes.

Place mixture in a food processor or blender and process until smooth and creamy. Return to saucepan. Dissolve cornstarch in milk and stir into avocado mixture.

Bring soup slowly to a boil and cook until thickened to desired consistency.

1 SERVING

280 CALORIES	18 g CARBOHYDRATE	7 g PROTEIN
20 g FAT	2.9 g FIBER	15 mg CHOLESTEROL

CREAM OF ENDIVE SOUP

6 SERVINGS

6	Belgian endives	6
I tbsp	butter or margarine	15 mL
3	medium potatoes, peeled and chopped	3
2	small turnips, peeled and chopped	2
2	leeks, white part only, cleaned and chopped	2
2	onions, peeled and chopped	2
6 cups	chicken stock	1.5 liters
	salt and pepper	
	chopped fresh parsley or herbs for garnish	

Wipe endives clean, but do not wash. Core out the base of each, which tends to have a bitter taste. Cook endives about 25 minutes in boiling salted water. Drain and chop endives coarsely.

Melt butter in a skillet. Add chopped endives and cook, stirring, about 3 minutes. Remove endives and set aside.

Combine remaining vegetables and chicken stock in a large saucepan. Cover and cook gently about 20 to 25 minutes.

Remove vegetables from liquid and process them, along with chopped endives, in food processor until smooth. Stir into liquid in saucepan and season to taste. Garnish with parsley or herb of your choice.

~

NUTRITION TIP

To reduce cholesterol , cook the endives in olive oil instead of butter, and carefully skim any fat from the top of the chicken stock.

1 SERVING		
114 CALORIES	21g CARBOHYDRATE	3g PROTEIN
2g FAT	3.1g FIBER	5mg CHOLESTEROL

MINESTRONE

4 TO 6 SERVINGS

2	carrots, peeled	2
2	turnips, peeled	2
1/2	rutabaga, peeled	1/2
2	potatoes, peeled	2
4	slices bacon, finely chopped	4
I	onion, finely chopped	I
I	garlic clove, crushed	I
1/4 cup	tomato paste	50 mL
7 cups	water	1.75 liters
I tbsp	liquid vegetable stock concentrate	15 mL
1/3 cup	diced tomatoes	75 mL
1/3 cup	rice, cooked	75 mL
1/3 cup	green beans, cut up and blanched	75 mL
I tbsp	chopped fresh parsley	15 mL
	salt and pepper	

Cut carrots in 4 lengthwise, then slice thinly crosswise. Cut turnips, rutabaga and potatoes into pieces of roughly the same size as carrots. Keep chopped potatoes in cold water to avoid darkening.

Place bacon and onion in a large saucepan. Cook over low heat 5 minutes, stirring from time to time. Stir in carrots, turnips and rutabaga. Cook 5 minutes over medium heat.

Add garlic and tomato paste and stir to coat vegetables well.

Add water, vegetable stock concentrate and potatoes. Let simmer 20 minutes.

Add tomatoes, rice, green beans and parsley. Season to taste. Serve very hot.

~

NUTRITION TIP

You can turn this soup into a meal in a bowl by stirring in a can or two of drained and rinsed kidney beans or cannellini beans. A sprinkling of grated Parmesan cheese adds extra flavor.

1 SERVING		
118 CALORIES	22g CARBOHYDRATE	3g PROTEIN
2g FAT	3.6g FIBER	3mg CHOLESTEROL

PANTRY FISH CHOWDER

4 SERVINGS

I tbsp	butter or margarine	15 mL
I	small carrot, diced	I
I	celery stalk, diced	I
1/2	onion, finely chopped	1/2
2 tbsp	all-purpose flour	30 mL
I tbsp	ground turmeric	15 mL
10 oz	can clams, with their liquid	284 g
7 oz	can waterpacked tuna, drained and flaked	200 g
7 oz	can salmon, drained and flaked	200 g
1/2 cup	canned corn kernels, drained	125 mL
2 cups	fish stock	500 mL
I	bay leaf	I
I tbsp	cornstarch, dissolved in a little water	15 mL
	salt and pepper	

COOK'S TIP

This is an easy soup to make using ingredients from your pantry. If you don't have fish stock, use chicken stock or a few dissolved stock cubes.

Melt butter in a large saucepan. Add carrot, celery and onion. Cook about 5 minutes over medium heat, or until onion is soft.

Sprinkle in flour and turmeric. Stir well.

Stir in clams with their juice, tuna, salmon, corn, fish stock and bay leaf. Simmer over low heat, about 20 minutes.

Remove bay leaf, stir in dissolved cornstarch, and season to taste.

1 Cook chopped carrot, celery and onion until soft.

2 Sprinkle in flour and turmeric.

3 Add clams with their juice, tuna, salmon, corn, stock and bay leaf.

4 Stir in dissolved cornstarch and season to taste.

1 SERVING		
307 CALORIES	16g CARBOHYDRATE	36g PROTEIN
11g FAT	1.3g FIBER	75mg CHOLESTEROL

*The "bonne femme"
or smart housewife
for whom this classic
French soup is named
knew how to turn
odds and ends from the
garden into a nutritious
and delicious soup.
Follow her example
and substitute vegetables
you have on hand,
such as zucchini
or green beans.*

SOUPE BONNE FEMME

~

6 SERVINGS

1 tbsp	butter or margarine	15 mL
1	garlic clove, chopped	1
1 cup	chopped celery with leaves	250 mL
2	leeks, white part only, sliced	2
2	potatoes, peeled and diced	2
1	small turnip, peeled and diced	1
1	cucumber, peeled, seeded and diced	1
8 cups	vegetable stock	2 liters
1/4 tsp	celery seed	1 mL
1 cup	frozen peas, thawed	250 mL

CROUTONS

2	slices wholewheat bread, diced	2
1 tbsp	melted butter or margarine	15 mL
1 tbsp	finely chopped fresh chives	15 mL

Preheat oven to 300°F (150°C).

Melt butter in a large saucepan.
Add garlic, celery, leeks, potatoes, turnip,
and cucumber. Cook 3 to 4 minutes.

Add vegetable stock and celery seed. Cover
and cook about 25 minutes over medium
heat. Add peas and cook 10 minutes more.

Meanwhile, toss diced bread in a bowl
with melted butter and chives. Spread out
on a cookie sheet and toast in oven about
15 minutes, stirring from time to time.

Pour soup into preheated soup bowls
and serve very hot. Serve with croutons
to sprinkle on top.

~

1 SERVING		
171 CALORIES	23g CARBOHYDRATE	4g PROTEIN
7g FAT	5.9g FIBER	17mg CHOLESTEROL

JULIENNE OF VEGETABLE AND NOODLE SOUP

4 SERVINGS

I	carrot, peeled	I
¹/₂ cup	snow peas	125 mL
I	leek, white part only	I
¹/₂ cup	white cabbage	125 mL
I	red pepper	I
6 cups	chicken stock	1.5 liters
3 oz	vermicelli noodles	90 g
I cup	bean sprouts	250 mL

Cut the carrot, snow peas, leek, cabbage and red pepper into julienne strips. Keep vegetables separate.

Bring chicken stock to a boil in a large saucepan. (Skim off any grease before adding vegetables.)

Stir ingredients into the stock in the following order: carrot, snow peas, vermicelli, leek, cabbage, bean sprouts, and red pepper. Return to a boil.

Remove immediately from heat and let stand 10 minutes, covered, before serving.

COOK'S TIP

Julienned vegetables are cut into thin, even strips about ¼ inch (.5 cm) thick. Their thin shape means they cook almost instantly, while retaining their distinct flavors.

1 SERVING		
116 CALORIES	24g CARBOHYDRATE	5g PROTEIN
0g FAT	2.2g FIBER	0mg CHOLESTEROL

MEDITERRANEAN SOUP AU PISTOU

4 SERVINGS

COOK'S TIP

The combination of basil, garlic and olive oil adds a classically Mediterranean touch to this healthy soup. Don't substitute dried basil for fresh!

6 cups	chicken stock	1.5 liters
³/4 cup	peeled diced carrots	175 mL
³/4 cup	diced celery	175 mL
³/4 cup	diced leeks	175 mL
³/4 cup	green beans cut in 1-inch (2.5-cm) pieces	175 mL
1	small onion, chopped	1
¹/4 cup	chopped fresh basil	50 mL
2	garlic cloves, finely chopped	2
1 tbsp	olive oil	15 mL
2	tomatoes, peeled, seeded and diced	2
	salt and pepper	
	grated Parmesan cheese	

In a large saucepan, simmer the chicken stock, carrots, celery, leeks, green beans and onion for about 20 minutes.

Blend together the basil, garlic and olive oil with a little of the hot vegetable broth to make a fairly smooth paste.

Stir diced tomatoes into the soup and ladle into bowls. Sprinkle Parmesan and a little of the basil mixture into each bowl, or let guests add their own garnishes to taste.

1 SERVING		
114 CALORIES	12g CARBOHYDRATE	3g PROTEIN
6g FAT	2.7g FIBER	2mg CHOLESTEROL

SPICY ORIENTAL SHRIMP SOUP

4 SERVINGS

3 cups	chicken stock	750 mL
1 cup	sliced fresh mushrooms	250 mL
10 oz	can drained sliced bamboo shoots	284 mL
5 oz	can baby clams, drained	140 g
1 cup	small peeled shrimp	250 mL
2 tbsp	cornstarch, dissolved in a little water	30 mL
1/2 tsp	crushed hot red pepper	2 mL
2 tbsp	white wine vinegar	30 mL
1	egg, beaten	1
2	green onions, chopped	2
	salt and freshly ground pepper	

Bring chicken stock to a boil in a large saucepan. Add mushrooms. Let simmer 5 minutes.

Add bamboo shoots, clams and shrimp. Stir in dissolved cornstarch. Simmer until slightly thickened.

Season with crushed hot pepper, vinegar, and salt and pepper to taste. Whisk in the beaten egg with a fork so that it forms long strands.

Sprinkle with green onions to serve.

COOK'S TIP

Do not allow the soup to boil once you have whisked in the egg; the egg should set in long tender strands, but not overcook.

1 SERVING		
131 CALORIES	8 g CARBOHYDRATE	18 g PROTEIN
3 g FAT	0.7 g FIBER	147 mg CHOLESTEROL

CONSOMMÉ WITH SPICY MEAT-STUFFED WONTONS

~

4 SERVINGS

COOK'S TIP

This soup may appear complicated, but with a food processor, it is a snap to make. Wonton wrappers can be purchased in most frozen food sections of supermarkets.

2	spicy-style raw Italian sausages, turkey or pork	2
6	large raw shrimp, peeled and deveined	6
5 oz	lean ground pork	150 g
2	green onions, chopped	2
1	garlic clove	1
1 tsp	light soy sauce	5 mL
1 tsp	dry sherry	5 mL
1 tsp	sesame oil	5 mL
1/4 tsp	ground white pepper	1 mL
20	wonton wrappers	20
4 cups	chicken stock	1 liter
2	green onions, finely chopped	2

Peel skin off sausages. Place sausage meat, shrimp and ground pork in food processor. Process to mix.

Add 2 green onions, garlic, soy sauce, sherry, sesame oil, and pepper. Process again until well combined.

Place 1 tsp (5 mL) meat mixture in center of each wonton wrapper. Baste edges with a little water and fold wrapper to make a triangle. Press to seal edges. Repeat with remaining wrappers and meat filling.

Heat chicken stock in a large saucepan and let boil 2 minutes.

Gently drop wontons into stock and let simmer 3 minutes. Serve soup sprinkled with chopped green onions.

~

1 Prepare wonton filling in the food processor.

2 Fold wonton wrappers over filling to make triangles. Seal edges well.

3 Heat the chicken stock.

4 Simmer stuffed wontons in the stock.

1 SERVING		
362 CALORIES	22g CARBOHYDRATE	28g PROTEIN
18g FAT	2.0g FIBER	137mg CHOLESTEROL

CHILLED MELON SOUP

4 SERVINGS

Chilling changes the consistency of soup. Cold soups are always better thick, but you can thin this soup with a little milk if necessary.

2	cantaloupes, halved and seeded	2
1 tbsp	chopped fresh mint	15 mL
3 tbsp	fresh lemon juice	45 mL
1/4 cup	plain low-fat yogurt	50 mL
1/4 cup	chicken stock	50 mL
	salt and freshly ground pepper	
	plain yogurt for garnish	
	grated lemon zest for garnish	

Scoop out the flesh from the cantaloupe halves and place in food processor. (You might want to reserve the cantaloupe shells to use as interesting soup bowls!)

Add mint, lemon juice, yogurt, chicken stock and seasonings to taste. Process until smooth. Cover and refrigerate until well chilled.

Serve in chilled bowls garnished with yogurt and lemon zest, if desired.

1 SERVING		
117 CALORIES	24g CARBOHYDRATE	3g PROTEIN
1 g FAT	1.9g FIBER	1 mg CHOLESTEROL

CHILLED YOGURT AND FENNEL SOUP

4 SERVINGS

4 cups	chicken stock	1 liter
¼ cup	quick-cooking rice	50 mL
2	egg yolks	2
1 cup	plain yogurt	250 mL
2 tbsp	finely chopped fresh fennel	30 mL
	salt and freshly ground pepper	

Bring chicken stock to a boil in a large saucepan. Stir in rice. Season to taste with salt and pepper. Cover and let simmer 5 minutes over low heat.

In a bowl, beat together egg yolks and yogurt until smooth. Stir in 3 tbsp (45 mL) of the hot chicken stock.

Remove stock saucepan from heat. Pour in egg yolk mixture and add fennel. Stir very well. Cover and let chill in refrigerator.

Serve in well-chilled bowls, with a little more fennel sprinkled on top.

COOK'S TIP

Always taste cold soups and adjust the seasonings after they are chilled. Chilling affects flavor.

1 SERVING		
96 CALORIES	10g CARBOHYDRATE	5g PROTEIN
4g FAT	0.3g FIBER	59mg CHOLESTEROL

GAZPACHO

4 SERVINGS

I	English cucumber, washed, seeded and coarsely chopped	I
4	garlic cloves, crushed	4
1/2 tsp	cumin seeds	2 mL
2 tbsp	red wine vinegar	30 mL
I tbsp	olive oil	15 mL
3	tomatoes, peeled and seeded	3
I	green pepper, seeded and chopped	I
4 cups	tomato juice	I liter
2 tbsp	liquid beef stock concentrate	30 mL
	freshly ground pepper	
	hot pepper sauce	
	chopped fresh parsley for garnish	

COOK'S TIP

Some people prefer this soup processed until it is very smooth. In this case, be sure to garnish it with some finely chopped fresh vegetables to provide some crunch appeal!

Place first 7 ingredients in food processor (in batches if necessary) and process until finely chopped, but not puréed.

Add tomato juice, beef stock concentrate, pepper and hot sauce. Stir to combine.

Pour into a large bowl, cover and refrigerate at least 4 hours to chill and combine flavors. Serve garnished with parsley and diced peppers or cucumber.

1 SERVING

132 CALORIES	20g CARBOHYDRATE	4g PROTEIN
4g FAT	4g FIBER	0mg CHOLESTEROL

LIGHT AND EASY MAIN DISHES

~

A few years ago, a newspaper article reported
that the average family ate the same 10 recipes
over and over throughout the year. If you are
one of those cooks, or one who makes special
meals for entertaining but falls back on the
same old standards on week nights,
this chapter is for you.

More often than not, some of the old standards
most of us make routinely are too high in fat.
Nutritionists now recommend that we keep
our fat intake to less than 30% to 35% of total
calories, which may rule out some of your
favorite recipes. Many of us are also being
advised to eat more fish and white meat,
such as chicken.

In this chapter, we have tried to address
these concerns by trimming the fat while
keeping the flavor in some old and new
favorites. The emphasis is on lower-fat
beef cuts, skinless chicken breasts and
a variety of fish and seafood.

Every recipe is quick and easy to make.
And because so many people have developed
a taste for ethnic foods such as Mexican
and Oriental, we have included
some lower-fat variations.

But one piece of advice — don't try to change
your family's diet all at once. Introduce a new
recipe every week or so, and test their reaction.
You are sure to find some recipes in this chapter
that will become new family favorites!

~

CRISPY CHICKEN CASSEROLE

4 SERVINGS

1	envelope onion soup mix	1
1½ cups	buttermilk	375 mL
1 tbsp	all-purpose flour	15 mL
2	garlic cloves, finely chopped	2
4	skinless chicken breast halves	4
2 cups	frozen mixed vegetables	500 mL
¼ cup	dry breadcrumbs	50 mL
1 tbsp	butter or margarine	15 mL
	paprika	

Preheat oven to 350°F (180°C).

In a bowl, combine onion soup mix, buttermilk, flour and garlic. Stir well.

Place chicken in a lightly greased baking pan just big enough to hold pieces in a single layer. Surround with frozen vegetables. Pour onion soup mixture over everything.

Combine crumbs and butter.

Bake chicken, covered, for 20 minutes. Remove cover. Sprinkle crumb mixture over chicken. Bake uncovered another 25 minutes, or until chicken is cooked through. (Chicken breasts on the bone require longer cooking than boneless ones.)

Sprinkle with paprika before serving. A squeeze of fresh lemon juice adds a nice flavor.

1 SERVING		
311 CALORIES	27g CARBOHYDRATE	35g PROTEIN
7g FAT	4.3g FIBER	87mg CHOLESTEROL

LEMONY BAKED CHICKEN

4 SERVINGS

2 cups	boiling water	500 mL
2	sachets of lemon tea	2
2	lemons	2
6	slices bread	6
1/3 cup	milk	75 mL
4	chicken drumsticks	4
1 tbsp	vegetable oil	15 mL
1/2 cup	white sugar	125 mL
2 tbsp	wine vinegar	30 mL
2 tbsp	light soy sauce	30 mL

Preheat oven to 400°F (200°C). Pour water over tea bags and let soak.

Grate zest of lemons. Chop lemons and reserve separately from zest.

Soak bread slices and lemon zest in milk. Break up well with a fork.

Using fingers, loosen skin from flesh of thick part of chicken legs. Stuff bread mixture under skin. Fasten closed with toothpicks. Brown legs on all sides in oil in a nonstick skillet. Remove chicken and place in baking pan.

Add sugar and vinegar to skillet. Heat over medium-high heat. Stir in tea, chopped lemons and soy sauce. Bring to a boil. Pour sauce over chicken.

Bake, uncovered, 40 minutes. Remove chicken and keep warm. Strain cooking juices into a saucepan. Reduce over medium heat 5 minutes. Serve over chicken, with mashed potatoes to soak up the sauce and a vegetable of your choice.

COOK'S TIP

Don't be put off by the lemon tea in the sauce; it's a low-calorie way to add depth of flavor and color. If you wish, add ½ cup (125mL) chopped cooked spinach to the stuffing mixture.

1 SERVING		
250 CALORIES	22g CARBOHYDRATE	18g PROTEIN
10g FAT	3.2g FIBER	50mg CHOLESTEROL

INDIAN-STYLE SIMMERED CHICKEN

4 SERVINGS

3 lbs	chicken pieces	1.3 kg
1 tbsp	vegetable oil	15 mL
28 oz	can tomatoes with herbs	796 mL
	salt and pepper	

MARINADE

2 tbsp	curry powder	30 mL
1 tbsp	ground cumin	15 mL
1 tsp	cayenne pepper	5 mL
2 tbsp	chopped fresh oregano	30 mL
1	garlic clove, chopped	1
2 tbsp	vegetable oil	30 mL

Combine all marinade ingredients in a bowl. Set aside.

Place chicken pieces in a deep plate or bowl. Coat pieces with marinade. Let marinate several hours, covered, in refrigerator.

Heat oil in a deep skillet and brown chicken pieces about 8 minutes, turning to brown all sides.

Pour off fat. Add tomatoes, cover and let simmer 20 minutes over medium heat. Season to taste before serving. Serve with rice and a green vegetable.

1 Prepare marinade.

2 Coat chicken pieces with marinade.

3 Brown chicken on all sides in hot oil.

4 Add tomatoes and let simmer.

1 SERVING

295 CALORIES	8 g CARBOHYDRATE	32 g PROTEIN
15 g FAT	1.5 g FIBER	53 mg CHOLESTEROL

CHICKEN SOUFFLÉ

4 SERVINGS

1 cup	fresh breadcrumbs	250 mL
1/2 cup	skim milk	125 mL
2 tsp	olive oil	10 mL
1/2	onion, finely chopped	1/2
1	celery stalk, finely chopped	1
1 cup	mushrooms, finely chopped	250 mL
3	eggs	3
3 cups	chopped cooked chicken (preferably white meat)	750 mL
1/2 cup	diced red pepper	125 mL
1/2 tsp	paprika	2 mL
	salt and pepper	

Preheat oven to 325°F (160°C). Grease a soufflé dish or baking pan.

Soak breadcrumbs in milk for 5 minutes.

Meanwhile, heat oil in a nonstick skillet. Cook onion, celery and mushrooms 5 minutes, or until onion is soft.

Separate egg yolks and whites. In a bowl, combine yolks, chicken, red pepper, breadcrumbs and onion mixture. Season with paprika, salt and pepper.

In a second bowl, beat egg whites until stiff. Fold them carefully into chicken mixture. Scrape mixture into prepared baking dish.

Bake 50 to 60 minutes, or until knife inserted in middle of soufflé comes out clean.

1 SERVING

351 CALORIES	26g CARBOHYDRATE	37g PROTEIN
11g FAT	1.1g FIBER	279mg CHOLESTEROL

CHICKEN WITH TOMATO COULIS

4 SERVINGS

2 cups	tomato juice	500 mL
1 tbsp	tomato paste	15 mL
1	pinch sugar	1
2 tbsp	commercial white sauce and gravy thickener	30 mL
4	skinless, boneless chicken breast halves	4
	chopped fresh parsley for garnish	

Preheat oven to 350°F (180°C).

Bring tomato juice, tomato paste and sugar to a boil in a saucepan. When the mixture starts to boil, stir in sauce thickener and remove from heat.

Place chicken pieces in a lightly greased baking pan. Bake 15 to 20 minutes, until no longer pink inside.

Place sauce on plates. Slice chicken and arrange over sauce. This dish goes well with green beans and steamed potatoes or white and wild rice.

COOK'S TIP

You can make this simple dish quite exotic by sprinkling the cooked chicken with chopped fresh basil and some orange zest. Sprinkle with freshly grated Parmesan.

1 SERVING

175 CALORIES	9g CARBOHYDRATE	28g PROTEIN
3g FAT	1.1g FIBER	73mg CHOLESTEROL

LEAN TURKEY CHOP SUEY

4 SERVINGS

³/₄ lb	skinless, boneless turkey breast meat	350 g
2 tbsp	vegetable oil	30 mL
I cup	cauliflower, in small florets	250 mL
I cup	broccoli, in small florets	250 mL
2	garlic cloves, finely chopped	2
3	celery stalks, sliced	3
I	red pepper, sliced	I
I	envelope onion soup mix	I
I cup	water	250 mL
I¹/₂ lbs	bean sprouts	675 g
I	can miniature corn, halved	I
I cup	frozen peas	250 mL
I tbsp	cornstarch, dissolved in a little water	15 mL

Slice turkey thinly and stir-fry in wok in 1 tbsp oil until rosy tint is gone.

Blanch cauliflower and broccoli 1 minute in boiling water. Drain and reserve.

Heat remaining oil in wok and stir-fry garlic, celery and red pepper 2 to 3 minutes. Stir in onion soup mix and water. Cook 2 to 3 minutes.

Add bean sprouts, corn, peas, cauliflower and broccoli. Cook until vegetables are tender-crisp. Add reserved turkey and stir in cornstarch to thicken.

COOK'S TIP

This is a good basic recipe in which you can change the ingredients for those you have on hand. Make a vegetarian version with sliced mushrooms and cubed tofu.

1 SERVING

344 CALORIES	37g CARBOHYDRATE	31g PROTEIN
8g FAT	7.5g FIBER	58 mg CHOLESTEROL

TURKEY BREAST WITH BASIL SAUCE

~

4 SERVINGS

COOK'S TIP

Basil tends to turn black after it is chopped if left to stand too long. For best results, chop it just before using.

1¼ lbs	skinless, boneless turkey breast	575 g
2 tbsp	vegetable oil	30 mL
2 tbsp	chopped dry French shallots	30 mL
1 tsp	chopped garlic	5 mL
½ cup	dry white wine (optional)	125 mL
1 cup	tomatoes, crushed	250 mL
1 cup	canned brown sauce	250 mL
¼ cup	chopped fresh basil	50 mL
	salt and pepper	

Cut turkey breast crosswise in 4 equal pieces. Heat oil in a large skillet and brown turkey pieces 2 minutes on each side.

Add shallots and cook until slightly softened. Add garlic. Stir in white wine and cook 1 to 2 minutes. Add tomatoes and brown sauce. Let simmer 12 to 15 minutes over medium heat.

Stir in basil and season to taste before serving. Serve with steamed potatoes to soak up the delicious sauce.

~

1 SERVING		
305 CALORIES	7g CARBOHYDRATE	49g PROTEIN
9g FAT	0.7g FIBER	102mg CHOLESTEROL

QUICK GRILLED TURKEY WITH PASTA

~

2 SERVINGS

¹/₂ lb	fresh or dried pasta	225 g
2	turkey tournedos	2
¹/₂ cup	sliced fresh mushrooms	125 mL
2 tsp	olive oil	10 ml
I	garlic clove, crushed	I
I cup	homemade or purchased plain spaghetti sauce	250 mL
	chopped fresh basil	
	freshly ground pepper	
	grated Parmesan cheese	

Cook pasta according to package directions.

Cook the turkey in a grill pan or a nonstick skillet about 10 to 12 minutes, or until both sides are nicely browned.

Meanwhile, heat oil in a second nonstick skillet. Add mushrooms and cook, stirring, until lightly browned. Add garlic, basil and pepper. Stir in spaghetti sauce and heat over low heat.

When pasta is cooked to taste, drain and stir in ¾ of mushroom sauce. Top each serving with a little more sauce and Parmesan. Serve with grilled turkey.

1 SERVING		
887 CALORIES	93g CARBOHYDRATE	50g PROTEIN
35g FAT	3.8g FIBER	256 mg CHOLESTEROL

TURKEY IN RED WINE

4 SERVINGS

1 tbsp	vegetable oil	15 mL
1¹/₂ lbs	boneless turkey breast, thinly sliced	675 g
2	slices bacon, finely chopped	2
1	onion, chopped	1
1	garlic clove, chopped	1
3 tbsp	all-purpose flour	45 mL
1 cup	dry red wine	250 mL
1 cup	chicken stock	250 mL
1 tbsp	tomato paste	15 mL
1 tbsp	chopped fresh basil	15 mL
1	bay leaf	1
	salt and pepper	

Preheat oven to 350°F (180°C). Heat oil in a nonstick skillet and cook turkey over medium-high heat until meat loses its pink color.

Remove turkey from skillet. Add bacon, onion and garlic. Cook 3 minutes.

Sprinkle in flour and stir. Add wine, chicken stock, tomato paste, basil, bay leaf, salt and pepper.

Mix well and stir in turkey. Pour mixture into a baking dish. Bake, covered, 25 minutes. Serve with vegetables of your choice.

1 SERVING		
277 CALORIES	7g CARBOHYDRATE	42g PROTEIN
9g FAT	0.6g FIBER	115mg CHOLESTEROL

TURKEY AND MUSHROOM BURGERS

4 SERVINGS

¹/₂ lb	fresh mushrooms	225 g
I	onion, coarsely chopped	I
¹/₂ tsp	pepper	2 mL
2 tbsp	vegetable oil	30 mL
I¹/₄ lbs	ground turkey	575 g
I tbsp	chicken stock or water	15 mL
¹/₂ cup	dry breadcrumbs	125 mL

SALSA

¹/₂	red bell pepper, diced	¹/₂
¹/₂	yellow bell pepper, diced	¹/₂
2	green onions, chopped	2
2 tsp	vegetable oil	10 mL

Process mushrooms and onion in food processor until chopped but not smooth. Add pepper.

Heat 1 tbsp (15 mL) oil in a skillet. Add mushrooms and cook 3 to 4 minutes. Remove from heat and strain off cooking liquid well (reserve liquid).

In a bowl, combine turkey, stock and breadcrumbs. Shape into 8 flat patties. Divide mushroom mixture among 4 patties and top with remaining patties. Reshape patties to enclose mushroom mixture well.

Cook burgers in remaining oil about 5 minutes on each side. Serve on toasted buns with salsa.

To make the salsa, cook peppers and onions rapidly in oil; they should remain crisp. Stir in reserved mushroom liquid and cook over high heat until liquid is reduced. Serve over cooked burgers.

~

	1 SERVING	
347 CALORIES	14g CARBOHYDRATE	39g PROTEIN
15g FAT	1.7g FIBER	100mg CHOLESTEROL

BRAISED
TOP ROUND OF BEEF

4 SERVINGS

1	carrot	1
1/2	onion	1/2
1	celery stalk	1
1	leek	1
1	bay leaf	1
1 tsp	dried thyme	5 mL
2	parsley sprigs	2
1 tsp	cracked peppercorns	5 mL
2 tbsp	vegetable oil	30 mL
1½ lbs	lean top round roast, fat trimmed	675 g
3 cups	beef stock	750 mL

COOK'S TIP

Braising is an excellent way to prepare the tougher cuts of meat, as the slow cooking tenderizes them. As a bonus, tough cuts are generally leaner.

Chop vegetables coarsely. Tie bay leaf, thyme, peppercorns and parsley into a piece of cheesecloth to make a bouquet garni.

In a large heavy casserole, heat oil over high heat and brown meat on all sides. Remove meat.

Add vegetables to pan and cook over high heat 2 to 3 minutes. Return meat to pan.

Add beef stock and bouquet garni. Turn down heat to low. Cover and cook 1½ hours.

When meat is tender, strain cooking juices into a gravy boat. Serve meat surrounded with steamed vegetables.

~

1 SERVING		
324 CALORIES	6g CARBOHYDRATE	39g PROTEIN
16g FAT	1.2g FIBER	85mg CHOLESTEROL

TERIYAKI FLANK STEAK

4 SERVINGS

COOK'S TIP

If you like your steak a bit spicier, add some finely chopped fresh ginger and crushed hot red pepper flakes to the marinade.

¹/₃ cup	light soy sauce	75 mL
²/₃ cup	sake (rice wine) or dry sherry	150 mL
¹/₃ cup	rice vinegar	75 mL
1 tbsp	sesame oil	15 mL
2	garlic cloves, finely chopped	2
1½ lbs	flank steak	675 g
1 tbsp	cornstarch, dissolved in a little water	15 mL
	freshly ground pepper	

In a bowl, combine soy sauce, sake, rice vinegar, sesame oil, garlic and pepper.

Marinate steak in mixture 4 to 6 hours, covered, in refrigerator. Drain steak and reserve marinade.

Cook steak 6 to 9 minutes on each side in a grill pan or heavy skillet.

Heat marinade in a saucepan over low heat. Stir in cornstarch to thicken.

To serve, cut steak thinly across the grain. Serve with heated teriyaki sauce and vegetables of your choice.

1 SERVING		
289 CALORIES	7g CARBOHYDRATE	36g PROTEIN
13g FAT	0g FIBER	56mg CHOLESTEROL

EASY BEEF BURRITOS

4 SERVINGS

1 lb	beef sirloin or top round	450 g
2 tbsp	fresh lime juice	30 mL
³/4 cup	Italian-style bottled salad dressing	175 mL
4	flour or corn tortillas	4
1	bunch watercress	1
2	avocados, peeled, pitted and sliced	2
¹/2 cup	sour cream or plain yogurt	125 mL
	freshly ground pepper	

Place the meat in a shallow dish. Sprinkle with lime juice and salad dressing. Cover and refrigerate 1 to 2 hours, turning meat at least once.

Wrap tortillas in aluminum foil and heat for a few minutes in preheated oven or toaster oven.

Cook steak on preheated grill or in a nonstick pan until cooked to desired degree of doneness, turning once.

Cut steak into thin strips on the diagonal. Season to taste with pepper and salt, if desired.

Place watercress on plates with steak strips and avocado slices on top. Serve with heated tortillas for wrapping the beef and salad, and with sour cream or yogurt.

~

COOK'S TIP

Commercial liquid-style salad dressings make easy meat marinades. You can choose oil-free versions, or make your own with vinegar, oil and seasonings of your choice.

1 SERVING		
705 CALORIES	13 g CARBOHYDRATE	35 g PROTEIN
57 g FAT	4.1 g FIBER	106 mg CHOLESTEROL

MEXICAN STIR-FRY TACOS

~

4 SERVINGS

4	tortillas	4
2 tbsp	vegetable oil	30 mL
1 tsp	garlic salt	5 mL
1 tsp	oregano	5 mL
1	sweet red pepper, cut in strips	1
1	medium onion, sliced	1
1	hot pepper, finely chopped	1
1 lb	lean flank steak, cut in thin strips	450 g
	hot sauce or Tabasco sauce	

Drape tortillas over 4 upside-down ovenproof bowls. Heat in preheated 350°F (180°C) oven 5 to 10 minutes. Tortillas should be crisp, but not browned.

Meanwhile, heat oil in a nonstick skillet. Add garlic salt, oregano, sliced pepper, onion, and chopped hot pepper. Cook, stirring, over medium-high heat until onion is slightly soft.

Add beef strips and cook to desired degree of doneness. Remove from heat.

Stuff mixture into tortilla shells. Serve with guacamole.

~

GUACAMOLE

~

2	avocados, peeled and mashed	2
1 tbsp	grated onion	15 mL
1	garlic clove, crushed (optional)	1
	juice of 1/2 lemon	
	hot sauce (optional)	

Combine all ingredients. Serve with tortilla chips.

~

1 SERVING (TACOS)		
293 CALORIES	17g CARBOHYDRATE	27g PROTEIN
13g FAT	1.7g FIBER	37mg CHOLESTEROL

1 SERVING (GUACAMOLE)		
60 CALORIES	4g CARBOHYDRATE	1g PROTEIN
8g FAT	1.3g FIBER	0mg CHOLESTEROL

BEEF IN RED WINE

4 SERVINGS

COOK'S TIP

This dish is delicious served with noodles or mashed potatoes, and with a steamed vegetable.

1¼ lbs	beef sirloin, cut in strips	575 g
¼ cup	all-purpose flour	50 mL
3 tbsp	butter, margarine or vegetable oil	45 mL
1 cup	sliced fresh mushrooms	250 mL
½ cup	dry red wine	125 mL
1	envelope onion soup mix	1
1 cup	water	250 mL
	pepper	

Toss beef strips in flour. Shake off excess.

Melt 2 tbsp (30 mL) butter in a nonstick skillet. Cook beef over medium-high heat, stirring frequently to brown all sides. Remove meat from pan.

In the same skillet, melt remaining butter and cook mushrooms 2 minutes over medium heat.

Add red wine and bring to a boil. Reduce heat and let simmer 1 minute. Stir in soup mix and water. Season with pepper. Let simmer 10 minutes.

Return beef to pan to reheat.

1 SERVING		
415 CALORIES	14g CARBOHYDRATE	47g PROTEIN
19g FAT	2.2g FIBER	133mg CHOLESTEROL

ORIENTAL BEEF STIR-FRY

4 SERVINGS

I tbsp	dry sherry	15 mL
I tbsp	light soy sauce	15 mL
I tbsp	sesame oil	15 mL
I tbsp	cornstarch	15 mL
I lb	beef sirloin tip	450 g
I tbsp	vegetable oil	15 mL
4	celery stalks, cut in small sticks	4
I	carrot, sliced diagonally	I
I tbsp	cornstarch	15 mL
¼ cup	water	50 mL
2 tbsp	beef stock	30 mL
	pepper	

In a bowl, combine sherry, soy sauce, sesame oil, 1 tbsp (15 mL) cornstarch and pepper. Add beef strips and let marinate 10 minutes.

Heat 2 tsp (10 mL) oil in a nonstick skillet or wok over high heat. Drain beef (reserving marinade) and stir-fry 2 minutes in oil. Remove beef and set aside. Heat remaining oil in the same pan. Add celery and carrot and stir-fry 1 minute. Add vegetables to beef.

Stir 1 tbsp (15 mL) cornstarch into water. Add beef stock and leftover marinade from beef. Pour mixture into pan and bring to a boil until thickened. Stir in meat and vegetables to reheat. Serve over rice.

1 SERVING		
278 CALORIES	8g CARBOHYDRATE	30g PROTEIN
14g FAT	1.2g FIBER	65mg CHOLESTEROL

HEARTY IRISH SOUP

4 SERVINGS

1 tbsp	vegetable oil	15 mL
1/2 lb	flank steak, thinly sliced	225 g
8 cups	beef stock	2 liters
1/4 cup	green or brown lentils	50 mL
1/4 cup	pearl barley	50 mL
2 cups	chopped cabbage	500 mL
2	onions, chopped	2
2	carrots, peeled and sliced	2
2	celery stalks, chopped	2
1	small rutabaga, peeled and diced	1
1	bay leaf	1
1/2 tsp	black pepper	2 mL
2 tbsp	chopped fresh parsley	30 mL
1 tsp	dried thyme	5 mL

Heat oil in a large saucepan. Add beef and cook until it loses its rosy color.

Add stock and bring to a boil.

Add remaining ingredients, reduce heat, and let simmer, covered, about 40 minutes, or until vegetables are tender. Adjust seasoning to taste before serving.

NUTRITION TIP

This hearty soup is low in fat and high in fiber, thanks to the lentils, barley and vegetables. Unlike other dried legumes, lentils do not require soaking or long cooking.

1 SERVING		
235 CALORIES	27g CARBOHYDRATE	16g PROTEIN
7g FAT	7.8g FIBER	19mg CHOLESTEROL

BEEF BRAISED WITH SPANISH ONIONS

4 SERVINGS

14 oz	can tomatoes, with juice	398 mL
2 cups	Spanish onions, sliced	500 mL
2	garlic cloves, finely chopped	2
1³/₄ lbs	lean boneless rolled roast	800 g
¹/₄ cup	water	50 mL
2	potatoes, with skins, scrubbed and sliced	2
1 tbsp	cornstarch dissolved in a little water	15 mL
	freshly ground pepper	

Preheat oven to 325°F (160°C).

Place tomatoes and liquid in an ovenproof casserole with lid. Spread with ½ the onions and garlic. Arrange roast on vegetables. Top with remaining onions and garlic. Season with pepper and pour in water; cover.

Roast in oven 2 ½ to 3 hours, or until meat is tender. Add potato slices 15 minutes before end of cooking time.

Place meat and vegetables on serving platter. Cover with foil and let stand 10 minutes to make slicing easier.

Add enough water to cooking juices to make 1 cup (250 mL). Stir in dissolved cornstarch and cook over medium heat 2 to 3 minutes. Serve meat thinly sliced with sauce.

COOK'S TIP

Feel free to add other vegetables such as sliced carrots or turnips with the tomatoes.

LIGHT & EASY MAIN DISHES

1 SERVING		
452 CALORIES	31g CARBOHYDRATE	55g PROTEIN
12g FAT	3.7g FIBER	115mg CHOLESTEROL

BEEF STIR-FRY
WITH YELLOW RICE

~

6 SERVINGS

1½ lbs	flank steak, thinly sliced	675 g
¼ cup	teriyaki sauce	50 mL
¼ cup	light soy sauce	50 mL
1 tbsp	liquid vegetable stock concentrate	15 mL
1 tbsp	sesame oil	15 mL
1½ cups	raw rice	375 mL
4 cups	boiling water	1 liter
1	bay leaf	1
½ tsp	ground turmeric	2 mL
1 tsp	sesame oil	5 mL
1	green bell pepper, cubed	1
1	red bell pepper, cubed	1
1 cup	snow peas, sliced diagonally	250 mL
1½ cups	peeled and cubed winter squash or pumpkin	375 mL
1 cup	water	250 mL
1 tsp	cornstarch, dissolved in a little water	5 mL

Marinate sliced beef in a mixture of teriyaki and soy sauces, and vegetable stock concentrate for 1 hour in refrigerator.

In a large saucepan, heat 1 tbsp (15 mL) sesame oil over medium heat. Add rice and stir well to coat rice grains. Add boiling water, bay leaf and turmeric.

Bring rice to a boil. Cover and let simmer over low heat about 20 minutes, or until rice is cooked. Remove bay leaf and keep rice warm.

Meanwhile, heat 1 tsp (5 mL) oil in nonstick wok or skillet. Add peppers, snow peas and squash. Stir-fry 2 minutes over medium-high heat.

Remove meat from marinade, draining well. Add to vegetables. Stir-fry 2 minutes. Pour mixture over rice on a serving plate.

Put marinade in wok and heat over high heat. Add water. Reduce heat to low and stir in dissolved cornstarch. Pour sauce over meat.

~

1 SERVING

378 CALORIES	41g CARBOHYDRATE	31g PROTEIN
10g FAT	3.7g FIBER	38mg CHOLESTEROL

LIGHT BEEF AND VEGETABLE CHILI

~

6 SERVINGS

COOK'S TIP

Substitute ground turkey for the beef, and experiment with different kinds of legumes – chickpeas, white kidney beans, or lentils.

I lb	lean ground beef	450 g
2	medium onions, chopped	2
I	garlic clove, chopped	I
I cup	chopped carrots	250 mL
I cup	chopped celery	250 mL
I cup	chopped green pepper	250 mL
28 oz	can whole tomatoes, crushed	796 mL
19 oz	can kidney beans, rinsed and drained	540 mL
I tbsp	crushed chili pepper	15 mL
I tbsp	lemon juice	15 mL
I tsp	cumin	5 mL
3 tbsp	chopped fresh parsley	45 mL
I cup	chicken stock or water	250 mL

Put ground beef in a large nonstick skillet and cook, stirring with a fork, over medium-high heat 5 minutes. Pour off all excess fat.

Stir in onions, garlic, carrots, celery and green pepper. Cook 4 to 5 minutes.

Add tomatoes, beans, chili, lemon juice, cumin and parsley. Cover and let simmer 8 to 10 minutes.

Add stock and cook until thickened to desired consistency.

~

1 SERVING		
289 CALORIES	29g CARBOHYDRATE	23g PROTEIN
9g FAT	5.1g FIBER	38mg CHOLESTEROL

HEALTHY MEATLOAF

4 SERVINGS

³/₄ cup	diced wholewheat bread	175 mL
¹/₂ cup	skim milk	125 mL
1 lb	lean ground beef or pork	450 g
¹/₂ cup	grated carrots	125 mL
¹/₄ cup	grated onion	50 mL
¹/₄ cup	finely chopped fresh parsley	50 mL
1	egg	1
	dried thyme	
	salt and freshly ground pepper	

Preheat the oven to 350°F (180°C).

In a bowl, soak the diced bread in milk for 5 to 10 minutes.

Add all remaining ingredients and mix well.

Pour into a lightly greased loaf pan. Bake 45 to 50 minutes. Serve with tomato sauce.

QUICK TOMATO SAUCE

1 cup	tomato juice	250 mL
¹/₂ tsp	chopped garlic	2 mL
1 tbsp	chopped fresh parsley	15 mL
1 tsp	dried basil	5 mL
2 tbsp	light cream cheese	30 mL

Cook tomato juice with garlic and herbs about 10 minutes over medium heat until slightly thickened. Stir in light cream cheese just before serving.

NUTRITION TIP

This meatloaf is a tasty way to add fiber to your diet. You could stir in some wheat germ or bran cereal as well, or increase the amount of vegetables.

1 SERVING		
279 CALORIES	10g CARBOHYDRATE	26g PROTEIN
15g FAT	1.6g FIBER	130mg CHOLESTEROL

ORANGE-SCENTED VEAL STIR-FRY

~

4 SERVINGS

1/3 cup	unsweetened orange juice	75 mL
2 tbsp	red wine vinegar	30 mL
2 tsp	grated orange zest	10 mL
1/4 cup	chicken stock	50 mL
1 tsp	cumin	5 mL
2 tsp	cornstarch	10 mL
2 tbsp	vegetable oil	30 mL
3/4 lb	boneless veal, cut in thin strips	350 g
2	zucchini, sliced	2
1	red or green bell pepper, sliced	1
1 1/2 tsp	grated fresh ginger	7 mL
	salt and freshly ground pepper	

COOK'S TIP

This easy stir-fry is elegant enough for company. Stir in chopped cashews and sprinkle with sesame seeds for added flavor.

Heat orange juice in a wok over high heat. When slightly reduced, add vinegar and orange zest.

Add chicken stock and cumin. Stir in cornstarch dissolved in a little cold water. Cook over medium heat until sauce is thickened and glossy. Remove sauce and set aside.

Wipe out wok and add oil; heat over high heat. Add veal and cook over high heat 2 minutes, stirring. Add zucchini, red pepper and ginger. Cook another 2 minutes, stirring constantly. Cook until veal loses any pink color. Stir in sauce to reheat. Season to taste. Serve with rice.

~

1 SERVING		
207 CALORIES	*7g CARBOHYDRATE*	*20g PROTEIN*
11g FAT	*1.6g FIBER*	*64mg CHOLESTEROL*

PORK TOURNEDOS WITH SAGE

~

4 SERVINGS

1 tbsp	vegetable oil	15 mL
4	pork tournedos, 5 oz (150 g) each	4
2	green onions, chopped	2
1/2 cup	dry white wine	125 mL
1 cup	chicken stock	250 mL
1 tbsp	Dijon mustard	15 mL
2 tbsp	chopped fresh sage	30 mL
1 tbsp	cornstarch, dissolved in a little water	15 mL
2 tbsp	sour cream	30 mL

Heat oil in a nonstick skillet over medium-high heat. Cook pork about 12 minutes, turning from time to time, until done to taste.

Remove pork and keep warm. Pour off excess fat from pan. Add onions and cook until soft. Stir in white wine.

Add chicken stock, mustard and sage. Stir in dissolved cornstarch. Stir in sour cream just before serving. Serve sauce over pork, with vegetables of your choice.

~

1 SERVING		
239 CALORIES	3g CARBOHYDRATE	23g PROTEIN
15g FAT	0.1g FIBER	58mg CHOLESTEROL

LIGHT & EASY MAIN DISHES

PORK CHOPS
WITH SWEET AND SOUR SAUCE
~

4 SERVINGS

COOK'S TIP

Trim all visible fat from pork chops and slash edges of chops to keep them from curling.

4	pork chops, about 4 oz (110 g) each	4
1 tbsp	olive oil	15 mL
1	red onion, chopped	1
12	mushrooms, quartered	12
1	green pepper, diced	1
19 oz	can diced tomatoes, drained	540 mL
1 tbsp	Worcestershire sauce	15 mL
2 tbsp	wine vinegar	30 mL
1/2 cup	tomato sauce	125 mL
1 tsp	hot pepper sauce	5 mL
2 tbsp	honey	30 mL
1/2 cup	vegetable or chicken stock	125 mL
1/4 tsp	dried thyme	1 mL
1 tsp	dried basil	5 mL

Preheat oven to 350°F (180°C).

In a nonstick skillet, brown chops on both sides in olive oil. Arrange chops in single layer in a baking dish.

Add onion, mushrooms and green pepper to skillet. Cook over medium-high heat 5 minutes. Pour over chops.

Put remaining ingredients in the skillet. Bring to a boil and pour over meat. Bake 1 hour, basting chops from time to time.

Serve with rice or pan-fried or mashed potatoes.

~

1 SERVING		
279 CALORIES	26g CARBOHYDRATE	19g PROTEIN
11g FAT	3.3g FIBER	47mg CHOLESTEROL

PORK FILET WITH RED PEPPER SAUCE

4 SERVINGS

1	red pepper, seeded	1
1	hot red pepper, seeded	1
3 tbsp	vegetable oil	45 mL
2 tbsp	lemon juice	30 mL
2	pork filets, ¾ lb (350 g) each	2
	freshly ground pepper	

In food processor, combine red pepper, hot red pepper, oil, lemon juice and pepper until smooth.

Pour pepper mixture into a shallow dish. Arrange filets in sauce and let marinate 3 hours in refrigerator.

Preheat oven to 350°F (180°C). Remove filets from marinade and brown them on both sides in a nonstick pan over medium-high heat, using a little oil if necessary. Place filets in a pan and finish cooking in the oven to taste.

Meanwhile, strain pepper marinade. Discard solids. Heat liquid over low heat until hot. Slice filets and serve with pepper sauce.

1 SERVING		
279 CALORIES	3g CARBOHYDRATE	24g PROTEIN
19g FAT	0.4g FIBER	63mg CHOLESTEROL

HAM WITH SPICY PEAR CHUTNEY

4 SERVINGS

COOK'S TIP

You can substitute pears packed in light syrup for the fresh pears. The chutney can be made ahead, and stored in clean, sealed jars in the refrigerator. A quick way to turn leftover baked ham into something special!

4	slices baked or broiled ham	4
5	fresh pears, peeled and cored	5
1/2 tsp	grated fresh ginger	2 mL
2 tbsp	molasses	30 mL
2/3 cup	white vinegar	150 mL
2	onions, finely chopped	2
1	garlic clove, finely chopped	1
1/2 tsp	chopped hot pepper or 1 pinch dried hot pepper	2 mL
8	juniper berries, crushed	8
1/2 tsp	ground cinnamon	2 mL
1/4 tsp	ground cloves	1 mL

In a food processor, chop 3 pears with the ginger and molasses. Pour into a saucepan and add vinegar, onions, garlic and spices.

Dice remaining 2 pears and add to mixture. Bring to a boil. Simmer 45 minutes over low heat.

Let cool before serving with cold baked ham or broiled ham slices. (Cook ham slices 5 to 10 minutes per side under preheated broiler.)

Leftover chutney will keep well refrigerated in a covered jar.

1 SERVING		
324 CALORIES	33g CARBOHYDRATE	30g PROTEIN
8g FAT	4.4g FIBER	71mg CHOLESTEROL

GLAZED SMOKED PORK SHOULDER

4 SERVINGS

1 tbsp	olive oil	15 mL
1	carrot, sliced	1
1	celery stalk, sliced	1
1/4 tsp	dried rosemary	1 mL
1	sprig fresh thyme	1
1	bay leaf	1
1/3 cup	dry white wine	75 mL
1/3 cup	unsweetened apple juice	75 mL
1/2 cup	chicken stock	125 mL
4	slices smoked pork shoulder, about 4 oz (110 g) each	4

Heat oil in a saucepan. Add carrot and celery and cook until softened, along with rosemary, thyme and bay leaf.

Add white wine, apple juice and chicken stock. Cook 5 minutes over low heat.

Meanwhile, grill smoked pork slices in a hot pan or under broiler until lightly browned.

Arrange meat in a single layer in a baking dish. Pour sauce over. Bake 5 minutes at 350°F (180°C). Serve remaining sauce over smoked pork, with vegetables of your choice.

COOK'S TIP

Smoked pork shoulder is leaner than ham. You can substitute ham steaks if you wish. If you grill the meat under the broiler, add some slices of sweet peppers and zucchini brushed lightly with oil to the broiler pan... delicious!

1 SERVING		
153 CALORIES	6g CARBOHYDRATE	18g PROTEIN
7g FAT	0.9g FIBER	49mg CHOLESTEROL

LAMB KEBABS

4 SERVINGS

1 lb	boneless lamb, in large cubes	450 g
1/4 cup	Dijon mustard	50 mL
2 tbsp	fresh lemon juice	30 mL
2 tbsp	vegetable oil	30 mL
1 tbsp	chopped fresh basil	15 mL
1/2 tsp	freshly ground pepper	2 mL
1	zucchini	1
2	thick slices bread	2
1/2 cup	dry breadcrumbs	125 mL

Toss together lamb cubes in a bowl with mustard, lemon juice, oil, basil and pepper. Let marinate a few hours or overnight in refrigerator.

Cut zucchini in 4 lengthwise, then in chunks crosswise. Cut bread in large cubes about same size as lamb.

Thread lamb, zucchini and bread cubes onto skewers. Roll in breadcrumbs.

Preheat oven to 400°F (200°C). Place brochettes on a broiler pan. Cook about 20 to 25 minutes, depending on degree of doneness you like. Serve with noodles and a salad.

~

1 Marinate lamb cubes with mustard, lemon juice, oil, basil and pepper.

2 Thread lamb on skewers alternating with bread cubes and zucchini.

3 Roll in breadcrumbs.

1 SERVING		
339 CALORIES	24g CARBOHYDRATE	27g PROTEIN
15g FAT	1.5g FIBER	75mg CHOLESTEROL

HEALTHY LAMB BURGERS

~

4 TO 6 SERVINGS

1 lb	lean ground lamb	450 g
3/4 cup	crumbled tofu	175 mL
2	green onions, chopped	2
1	garlic clove, finely chopped	1
1/4 cup	wheat germ	50 mL
1/2 tsp	curry powder	2 mL
1	pinch freshly ground pepper	1
	vegetable oil	

In a bowl, combine lamb and crumbled tofu with a fork.

Add remaining ingredients except oil. Mix well and shape into 4 to 6 patties.

In a skillet, cook patties in oil over medium-high heat until done as desired. Serve on toasted buns.

~

1 SERVING		
129 CALORIES	3g CARBOHYDRATE	18g PROTEIN
5g FAT	0.9g FIBER	49mg CHOLESTEROL

CRISPY LAMB CHOPS

4 SERVINGS

¹/₂ cup	cornflake cereal	125 mL
I	slice wholewheat bread	I
I	garlic clove, finely chopped	I
I tbsp	chopped parsley	15 mL
¹/₄ cup	Parmesan cheese	50 mL
8	loin lamb chops	8
2 tbsp	Dijon mustard	30 mL
2 tbsp	vegetable oil	30 mL
	pepper	

In food processor, combine cornflakes, bread, garlic, parsley and Parmesan. Set aside.

Pepper lamb chops, and coat with mustard. Coat well in breadcrumbs.

Preheat oven to 325°F (160°C). Heat oil in an ovenproof skillet. Brown chops 5 minutes on each side. Finish cooking in oven 10 minutes.

COOK'S TIP

Don't be put off by the amount of mustard in this recipe. It actually brings out the sweet taste of the lamb.

1 SERVING		
314 CALORIES	7g CARBOHYDRATE	31g PROTEIN
18g FAT	0.7g FIBER	92mg CHOLESTEROL

LEMONY SALMON STEAKS

4 SERVINGS

2 tbsp	vegetable oil	30 mL
4	salmon steaks, 5 oz (150 g) each	4
I tbsp	chopped dry French shallots	15 mL
¼ cup	dry white wine	50 mL
¼ cup	fresh lemon juice	50 mL
2 tbsp	chopped fresh coriander (optional)	30 mL
½ cup	plain low-fat yogurt	125 mL

Heat oil in a nonstick skillet. Cook salmon steaks about 10 minutes, turning to brown both sides. Remove and keep hot.

Add shallots to same pan and cook 1 minute. Stir in wine, then lemon juice and coriander. Cook until liquid is reduced by ⅓.

Stir in yogurt and heat through. Serve with salmon steaks, and vegetables.

1 Cook salmon steaks.

2 In same pan, cook shallots.

3 Stir in white wine.

4 Add lemon juice, coriander and yogurt.

1 SERVING

258 CALORIES	3g CARBOHYDRATE	30g PROTEIN
14g FAT	0g FIBER	79mg CHOLESTEROL

SALMON WITH CUCUMBER-POTATO PURÉE
~

2 SERVINGS

COOK'S TIP

For a special touch, serve these salmon filets in crisp filo shells (as shown). Simply drape squares of filo pastry in 2 small pie plates. Lay a cooked salmon filet in each. Bake in 300°F (150°C) oven 1 or 2 minutes.

2	salmon filets, 4 oz (110 g) each	2
	flour	
	vegetable oil	

PURÉE

2 cups	vegetable stock	500 mL
2	cucumbers, peeled, seeded and coarsely chopped	2
1	medium potato, peeled and coarsely chopped	1
1/3 cup	skim milk	75 mL
2 tbsp	grated Parmesan cheese	30 mL

To make the purée, cook cucumbers and potatoes in vegetable stock until liquid has completely evaporated. Mash vegetables and stir in milk and Parmesan. Keep warm.

Dip salmon pieces in flour and shake off excess. Heat oil in skillet over medium heat. Add salmon and cook on both sides until flesh flakes with a fork. Remove from pan and drain on paper towels. Serve with purée.

~

1 SERVING		
404 CALORIES	28g CARBOHYDRATE	28g PROTEIN
20g FAT	3.4g FIBER	61mg CHOLESTEROL

PORTUGUESE-STYLE COD

4 SERVINGS

1 tbsp	vegetable oil	15 mL
1	onion, sliced	1
1	red pepper, cut in strips	1
1	garlic clove, chopped	1
1	bay leaf	1
3	fresh tomatoes, chopped	3
1/2 cup	dry white wine	125 mL
4	cod filets, about 7 oz (200 g) each	4
	salt and pepper	

Heat oil in a large nonstick skillet over medium heat. Add onion, red pepper and garlic and cook until soft.

Add bay leaf and tomatoes. Season to taste and let simmer 5 minutes.

Stir in white wine. Arrange cod filets in a single layer on top of sauce. Cover and let simmer over very low heat 10 minutes, or until fish flakes easily with a fork. Serve with rice or pasta.

COOK'S TIP

Substitute any white fish, and use chopped canned tomatoes if you wish. If you decide to leave out the wine, add enough tomato juice to make the sauce fairly liquid, so the fish poaches.

1 SERVING		
257 CALORIES	7g CARBOHYDRATE	37g PROTEIN
9g FAT	1.7g FIBER	86mg CHOLESTEROL

TROUT IN RED WINE

4 SERVINGS

<table>
<tr><td>4</td><td>trout, 7 oz (200 g) each, cleaned</td><td>4</td></tr>
<tr><td>1 tbsp</td><td>olive oil</td><td>15 mL</td></tr>
<tr><td>1</td><td>carrot, coarsely chopped</td><td>1</td></tr>
<tr><td>1/2</td><td>celery stalk, coarsely chopped</td><td>1/2</td></tr>
<tr><td>1</td><td>dry French shallot, chopped</td><td>1</td></tr>
<tr><td>1 tsp</td><td>dried thyme</td><td>5 mL</td></tr>
<tr><td>1</td><td>bay leaf</td><td>1</td></tr>
<tr><td>1 1/4 cups</td><td>dry red wine</td><td>300 mL</td></tr>
<tr><td>1/2 cup</td><td>vegetable or fish stock</td><td>125 mL</td></tr>
<tr><td>1/2 tsp</td><td>cornstarch, dissolved in a little water</td><td>2 mL</td></tr>
</table>

COOK'S TIP

A fresh fish feels firm and elastic and has no fishy odor. The eyes should be bright and not sunken. Remove heads before cooking if you prefer.

Preheat oven to 400°F (200°C). Rinse trout and dry well with paper towels. Arrange in a greased baking dish. Bake 10 minutes.

Meanwhile, heat oil in a saucepan. Add carrot, celery, shallot, thyme and bay leaf. Cook over low heat 5 minutes.

Stir in red wine and stock. Pour mixture over trout. Return to oven for 5 minutes.

Pour cooking liquid and vegetables into saucepan. Cook over high heat to reduce by ½. Remove bay leaf and process until smooth in blender or food processor. Strain, reheat, and thicken with cornstarch mixture. Pour over fish to serve.

1 SERVING		
163 CALORIES	4g CARBOHYDRATE	21g PROTEIN
7g FAT	0.8g FIBER	57mg CHOLESTEROL

PERCH FILETS WITH CORN AND TOMATO

4 SERVINGS

4	perch filets, about 7 oz (200 g) each	4
1 tbsp	vegetable oil	15 mL
2 tbsp	lemon juice	30 mL
	all-purpose flour	
	salt and pepper	

Season filets to taste with salt and pepper. Dip them in flour on both sides, and shake off excess.

Heat oil in a nonstick skillet over medium-high heat. Cook filets on both sides until they flake easily with a fork. Sprinkle with lemon juice before serving.

~

CORN AND TOMATO
~

4 SERVINGS

4	bacon slices	4
28 oz	can diced tomatoes	796 mL
1 tsp	dried savory	5 mL
2	12 oz (341 mL) cans corn kernels	2
	pepper	

Cook bacon in a skillet until crisp. Discard fat. Crumble bacon and set aside.

Drain tomatoes and heat in same skillet about 5 minutes over medium-high heat with savory and pepper. Stir in drained corn and reserved crumbled bacon. Cook another 3 minutes to blend flavors. Serve hot.

~

1 SERVING		
229 CALORIES	7g CARBOHYDRATE	39g PROTEIN
5g FAT	0.2g FIBER	176mg CHOLESTEROL

1 SERVING		
236 CALORIES	42g CARBOHYDRATE	8g PROTEIN
4g FAT	5.7g FIBER	5mg CHOLESTEROL

FISH PARMENTIER

2 SERVINGS

2	cod filets, about 4 oz (110 g) each	2
1	sweet potato, peeled and thinly sliced	1
1	potato, peeled and thinly sliced	1
1 tbsp	vegetable oil	15 mL
	capers for garnish	

SAUCE

2 tsp	vegetable oil	10 mL
1	garlic clove, finely chopped	1
1	onion, diced	1
19 oz	can tomatoes, chopped	540 mL
1 tbsp	chopped fresh basil	15 mL
1 tbsp	chopped fresh parsley	15 mL
1/4 tsp	pepper	1 mL
1	pinch cayenne pepper	1
1 tsp	dried oregano	5 mL

NUTRITION TIP

The deep orange color of sweet potatoes indicates that they are a rich source of beta carotene.

Preheat oven to 350°F (180°C). Arrange filets in a baking pan. Alternate slices of potato and sweet potato over filets. Baste with oil. Bake 10 to 12 minutes.

Meanwhile, make the sauce: heat oil in a saucepan, add garlic and onion, and cook until onion is soft. Add remaining ingredients and cook 15 minutes.

Arrange fish on a serving plate with sauce, and garnish with capers.

1 Arrange fish in single layer in a baking pan.

2 Place potato and sweet potato slices on top.

3 Baste with oil and bake.

4 Prepare the sauce.

1 SERVING		
482 CALORIES	46g CARBOHYDRATE	25g PROTEIN
22g FAT	7.3g FIBER	48mg CHOLESTEROL

SALMON AND TOMATO LOAF

~

4 SERVINGS

NUTRITION TIP

*Be sure to mash up
the bones and vertebrae
of canned salmon
and include in the recipe.
They are an excellent
source of calcium.*

1 cup	canned salmon, drained	250 mL
1 cup	fresh breadcrumbs	250 mL
2	eggs, lightly beaten	2
⅔ cup	canned tomatoes, drained	150 mL
2 tbsp	chopped green pepper or pickles	30 mL
	chopped onion	
	salt, pepper and paprika	

Preheat oven to 350°F (180°C). In a bowl, combine all ingredients in the order given, mixing well. Pour into a greased 5 x 9 inch (12.5 x 23 cm) loaf pan.

Place pan in a larger pan. Pour water in larger pan to halfway up sides of loaf pan.

Bake 30 to 40 minutes, or until firm.

Serve hot, with a tomato sauce if desired. Or chill and slice to serve cold with salad.

~

1 SERVING		
227 CALORIES	25g CARBOHYDRATE	16g PROTEIN
7g FAT	1.2g FIBER	153mg CHOLESTEROL

LIGHT AND CRISPY FISH STICKS

2 SERVINGS

I	egg	I
2 tbsp	all-purpose flour	30 mL
2	fish filets (your choice), cut into strips	2
3 cups	cornflakes, crushed	750 mL
	salt and freshly ground pepper	
	vegetable oil or spray	
	lemon wedges	

Preheat oven to 375°F (190°C). Break egg into a shallow bowl and beat lightly with a fork.

In a bowl, combine flour with salt and pepper. Place crushed cornflakes in another bowl.

Lightly oil a baking sheet.

Dip each fish strip in seasoned flour, then in egg. Coat with crushed cornflakes. Place on baking sheet. Do not let pieces overlap. Bake 15 minutes.

~

COOK'S TIP

These fish sticks are so easy to make, you may never buy frozen prepared fish again! And they have the added virtue of being crispy without deep-frying.

1 SERVING		
447 CALORIES	45g CARBOHYDRATE	42g PROTEIN
11g FAT	1.4g FIBER	225mg CHOLESTEROL

GRILLED SCALLOPS

4 SERVINGS

¹/₄ cup	all-purpose flour	50 mL
I tbsp	chopped fresh tarragon	15 mL
I	pinch ground white pepper	I
I lb	scallops	450 g
2 tbsp	vegetable oil	30 mL
3	tomatoes, peeled, seeded and diced	3
¹/₄ tsp	garlic salt	I mL
2	green onions, finely chopped	2

COOK'S TIP

Do not overcook scallops; they become rubbery. Fresh scallops will keep only 1 or 2 days in the refrigerator, but freeze well. If you use frozen scallops, do not thaw before cooking.

In a bowl, combine flour, tarragon, and pepper. Toss scallops in flour and shake off excess.

Heat oil in a nonstick skillet. Add scallops and fry on both sides over medium-high heat just until interior is no longer translucent. Remove scallops from skillet.

In the same skillet, cook tomatoes, garlic salt and green onions 10 minutes over medium heat. Season to taste with salt and pepper. Serve scallops on a bed of tomato sauce.

~

1 Combine flour, tarragon and pepper. Coat scallops in mixture.

2 Fry scallops on both sides in oil. Set aside.

3 Cook tomatoes, garlic salt and green onions.

4 Serve scallops on top of tomato sauce.

1 SERVING

173 CALORIES	12g CARBOHYDRATE	20g PROTEIN
5g FAT	1.0g FIBER	37mg CHOLESTEROL

FETTUCINE WITH SCALLOPS

4 SERVINGS

1½ cups	scallops	375 mL
1 tsp	cardamom seeds	5 mL
1 tbsp	vegetable oil	15 mL
½	red onion, finely chopped	½
1 cup	dry white wine	250 mL
½ cup	15% cream	125 mL
1 tsp	cornstarch, dissolved in a little water	5 mL
½ cup	plain yogurt	125 mL
1 lb	fettucine, cooked	450 g
2 tbsp	chopped fresh chives	30 mL

Cut each scallop in 2 or 3 pieces, depending on size. (Small bay scallops can be left whole). Tie cardamom seeds in a small piece of cheesecloth.

In a large skillet, heat oil. Add scallops and cook over high heat 2 minutes, stirring from time to time. Lower heat to medium. Add onion and cook 2 minutes. Remove scallops and keep warm.

Stir wine into same skillet. Add cardamom and cook to reduce liquid by ½. Add cream and cornstarch mixture. Bring to a boil. Remove cardamom. Stir in yogurt and serve at once over hot drained fettucine. Garnish with scallops and chives.

~

	1 SERVING	
515 CALORIES	83g CARBOHYDRATE	21g PROTEIN
11g FAT	0.2g FIBER	36mg CHOLESTEROL

TORTIGLIONI WITH CLAM SAUCE

4 SERVINGS

2 tbsp	olive oil	30 mL
2	garlic cloves, finely chopped	2
2	cans baby clams, drained	2
¼ cup	chopped fresh parsley	50 mL
2 tsp	chopped fresh basil	10 mL
1 lb	tortiglioni, cooked	450 g
	pepper	
	grated Parmesan	

Heat oil in a saucepan over medium-high heat.
Cook garlic and drained clams 2 to 3 minutes.

Stir in parsley, basil and pepper. Let simmer
5 to 8 minutes. Stir in hot drained pasta.

Serve topped with grated Parmesan.

COOK'S TIP

You can use any short pasta variety for this recipe: macaroni, penne or fusilli.

1 SERVING		
589 CALORIES	83g CARBOHYDRATE	35g PROTEIN
13g FAT	0g FIBER	67mg CHOLESTEROL

SPAGHETTI ALFREDO

4 SERVINGS

I cup	15% cream	250 mL
2 tbsp	dry white wine or unsweetened apple juice	30 mL
I tbsp	liquid chicken stock concentrate	15 mL
1/2 cup	grated Parmesan cheese	125 mL
I cup	diced cooked ham	250 mL
I lb	spaghetti, cooked and drained	450 g
	chopped fresh parsley for garnish	

Heat cream in a saucepan with white wine and chicken stock concentrate over medium-low heat about 5 minutes.

Stir in grated cheese until melted. Add ham and reduce heat to low.

Add drained spaghetti to mixture and toss well. Sprinkle with parsley to serve.

~

1 SERVING		
556 CALORIES	81g CARBOHYDRATE	22g PROTEIN
16g FAT	0.3g FIBER	56mg CHOLESTEROL

PASTA WITH PEPPERONI AND OREGANO

4 SERVINGS

10	slices pepperoni or salami	10
I tbsp	olive oil	15 mL
I	garlic clove, finely chopped	I
1/4 cup	dry white wine	50 mL
I tbsp	chopped fresh oregano	15 mL
1/4 cup	chopped black olives	50 mL
I lb	spaghetti, cooked	450 g
3/4 cup	dry breadcrumbs	175 mL
	grated Parmesan cheese (optional)	

Cut pepperoni into thin strips. Heat oil in a skillet, and cook pepperoni and garlic over medium-high heat 3 minutes.

Stir in wine, oregano and olives. Reduce heat. Stir in hot drained pasta. If mixture seems too dry for your liking, stir in a spoonful or 2 of pasta cooking liquid. Stir in breadcrumbs. Sprinkle with Parmesan cheese before serving.

COOK'S TIP

The breadcrumbs add a terrific texture to this spicy pasta. Use wholewheat crumbs for extra fiber.

1 SERVING		
615 CALORIES	93g CARBOHYDRATE	18g PROTEIN
19g FAT	0.7g FIBER	23mg CHOLESTEROL

ADRIATIC PIZZA

4 SERVINGS

1	garlic clove, chopped	1
3	bacon slices, chopped	3
7 oz	can waterpacked tuna, drained and flaked	200 g
2	large tomatoes, peeled, seeded and chopped	2
1/2 cup	chopped black olives	125 mL
1/4 cup	chopped fresh parsley	50 mL
1/4 cup	chopped fresh basil	50 mL
4	precooked individual pizza shells	4
1 cup	grated skim milk mozzarella	250 mL
	freshly ground pepper	

Preheat oven to 350°F (180°C).

Heat bacon and garlic together in a nonstick skillet over high heat until bacon is cooked. Drain off fat.

Stir in tuna and pepper to taste. Stir in tomatoes, olives, parsley and basil.

Spread mixture over pizza shells. Bake 10 to 15 minutes. Top with grated mozzarella towards end of cooking time.

1 SERVING		
371 CALORIES	37g CARBOHYDRATE	31g PROTEIN
11g FAT	3.1g FIBER	29mg CHOLESTEROL

VEGETABLE AND BACON PIZZA

~

4 SERVINGS

3	slices bacon	3
1/2 cup	broccoli florets	125 mL
1/2 cup	cauliflower florets	125 mL
1 cup	mushrooms, quartered	250 mL
2 tsp	olive oil	10 mL
3 tbsp	butter, margarine or oil	45 mL
1/4 cup	all-purpose flour	50 mL
2 cups	skim milk	500 mL
1	pinch ground nutmeg	1
1	precooked pizza shell	1
1 cup	grated Emmenthal or Swiss cheese	250 mL
	pepper	

Preheat oven to 400°F (200°C).
Cook bacon until crisp. Drain well,
crumble and set aside.

Cook broccoli and cauliflower in boiling
salted water until tender-crisp. Drain and
set aside.

Cook mushrooms in olive oil until lightly
browned. Set aside.

Heat butter or oil in a saucepan. Stir
in flour, mixing well. Cook 1 minute.
Gradually stir in milk and nutmeg.
Cook until thickened. Pour into a bowl
and let cool.

Spread cooled white sauce over pizza shell.
Top with vegetables, grated cheese and
bacon. Bake 10 minutes. Serve very hot.

~

COOK'S TIP

*If you really want
to save time, use
a packaged white
or béchamel sauce
instead of making
your own.*

1 SERVING		
537 CALORIES	46g CARBOHYDRATE	23g PROTEIN
29g FAT	3.1g FIBER	59mg CHOLESTEROL

SEAFOOD SALAD WITH ROSY DRESSING

~

2 SERVINGS

2	large oranges, skin and membranes removed, seeded	2
I cup	imitation crabmeat	250 mL
2	green onions, chopped	2
	lettuce leaves	
	fresh lemon juice	

DRESSING

I cup	plain low-fat yogurt	250 mL
1/4 cup	tomato juice	50 mL
I tbsp	chopped fresh parsley	15 mL
I to 2 tbsp	dry white vermouth	15 to 30 mL
2 to 3	drops Tabasco sauce	2 to 3
3 tbsp	chopped pitted black olives	45 mL

COOK'S TIP

Imitation crabmeat is made from Alaska pollack flavored with crab. It is low in fat, and freezes well, so it is easy to keep on hand. The dressing is equally delicious with fresh crab or shrimp.

Combine all dressing ingredients in a bowl. Mix well and set aside.

Arrange lettuce leaves on individual plates. Arrange imitation crabmeat on top, sprinkled lightly with lemon juice.

Pour dressing over and garnish with green onions.

~

I SERVING

280 CALORIES	26g CARBOHYDRATE	26g PROTEIN
8g FAT	3.0g FIBER	24mg CHOLESTEROL

TABOULI WITH SHRIMP

2 SERVINGS

NUTRITION TIP

*Bulgur is a good way
to add fiber and
grain to your diet.*

2 cups	chicken stock	500 mL
1 cup	bulgur	250 mL
2 cups	chopped fresh parsley	500 mL
1/2 cup	chopped fresh mint	125 mL
1	onion, finely chopped	1
3	green onions, chopped	3
3	tomatoes, diced	3
1/2 cup	fresh lemon juice	125 mL
1/4 cup	virgin olive oil	50 mL
1 to 2 cups	chopped, cooked and peeled small shrimp	250 to 500 mL
	freshly ground pepper	

Bring chicken stock to a boil in a large saucepan. Stir in bulgur and remove from heat. Let stand 2 hours at room temperature.

Drain bulgur well; place in a large bowl. Add parsley, mint, onion, green onions, tomatoes and ground pepper.

Shake together lemon juice and oil in a covered jar. Pour over salad. Toss well. Toss in shrimp. Let marinate 2 to 3 hours, refrigerated. Serve chilled.

1 SERVING		
594 CALORIES	60g CARBOHYDRATE	30g PROTEIN
26g FAT	7.0g FIBER	156mg CHOLESTEROL

LIGHT GOURMET POTATO SALAD

2 SERVINGS

1	cucumber	1
2	potatoes, boiled in their skins	2
1	onion	1
1	apple, green or red	1
4	hardboiled eggs	4
¹/₄ cup	plain yogurt	50 mL
2 tbsp	unsweetened apple juice or cider	30 mL
	salt and freshly ground pepper	
	lettuce and radicchio leaves	

Peel and dice the cucumber, potatoes, and onion. Core and dice the apple. Place in a large bowl.

Peel and slice eggs. Add to vegetables.

Combine yogurt, apple juice, salt and pepper in a small bowl. Pour over eggs and vegetables. Toss gently. Serve over lettuce and radicchio leaves.

COOK'S TIP

For a more substantial cold meal, serve this potato salad with cold cooked asparagus and cold sliced ham. Or wrap cooked fresh asparagus spears in thin slices of prosciutto.

1 SERVING		
390 CALORIES	48g CARBOHYDRATE	18g PROTEIN
14g FAT	5.4g FIBER	550mg CHOLESTEROL

CORN AND TUNA SALAD

4 SERVINGS

COOK'S TIP

Instead of the vegetable oil, use walnut oil. It is expensive, but adds a delightful flavor.

7 oz	can waterpacked tuna	200 g
2 tbsp	vegetable oil	30 mL
4 tbsp	white wine vinegar	60 mL
2 tbsp	chopped fresh parsley	30 mL
12 oz	can corn kernels	341 mL
4	large lettuce leaves, your choice	4
4	hardboiled eggs	4
	salt and pepper	

Drain tuna and flake well.

Make a dressing by mixing together oil, vinegar, parsley, salt and pepper.

In a bowl, stir together drained corn kernels, half of dressing, and flaked tuna. Arrange mixture on lettuce leaves on plates. Garnish with sliced hardboiled eggs and remaining dressing.

LIGHT & EASY MAIN DISHES

1 SERVING		
273 CALORIES	16g CARBOHYDRATE	23g PROTEIN
13g FAT	1.7g FIBER	282mg CHOLESTEROL

SWISS SALAD PLATE

4 SERVINGS

1¹/₂ cups	fresh mushrooms, quartered	375 mL
¹/₂ cup	diced Swiss cheese	125 mL
¹/₂ cup	diced Emmenthal cheese	125 mL
1 cup	lean cooked ham, in strips	125 mL
1¹/₂ cups	asparagus spears, cooked fresh or canned	375 mL
4	tomatoes, peeled and cut in wedges	4
1	green pepper, in strips	1
	lettuce leaves	

DRESSING

¹/₄ cup	olive oil	50 mL
2 tbsp	red wine vinegar	30 mL
	freshly ground pepper	

In a large bowl, toss together mushrooms, cheeses and ham.

Mix together dressing ingredients in a small bowl.

Arrange lettuce leaves on plates with asparagus, tomatoes and green pepper. Mound cheese mixture on top. Pour dressing over.

1 SERVING

318 CALORIES	12g CARBOHYDRATE	18g PROTEIN
22g FAT	3.2g FIBER	44mg CHOLESTEROL

SPINACH AND GRAPE SALAD

4 SERVINGS

I cup	cooked rice	250 mL
2 cups	spinach, washed, stemmed and torn up	500 mL
I	red onion, sliced	I
3	green onions, chopped	3
2 cups	bean sprouts	500 mL
I cup	red grapes, halved	250 mL
I cup	green grapes, halved	250 mL
I tbsp	chopped fresh parsley	I5 mL
1/4 cup	walnuts or pecans	50 mL
1/4 tsp	pepper	I mL
	chopped fresh thyme	

DRESSING

1/2 cup	plain low-fat yogurt	125 mL
1/3 cup	unsweetened orange juice	75 mL
2 tbsp	vegetable oil	30 mL
I	garlic clove, finely chopped	I
2 tbsp	maple syrup	30 mL
3 to 4	drops Tabasco sauce	3 to 4

COOK'S TIP

To make a more substantial main dish salad, add some shredded cooked chicken.

Combine spinach and rice in a large bowl. Add red onion, green onions, sprouts, and grapes. Toss well.

Add herbs, nuts and pepper. Toss again.

Combine dressing ingredients in a second bowl. Pour over salad just before serving, tossing well.

1 SERVING		
320 CALORIES	46g CARBOHYDRATE	7g PROTEIN
12g FAT	3.2g FIBER	2mg CHOLESTEROL

COLD CHICKEN SALAD PIZZA

4 SERVINGS

¹/₂ cup	light mayonnaise	125 mL
¹/₂ cup	2% cottage cheese	125 mL
1 tbsp	liquid vegetable stock concentrate	15 mL
1	large Italian style flat bread or cooked pizza shell	1
2	tomatoes, sliced	2
1	red onion, thinly sliced	1
4	canned artichoke hearts, drained and sliced	4
1¹/₂ cups	diced cooked chicken	375 mL
2 tbsp	chopped fresh tarragon	30 mL
¹/₄ tsp	white pepper	1 mL
2 tbsp	capers	30 mL
	sliced olives	

COOK'S TIP

This makes a quick and nutritious hot weather meal.

In a bowl, combine mayonnaise, cottage cheese and stock concentrate. Spread over flat bread or cooked pizza shell.

Arrange tomato slices over mayonnaise mixture. Top with onion slices separated into rings, artichokes and chicken.

Sprinkle with tarragon and pepper. Decorate with capers and olives, if desired.

1 Combine mayonnaise, cottage cheese, and stock concentrate.

2 Spread mixture over flat bread.

3 Arrange vegetables and chicken on top.

4 Sprinkle with capers and olive slices, if desired.

1 SERVING

456 CALORIES	53g CARBOHYDRATE	25g PROTEIN
16g FAT	3.9g FIBER	41mg CHOLESTEROL

VEGETARIAN MEALS

~

Many of us are thinking of cutting down on meat. Or perhaps we have a teenager who has decided to go vegetarian, or we are entertaining non-meat eaters. But if you were raised with the idea that a square meal has to include meat, potatoes and a vegetable, the idea of a meal without meat can present a problem.

Well, the first thing to do is relax! Cutting down on meat can be as simple as reducing your portion sizes, and adding an extra vegetable or some whole-grain bread at each meal. Then try making one or two meatless meals each week — featuring something your family already likes, such as spaghetti or pizza, which easily convert to meatless versions. You will find some easy ideas in this chapter.

Most North Americans consume more protein than they need. As long as you continue to eat yogurt, milk, low-fat cheeses, dried beans and peas, nuts and peanut butter, and whole-grain breads and cereals, you really don't have to worry about getting enough protein. On the other hand, packing your meal with cheese and eggs to make up for the lack of meat will provide way too much fat!

If someone in your family becomes serious about a vegetarian diet, look for a cookbook that explains how to combine foods like nuts and grains, or beans and rice, to provide complete protein. In the meantime, this chapter will provide vegetarian meal ideas your whole family should enjoy!

~

ASPARAGUS
IN PASTRY SHELLS

4 SERVINGS

14 oz	puff pastry	400 g
1	egg yolk, beaten	1
2 tbsp	milk	30 mL
20	fresh asparagus spears, trimmed	20
	salt and freshly ground pepper	

CHEESE SAUCE

1 tbsp	butter or margarine	15 mL
1 tbsp	all-purpose flour	15 mL
2	dry French shallots, finely chopped	2
1/4 cup	dry white wine	50 mL
1 1/2 cups	skim milk	375 mL
1/2 cup	freshly grated Parmesan	125 mL

Preheat oven to 400°F (200°C). Roll out puff pastry to ¼ inch (0.5 cm) thick.

Cut pastry into 4 equal rectangles. Arrange on a baking sheet, and brush tops with beaten egg yolk mixed with 2 tbsp (30 mL) milk. Bake 15 to 20 minutes or until golden brown.

Meanwhile, make sauce: melt butter in a saucepan. Stir in flour and shallots. Cook 1 minute over medium-low heat, but do not let brown.

Stir in wine and cook until partially reduced. Gradually whisk in milk and Parmesan. Cook slowly until thickened and creamy. Season to taste.

Steam asparagus in boiling salted water until tender-crisp. Drain well and layer between split pastry rectangles. Cover with sauce to serve.

1 SERVING

603 CALORIES	40g CARBOHYDRATE	14g PROTEIN
43g FAT	1.3g FIBER	72mg CHOLESTEROL

STUFFED CABBAGE ROLLS

4 SERVINGS

³/₄ cup	long grain brown rice	175 mL
1 tbsp	olive oil	15 mL
¹/₂	onion, finely chopped	¹/₂
1	carrot, grated	1
4	mushrooms, chopped	4
4	eggs, beaten	4
2 tbsp	grated Parmesan cheese	30 mL
8	large cabbage leaves	8
¹/₄ cup	vegetable stock	50 mL
2 tbsp	tamari sauce	30 mL
	Tabasco sauce	
	salt and pepper	

Cook rice in 6 cups (1.5 liters) boiling salted water
for 45 minutes, or until tender. Drain and set aside.

Heat oil in a nonstick skillet over medium-high heat.
Add onion, carrot and mushrooms. Stir-fry until tender.

Combine cooked drained rice with cooked vegetables
and beaten eggs. Season with Tabasco, Parmesan and
salt and pepper. Cover and set aside.

Blanch cabbage leaves in boiling water until pliable.
Lay out, curved side down, on work surface. Divide rice
mixture among leaves. Roll up leaves, folding in ends
to form a package.

Place rolls seam side down in a baking dish. Combine
vegetable stock and tamari. Pour over cabbage rolls. Bake
in 300°F (150°C) oven about 30 minutes, or until tender.

1 SERVING		
263 CALORIES	29g CARBOHYDRATE	12g PROTEIN
11g FAT	5.1g FIBER	275mg CHOLESTEROL

MUSHROOM CRÊPES WITH CHEESE SAUCE

4 SERVINGS

2 tbsp	butter or margarine	30 mL
3 cups	sliced fresh mushrooms	750 mL
1/4 cup	dry white wine	50 mL
1/2	envelope mushroom sauce mix	1/2
1/3 cup	whipping cream	75 mL
2 tbsp	chopped fresh parsley	30 mL
4	thin crêpes, 8 inches (20 cm) in diameter	4

SAUCE

2 tbsp	butter or margarine	30 mL
2 tbsp	all-purpose flour	30 mL
1 1/2 cups	2% milk	375 mL
1	onion, peeled and studded with 1 clove	1
1	bay leaf	1
1/3 cup	grated Gruyère cheese	75 mL

Melt butter in a large saucepan and add mushrooms. Cook over medium-high heat until slightly browned.

Mix together wine and sauce mix. Stir into mushrooms. Stir in cream and simmer mixture until thickened. Add parsley. Fill crêpes with mushroom mixture and roll up. Keep warm.

To make the sauce: melt butter in a saucepan. Stir in flour and cook 3 to 4 minutes over medium-low heat. Gradually whisk in milk, then add onion and bay leaf. Simmer over low heat 10 to 15 minutes. Remove onion.

Add grated cheese. When sauce is smooth, pour it over crêpes. Brown lightly under preheated broiler, if desired. Serve with a vegetable of your choice.

~

COOK'S TIP

Use frozen crêpes from the supermarket, or make your own using the recipe on page 364, but leaving out the sugar.

1 SERVING		
443 CALORIES	37g CARBOHYDRATE	13g PROTEIN
27g FAT	1.7g FIBER	107mg CHOLESTEROL

CORN PANCAKES

2 TO 4 SERVINGS

COOK'S TIP

This versatile recipe can be served for brunch or lunch, or dressed up with a green vegetable and salad for a light supper.

¹/₂ cup	yellow cornmeal	125 mL
¹/₂ cup	wholewheat flour	125 mL
2	eggs	2
³/₄ cup	2% milk	175 mL
1 tsp	Dijon mustard	5 mL
1¹/₂ cups	canned or frozen corn kernels	375 mL
¹/₂ cup	grated cheddar cheese	125 mL
1 tbsp	chopped fresh parsley	15 mL
	salt and pepper	
	vegetable oil, for frying	

In a large bowl, beat together the cornmeal, flour, eggs, milk and mustard.

Stir in the corn kernels, cheese and parsley. Season to taste.

Heat 1 tbsp (15 mL) oil over medium-high heat in a skillet. Drop in spoonfuls of batter so that they do not touch. Turn when the pancakes are browned on the bottom, and cook the other side. Repeat with remaining batter, adding more oil if necessary.

1 SERVING		
349 CALORIES	34g CARBOHYDRATE	14g PROTEIN
13g FAT	3.6g FIBER	153mg CHOLESTEROL

CAMEMBERT AND RED PEPPER OMELET

2 SERVINGS

4 tsp	butter or margarine	20 mL
1	garlic clove, chopped	1
1	red bell pepper, diced	1
2 tbsp	chopped fresh basil	30 mL
3 oz	Camembert cheese	90 g
4	eggs, lightly beaten	4
	freshly ground pepper	

Melt 2 tsp (10 mL) butter in a small nonstick skillet. Add garlic and red pepper, and cook over low heat 5 minutes. Stir in basil and pepper to taste. Set mixture aside.

Remove rind from cheese and discard. Slice cheese thinly.

Melt 1 tsp (5 mL) butter in same skillet over medium heat. Pour in half of beaten eggs. Cook 2 to 3 minutes or until nearly cooked but still moist in center.

Spread half of cheese and pepper mixture on one side of omelet. Fold over and cook until cheese melts. Keep omelet warm while you prepare second omelet.

COOK'S TIP

Omelets cook so quickly that, for visual appeal, it is really worthwhile to make two small omelets rather than 1 large one.

1 SERVING

388 CALORIES	3g CARBOHYDRATE	22g PROTEIN
32g FAT	0.7g FIBER	604mg CHOLESTEROL

VEGETABLE OMELET

4 SERVINGS

8	egg whites	8
4	egg yolks	4
1/3 cup	skim milk	75 mL
2 tbsp	chopped fresh parsley	30 mL
1/3 cup	curd cheese	75 mL
1 tbsp	butter or margarine	15 mL
1/2 cup	sliced fresh mushrooms	125 mL
1/2 cup	cooked broccoli florets	125 mL
1/3 cup	grated carrot	75 mL
1/3 cup	diced red or green bell pepper	75 mL
	salt and pepper	

COOK'S TIP

For a prettier presentation, make individual omelets by dividing the ingredients, and cooking one at a time using the same procedure.

In a bowl, beat together the egg whites, yolks and milk. Season to taste. Stir in parsley and cheese. Set aside.

Heat butter in a nonstick skillet and cook mushrooms over high heat until lightly browned.

Pour egg mixture over mushrooms. Arrange broccoli, carrot and red pepper on top.

Continue cooking over low heat until egg is set. Or place in a 350°F (180°°C) oven until done to taste. Fold omelet in half, slide out of pan and serve piping hot.

1 SERVING		
261 CALORIES	6g CARBOHYDRATE	21g PROTEIN
17g FAT	1.0g FIBER	453mg CHOLESTEROL

MEXICAN SCRAMBLED EGG TACOS

2 TO 4 SERVINGS

1 tbsp	butter or margarine	15 mL
1	tomato, peeled, seeded and chopped	1
¹/₄ cup	red or green bell pepper, diced	50 mL
¹/₄ cup	chopped green onions	50 mL
¹/₂	jalapeño pepper, finely chopped	¹/₂
1	pinch ground cumin	1
6	eggs	6
2 tbsp	plain yogurt or milk	30 mL
4	taco shells	4
4	lettuce leaves	4

Melt butter in a nonstick skillet.
Add tomato, bell pepper, green onion,
jalapeño and cumin. Cook 2 minutes.
Pour off excess liquid.

Beat together eggs and yogurt in a bowl.
Pour into skillet with vegetables.
Cook, stirring, until eggs are cooked
to taste.

Spoon into taco shells and garnish
with lettuce leaves.

~

COOK'S TIP

*To make an easy quick
meal, serve these tacos
with a salad made
of drained rinsed
kidney beans or chick
peas flavored with
chopped onion, celery,
green pepper and a light
vinaigrette.*

1 SERVING

214 CALORIES	11g CARBOHYDRATE	11g PROTEIN
14g FAT	0.9g FIBER	419mg CHOLESTEROL

SPANISH OMELET

4 SERVINGS

I tbsp	vegetable oil	I5 mL
2	green onions, chopped	2
I	green bell pepper, diced	I
I	red bell pepper, diced	I
2	garlic cloves, finely chopped	2
28 oz	can tomatoes, drained and chopped	796 mL
2 tbsp	chopped fresh basil	30 mL
2 tbsp	chopped fresh oregano	30 mL
I tbsp	butter or margarine	I5 mL
6	eggs, lightly beaten	6
	salt and pepper	

COOK'S TIP

*Omelets are richer
and creamier if they
are not overcooked.
The eggs will keep
cooking slightly even
after removed from heat.*

Heat oil in a skillet and add green onions, peppers
and garlic. Cook over high heat until soft.

Stir in tomatoes, basil and oregano. Let simmer 15 minutes
over medium-low heat. Season to taste and set aside.

Melt butter in an omelet pan or nonstick skillet over
medium heat. Pour in eggs. Cook just until partially set.

Stir in tomato mixture. Continue cooking over low heat
2 to 3 minutes until done to taste.

1 SERVING		
232 CALORIES	*11g CARBOHYDRATE*	*11g PROTEIN*
16g FAT	*2.0g FIBER*	*418mg CHOLESTEROL*

GOURMET VEGETABLE QUICHE

4 SERVINGS

I	uncooked pastry shell	I
4	eggs	4
2 cups	skim milk	500 mL
I	pinch cayenne pepper	I
I	pinch ground nutmeg	I
2 tsp	butter or margarine	10 mL
1/2 cup	sliced mushrooms	125 mL
1/4 cup	sliced zucchini	50 mL
1/2	red or green bell pepper, diced	1/2
1/2	onion, chopped	1/2
1/4 cup	corn kernels	50 mL

COOK'S TIP

Chopped fresh basil or summer savory can be stirred into the vegetable mixture if you wish.

Preheat oven to 375°F (190°C). Line a 9-inch (23 cm) quiche or pie plate with shortcrust pastry. Set aside.

In a bowl, beat together eggs, milk, cayenne and nutmeg. Set aside in refrigerator.

Heat butter in a nonstick skillet over medium heat. Add mushrooms, zucchini, red pepper and onion; cook about 10 minutes.

Meanwhile, bake pastry shell 10 minutes. Spread cooked vegetables and corn kernels in pie shell. Pour milk mixture over, and bake 30 to 40 minutes, or until set. Serve hot or cold.

1 SERVING		
587 CALORIES	51g CARBOHYDRATE	17g PROTEIN
35g FAT	1.9g FIBER	281mg CHOLESTEROL

VEGETARIAN QUICHE

4 TO 6 SERVINGS

I	uncooked pastry shell	I
3	eggs	3
1½ cups	milk or soya milk	375 mL
I cup	diced plain tofu	250 mL
½ cup	grated carrots	125 mL
½ cup	grated zucchini	125 mL
I cup	cooked or canned lentils, rinsed and drained	250 mL
2 tbsp	chopped fresh chervil	30 mL
	salt and pepper	

Preheat oven to 350°F (180°C). Line pie plate or quiche pan with shortcrust pastry.

In a bowl, beat eggs together with milk. Stir in remaining ingredients.

Pour mixture into pastry shell. Bake 30 to 35 minutes, or until center is set when poked with a knife. Serve hot or cold with a mixed salad.

COOK'S TIP

If you are cooking for someone who has a lactose intolerance, soya milk can be used in almost any recipe in place of cow's milk.

1 SERVING		
441 CALORIES	39g CARBOHYDRATE	15g PROTEIN
25g FAT	2.5g FIBER	145mg CHOLESTEROL

RATATOUILLE PIZZA

4 SERVINGS

COOK'S TIP

This recipe is full of rich Mediterranean flavors. Vary it by adding other flavors typical of the region, such as roasted peppers, black olives, tuna or anchovies.

1	small eggplant	1
1	onion	1
1	zucchini	1
2 tbsp	olive oil	30 mL
2	garlic cloves, finely chopped	2
2	tomatoes, chopped	2
1¹/₂ cups	sliced fresh mushrooms	375 mL
¹/₂ tsp	dried oregano	2 mL
¹/₂ tsp	dried thyme	2 mL
¹/₂ tsp	pepper	2 mL
1	cooked pizza shell	1
1¹/₂ cups	grated partially skim milk mozzarella	375 mL

Preheat oven to 350°F (180°C). Cut eggplant and onion in half lengthwise, then crosswise in thin slices. Cut zucchini in thin slices.

Heat oil in a large nonstick skillet over medium heat. Add eggplant, onion, zucchini and garlic. Cook until slightly softened.

Add tomatoes, mushrooms, herbs and pepper. Let simmer 5 minutes.

Spread mixture over pizza shell. Top with cheese. Bake 15 to 20 minutes or until cheese melts.

1 SERVING		
417 CALORIES	45g CARBOHYDRATE	21g PROTEIN
17g FAT	6.3g FIBER	24mg CHOLESTEROL

TAGLIATELLE WITH ROASTED GARLIC PURÉE

4 SERVINGS

1 tbsp	butter or margarine	15 mL
1 tbsp	olive oil	15 mL
2	onions, thinly sliced	2
6	garlic cloves, chopped	6
1 tbsp	all-purpose flour	15 mL
1/4 cup	chicken stock	50 mL
1 lb	tagliatelle, cooked and drained	450 g
1/3 cup	grated Parmesan cheese	75 mL
	salt and freshly ground pepper	

Heat butter together with oil in a saucepan. Add onions and garlic and cook over medium heat about 5 minutes, until soft. Stir in flour until well blended.

Add chicken stock and season to taste. Cover and let simmer 30 minutes over very low heat.

Purée mixture in blender or food processor until smooth. Pour into a large bowl. Add hot drained pasta and cheese. Toss very well before serving.

COOK'S TIP

Be careful not to brown the garlic, or it will have a bitter taste. The long gentle cooking in oil brings out the sweet rich flavor of the garlic, but eliminates its pungency.

1 SERVING		
461 CALORIES	82g CARBOHYDRATE	13g PROTEIN
9g FAT	1.0g FIBER	13mg CHOLESTEROL

PASTA WITH ROASTED RED PEPPER SAUCE

4 SERVINGS

3	red bell peppers	3
1 tbsp	olive oil	15 mL
1/2	red onion, sliced	1/2
1	tomato, chopped	1
1/2 cup	dry white wine	125 mL
1 1/2 cups	vegetable stock	375 mL
1	pinch sugar	1
1 lb	funghini or other small pasta shapes	450 g
	olive oil	

Place peppers under a preheated broiler and roast, turning from time to time, until skin is blackened on all sides. Wrap peppers in foil or a paper bag until cool. Rub off charred skin, cut open and remove seeds.

Heat 1 tbsp oil in a saucepan over medium-low heat. Add onion, tomato and roasted peppers. Cook 15 minutes.

Stir in wine, stock, and sugar. Simmer 20 minutes.

Meanwhile, cook pasta to taste; drain. In a large bowl, toss pasta with enough olive oil to coat lightly.

Purée pepper and tomato mixture in blender or food processor. Pour over pasta, toss and serve hot.

~

1 SERVING		
452 CALORIES	84g CARBOHYDRATE	11g PROTEIN
8g FAT	1.8g FIBER	0mg CHOLESTEROL

QUICK NOODLES WITH HERBS

2 SERVINGS

¹/₂ lb	egg noodles	225 g
19 oz	can diced tomatoes	540 mL
2 tbsp	chopped fresh herbs (sage, oregano, basil, tarragon, thyme, etc.)	30 mL
2 tbsp	chopped fresh parsley	30 mL
2 tbsp	olive oil	30 mL
2	garlic cloves, peeled	2
	salt and freshly ground pepper	

Cook the noodles according to package directions. Drain and keep warm.

In a bowl, combine tomatoes, herbs and parsley; season to taste.

Heat oil in a skillet over medium-low heat. Add garlic cloves and brown on all sides to flavor the oil. Discard garlic. Stir tomato mixture into oil.

Stir in hot drained noodles and toss gently. Serve at once in heated plates, with grated cheese if you wish.

COOK'S TIP

This dish is good made with any combination of fresh chopped herbs, but less successful with dried ones. If you only have parsley on hand, increase the amount, as well as the amount of garlic.

1 SERVING		
560 CALORIES	91 g CARBOHYDRATE	13 g PROTEIN
16 g FAT	3.5 g FIBER	0 mg CHOLESTEROL

PASTA BAKE FLORENTINE

~

4 SERVINGS

1 lb	pasta, your choice	450 g
1 tbsp	olive oil	15 mL
2	garlic cloves, chopped	2
2	leeks, white part only, slivered	2
1	red bell pepper, in julienne strips	1
1	green bell pepper, in julienne strips	1
10 oz	package fresh spinach, stems removed, torn up	284 g
1/4 tsp	pepper	1 mL
1/4 cup	cottage cheese	50 mL
1/4 cup	diced feta cheese	50 mL
1/2 cup	vegetable stock	125 mL
2 tbsp	grated Parmesan cheese	30 mL

Cook pasta according to package directions. Do no overcook. Drain and set aside.

Heat oil in a large nonstick skillet over medium heat. Cook garlic and leeks until soft. Add red and green pepper. Cook until soft.

Rinse spinach and place in a large saucepan with 1 tbsp (15 mL) water. Add pepper; heat over high heat, covered, just until spinach wilts. Remove from heat.

In a small bowl, combine cottage cheese and feta with vegetable stock.

Arrange cooked pasta in a baking dish. Combine vegetables and spinach, and arrange over pasta. Top evenly with cheese mixture. Sprinkle with Parmesan.

Heat in a hot oven until warmed through and top is golden.

~

1 SERVING		
475 CALORIES	88g CARBOHYDRATE	15g PROTEIN
7g FAT	3.3g FIBER	9mg CHOLESTEROL

LINGUINI WITH BLUE CHEESE

4 SERVINGS

2 tsp	olive oil	10 mL
2 tbsp	chopped green onion	30 mL
1 tbsp	dried oregano or marjoram	15 mL
¼ cup	dry white wine	50 mL
¼ cup	15% cream	50 mL
1 cup	crumbled blue cheese	250 mL
1 lb	linguini, cooked and drained	450 g

Heat oil in a large saucepan; stir in onions. Cook over medium heat 1 to 2 minutes. Stir in oregano and white wine; cook to reduce by ⅓.

Add cream and stir in crumbled blue cheese. Simmer over low heat until cheese is more or less melted. Add hot drained pasta to pan and toss gently. If sauce is too thick, stir in a little of the pasta cooking water. Serve at once on heated plates.

COOK'S TIP

This dish is rich and flavorful. If you wish, you can cut the amount of blue cheese by ½ or more, and serve the linguini topped with a poached egg instead. Or for a delicious variation, add a can of drained, coarsely chopped artichokes when you add the cream.

1 SERVING		
510 CALORIES	79g CARBOHYDRATE	17g PROTEIN
14g FAT	0.3g FIBER	29mg CHOLESTEROL

INTERNATIONAL INSPIRATIONS

~

If you are like most good cooks, you love eating in fine restaurants. And you probably find yourself wishing you could recreate some of those restaurant meals at home.

The recipes in this chapter have been gathered from some top Italian, French, Cajun, Chinese, and Indian chefs, among others, to show you how easy it is to make gourmet-quality meals in your own kitchen. We think you will be surprised to discover just how quick some of these creations are to prepare.

No matter what their background, professional chefs agree on some basic principles. Ingredients must be top-quality and fresh. And presentation, including garnishes and accompaniments, is as important as the main dish when it comes to making an impression.

This chapter contains lots of tips and advice on garnishes and accompaniments, and suggestions on where to find, or how to substitute for, unusual ingredients.

Mostly, though, you will see how common ingredients, when artfully presented, can make the difference between an ordinary meal and a memorable one.

~

CASHEW CHICKEN WITH CHINESE PANCAKES

4 SERVINGS

1/4 cup	corn syrup	50 mL
1 tsp	sesame oil	5 mL
3 tbsp	light soy sauce	45 mL
1 tbsp	grated fresh ginger	15 mL
2	garlic cloves, finely chopped	2
1/2 tsp	crushed hot pepper	2 mL
3/4 lb	boneless chicken breast, cut in strips	350 g
2 tbsp	vegetable oil	30 mL
1/2 cup	unsalted cashews	125 mL
1/2	onion, sliced	1/2
1 1/2 cups	broccoli florets	375 mL
1/2	red bell pepper, cut in strips	1/2
1/2 cup	water	125 mL
14 oz	can miniature corn	398 mL
1 1/2 cups	snow peas, sliced diagonally	375 mL
1 cup	bean sprouts	250 mL
2 tbsp	cornstarch	30 mL
2 tsp	powdered chicken stock	10 mL

In a medium bowl, combine corn syrup, sesame oil, soy sauce, ginger, garlic and hot pepper. Marinate chicken in this mixture 30 minutes. Drain chicken and reserve marinade.

Heat oil in a large wok or skillet over medium heat. Cook cashews 1 minute or until golden. Remove and set aside cashews.

Add chicken and stir-fry 2 to 3 minutes. Add onion, broccoli, and red pepper. Cook 1 to 2 minutes. Add water, drained corn, snow peas and bean sprouts. Cover and cook 3 to 4 minutes or until vegetables are tender-crisp.

Dissolve cornstarch and chicken stock powder in reserved marinade. Stir into wok. Let simmer 1 minute to thicken. Sprinkle with cashews to serve.

GREEN ONION PANCAKES

5	slices bacon	5
1/4 cup	hot water	50 mL
3/4 cup	all-purpose flour	175 mL
1/3 cup	chopped green onions	75 mL
1 tbsp	vegetable oil	15 mL
	salt and freshly ground pepper	

Cook bacon until crisp in a nonstick skillet. Drain on paper towels and crumble.

In a bowl, combine water, flour, green onions, crumbled bacon and salt and pepper. Knead 5 minutes, adding a little more flour if dough is too sticky to handle. Divide dough into 8 equal balls. Roll out each with a rolling pin as thinly as possible.

Heat oil in a skillet over medium heat, and cook pancakes until golden on both sides, about 2 minutes. Serve hot with cashew chicken or as an appetizer.

1 SERVING

643 CALORIES	70g CARBOHYDRATE	39g PROTEIN
23g FAT	6.9g FIBER	66mg CHOLESTEROL

TROPICAL CHICKEN SATAY

4 SERVINGS

12	long strips of boneless chicken breast, about 2 oz (60 g) each	12
12	bamboo skewers, soaked 20 minutes in water	12

MANGO CHUTNEY

1/3 cup	rice vinegar	75 mL
1 tbsp	sugar	15 mL
1	mango, peeled and diced	1

TROPICAL FRUIT SAUCE

1/3 cup	canned coconut milk	75 mL
1	mango, peeled and coarsely chopped	1
1 cup	coarsely chopped fresh or canned pineapple	250 mL
1/2 tsp	cornstarch, dissolved in a little water	2 mL
1/3 cup	plain yogurt	75 mL

Preheat oven to 350°F (180°C). Thread chicken strips lengthwise on skewers.

Place rice vinegar and sugar in a small saucepan and bring to a boil. Reduce heat to low, add diced mango, and let simmer 15 minutes. Keep warm.

Meanwhile, make the sauce. In another saucepan, cook coconut milk, chopped mango and pineapple over low heat 20 minutes. Purée in blender or food processor until smooth. Return to saucepan over low heat. Stir in dissolved cornstarch and yogurt. Keep warm.

Bake skewered chicken 10 minutes in oven. Serve with chutney and fruit sauce.

COOK'S TIP

Continue the tropical theme by serving this dish with rice flavored with a little curry powder, raisins and slivered almonds.

1 SERVING		
358 CALORIES	32g CARBOHYDRATE	44g PROTEIN
6g FAT	2.6g FIBER	116mg CHOLESTEROL

TANDOORI CHICKEN AND SHRIMP

4 SERVINGS

1 tsp	dry mustard	5 mL
2 tsp	grated fresh ginger	10 mL
1/2 tsp	cumin seeds	2 mL
1/2 tsp	ground coriander	2 mL
1/2 tsp	turmeric	2 mL
1 tsp	lemon juice	5 mL
1/4 tsp	chili powder	1 mL
2 tsp	tomato paste	10 mL
1/3 cup	vegetable oil	75 mL
2/3 cup	plain yogurt	150 mL
8	chicken drumsticks, skin removed	8
8	large raw shrimp, peeled and deveined	8

In a bowl, combine mustard, ginger, cumin, coriander, turmeric, lemon juice and chili powder. Mix well.

Gradually stir in tomato paste and half the oil. Stir until smooth. Stir in remaining oil and yogurt. Set aside.

Using a fork or skewer, poke holes in the drumsticks on all sides so they absorb flavorings. Place drumsticks in a glass dish with shrimp. Pour marinade mixture over and stir well. Cover and refrigerate 30 minutes.

Preheat oven to 350°F (180°C).

Drain drumsticks and shrimp. Arrange on a baking sheet. Bake 30 to 35 minutes. Halfway through cooking time, remove shrimp and keep warm. Turn chicken to brown other side. Serve with Basmati or white rice flavored with currants, grated coconut and sliced bananas, if desired.

1 SERVING		
399 CALORIES	3g CARBOHYDRATE	30g PROTEIN
23g FAT	0g FIBER	107mg CHOLESTEROL

SPICY CHICKEN WINGS TANDOORI
WITH MINT DIPPING SAUCE

2 SERVINGS

COOK'S TIP

These wings can also be cooked on the barbecue. Brush some eggplant, pineapple and apple slices with melted butter and grill them at the same time. With a herbed rice pilaf, it makes a quick and exotic meal.

12	chicken wings, skin removed	12
	MARINADE	
1/2 tsp	ground ginger	2 mL
1 tsp	ground coriander	5 mL
2 tsp	ground cumin	10 mL
1 tbsp	white vinegar	15 mL
1	garlic clove, chopped	1
1 tsp	paprika	5 mL
2 tsp	turmeric	10 mL
1/4 cup	plain low-fat yogurt	50 mL
	DIPPING SAUCE	
1/2 cup	plain low-fat yogurt	125 mL
1 tbsp	liquid honey	15 mL
1/2 tsp	chopped fresh mint	2 mL

Combine all marinade ingredients in a bowl. Pour into a shallow dish.

Place chicken wings in marinade, coating all surfaces, and refrigerate 8 hours or overnight.

Shortly before serving, combine dipping sauce ingredients in a small bowl. Preheat oven to 350°F (180°C).

Drain chicken wings and bake until tender (about 30 minutes, although time will depend on their size). Serve with yogurt dipping sauce.

1 Mix together marinade ingredients.

2 Marinate chicken wings.

3 Combine dipping sauce ingredients.

4 Bake wings until tender.

1 SERVING		
379 CALORIES	12g CARBOHYDRATE	58g PROTEIN
11g FAT	0g FIBER	178mg CHOLESTEROL

FRENCH TARRAGON CHICKEN

4 SERVINGS

2 to 3 lb	whole chicken	1 to 1.5 kg
3	carrots, coarsely chopped	3
2	leeks, white part only, chopped	2
1/2	onion, sliced	1/2
2 tbsp	chopped fresh or dried tarragon	30 mL
1	bay leaf	1
1	clove	1
6	parsley sprigs	6
2 tbsp	cornstarch, dissolved in a little water	30 mL
1 cup	plain low-fat yogurt	250 mL
1 cup	light sour cream	250 mL

Rinse chicken in cold water. Place in a saucepan and cover with just enough cold water to cover. Bring to a boil. Remove chicken from liquid. Reserve 2 cups (500 mL) cooking liquid.

Return chicken to saucepan. Add vegetables, herbs and spices, and reserved cooking liquid. Liquid should cover ¾ of the chicken. Bring to a boil, then reduce heat and let simmer about 1 hour, or until joints of chicken move easily.

Remove chicken from pan and keep warm.

Strain cooking liquid, and discard vegetables. Return liquid to pan and heat over low heat. Stir in dissolved cornstarch, yogurt and sour cream. Heat until thickened to sauce consistency.

To serve, cut chicken in serving pieces, remove skin, and coat pieces with tarragon sauce. Serve with steamed zucchini, celery root, and a rice pilaf, if desired.

1 SERVING		
285 CALORIES	17g CARBOHYDRATE	34g PROTEIN
9g FAT	0g FIBER	109mg CHOLESTEROL

CHICKEN BREASTS STUFFED WITH SPINACH AND HAZELNUTS

4 SERVINGS

4	skinless, boneless chicken breast halves	4
¹/₂ cup	grated Gruyère cheese	125 mL
¹/₄ cup	chopped hazelnuts	50 mL
¹/₂ cup	packed, chopped fresh spinach	125 mL
¹/₄ cup	all-purpose flour	50 mL
2	eggs, lightly beaten	2
I	pinch ground nutmeg	I
¹/₄ cup	dry breadcrumbs	50 mL
2 tbsp	vegetable oil	30 mL
	freshly ground pepper	

Preheat oven to 350°F (180°C).

Cut a long slit in the side of each breast half to make a deep pocket. Set aside.

In a bowl, stir together grated cheese, hazelnuts and spinach. Stuff chicken pieces with mixture. Coat outside with flour.

In a bowl, beat eggs together with nutmeg and pepper. Dip chicken in egg mixture, then coat evenly with breadcrumbs.

Heat oil in a nonstick skillet over medium-high heat. Brown chicken on both sides. Place chicken in single layer in baking dish. Finish cooking in oven about 15 to 20 minutes, or until chicken is no longer pink inside.

COOK'S TIP

These stuffed chicken breasts look absolutely spectacular cut into slices so that the layers show, and arranged on a bed of fresh tomato sauce. In fact, this is a handy chef's trick for showing off any stuffed or layered dish.

1 SERVING		
386 CALORIES	10g CARBOHYDRATE	37g PROTEIN
22g FAT	0.7g FIBER	226mg CHOLESTEROL

DUCK BREASTS WITH BLACKCURRANT SAUCE

2 SERVINGS

COOK'S TIP

Don't be put off by the amount of garlic in this recipe; the cooking technique turns it into a mellow vegetable with no hint of its usual pungency.

1 cup	unpeeled garlic cloves	250 mL
2	potatoes, peeled and sliced	2
2 cups	2% milk	500 mL
2	blackcurrant tea bags	2
2	boneless duck breasts	2
2 tbsp	coarse salt	30 mL
1 tbsp	coarsely crushed peppercorns	15 mL
2 tbsp	blackcurrant vinegar or raspberry vinegar	30 mL
1/4 cup	blackcurrant jelly	50 mL

Preheat oven to 350°F (180°C). Place garlic, unpeeled, in a saucepan with enough cold water to cover. Bring to a boil, then remove from heat and let cool enough to handle.

Peel garlic cloves and place cloves in a saucepan with potatoes and milk. Cook over medium heat about 30 minutes, until tender. Drain, and mash potatoes together with garlic.

Place tea bags in 2 cups (500 mL) boiling water to steep. Set aside.

Rub fatty side of duck breasts with salt and peppercorns. Heat a heavy skillet over medium heat, and add duck breasts, fat side down. Cook 2 ½ minutes. Turn and cook 1 minute. Place duck breasts in a baking dish.

Return skillet to burner on medium heat. Stir in vinegar, then add tea. Bring to a boil and cook until reduced by half. Lower heat and stir in jelly until sauce is smooth.

Finish cooking duck breasts in oven 5 minutes. Do not overcook; they should be rosy inside when done. Slice breasts lengthwise to serve, topped with blackcurrant sauce and accompanied by garlicky potato purée.

~

1 SERVING		
628 CALORIES	77g CARBOHYDRATE	53g PROTEIN
12g FAT	4.0g FIBER	147mg CHOLESTEROL

WARM DUCK BREAST SALAD
WITH RASPBERRY VINEGAR

2 SERVINGS

2	boneless duck breast halves	2
1 tbsp	prepared mustard	15 mL
1 tbsp	vegetable oil	15 mL
8	Boston lettuce leaves	8
4	escarole or curly lettuce leaves	4
4	radicchio leaves	4
1	Belgian endive, cleaned and sliced	1
1	green apple, cored and cut in thin strips	1
	freshly ground pepper	

DRESSING

1/4 cup	raspberry vinegar	50 mL
1 tsp	crushed pink peppercorns	5 mL
1/4 cup	unsweetened apple juice	50 mL
2 tbsp	canola oil	30 mL
	salt and pepper	

Preheat oven to 350°F (180°C). Score skin of duck breasts in a diamond pattern with a sharp knife. Baste skin with mustard. Season with pepper.

Heat oil in an ovenproof skillet. Brown one side of duck over high heat. Turn and brown other side. Roast about 10 minutes in oven. Interior should be rosy pink. Remove duck from skillet and let stand 10 minutes.

Pour off and discard cooking juices from skillet. Heat skillet and stir in vinegar to deglaze. Add peppercorns and ground pepper. Stir in apple juice and oil. Remove from heat and let cool slightly.

Clean lettuce and arrange on plates with endive and apple. Remove skin from duck breasts, then slice meat thinly. Arrange slices over salad, and pour warm dressing on top.

~

1 SERVING		
352 CALORIES	17g CARBOHYDRATE	17g PROTEIN
24g FAT	2.9g FIBER	64mg CHOLESTEROL

TURKEY BREAST STUFFED WITH RED CABBAGE

~

4 SERVINGS

1 tsp	vegetable oil	5 mL
1 tbsp	butter or margarine	15 mL
¹/₂	head red cabbage, thinly sliced	¹/₂
¹/₄ cup	port wine or red wine	50 mL
¹/₄ cup	honey	50 mL
1	boneless turkey breast	1
2 cups	chicken stock	500 mL
	salt and pepper	

Preheat oven to 350°F (180°C).

Heat oil and butter over high heat in a large casserole or nonstick skillet. Add cabbage and stir-fry until glossy. Stir in port wine and honey. Lower heat to medium-low and simmer 10 to 15 minutes. Place in a bowl and let cool.

With a sharp knife, make a long incision lengthwise through the turkey breast to make a deep pocket. Fill with cabbage mixture. Place in a roasting pan. Pour chicken stock over. Cover and roast about 1 hour, or until turkey is cooked through.

Pour cooking juices into a saucepan. Season to taste and cook cover high heat until reduced by half. Serve sauce over slices of turkey breast, with vegetables of your choice.

~

1 Stir-fry cabbage over high heat. Stir in port and honey.

2 Cut a long slit down the middle of the turkey breast.

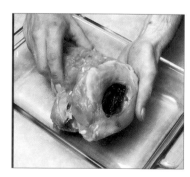

3 Stuff with cabbage mixture.

1 SERVING		
410 CALORIES	22g CARBOHYDRATE	58g PROTEIN
10g FAT	2.3g FIBER	137mg CHOLESTEROL

EASY INDIVIDUAL BEEF WELLINGTON

6 SERVINGS

COOK'S TIP

Serve with plain steamed green beans and potatoes, or with steamed corn and sweet peppers moistened with a touch of balsamic vinegar.

1 tbsp	butter or margarine	15 mL
2 lbs	beef filet, cut crosswise into six 1-inch (2.4 cm) thick medallions	1 kg
1/2 lb	chicken livers, trimmed and coarsely chopped	225 g
1 1/3 cups	sliced mushrooms	325 mL
8 oz	puff pastry	225 g
1	egg, beaten	1

Melt butter in a nonstick skillet. Brown beef medallions on both sides 2 minutes over high heat. Set beef aside.

In the same skillet, cook chicken livers 2 minutes, stirring. Add mushrooms and cook 3 minutes. Let livers and mushrooms cool.

Roll pastry out in a rectangle 8 x 16 inches (20 x 40 cm). Cut into 6 equal rectangles. Divide liver and mushroom mixture among rectangles. Top each with a beef medallion. Fold up pastry to make envelopes. Place on a baking sheet, brush with egg, and refrigerate 1 hour.

Preheat oven to 400°F (200°C). Remove pastries from refrigerator and place immediately in hot oven. Bake 20 minutes.

1 SERVING		
460 CALORIES	12g CARBOHYDRATE	40g PROTEIN
28g FAT	0.2g FIBER	142mg CHOLESTEROL

HONEYED POT ROAST

4 SERVINGS

2 lbs	lean, boneless beef roast	1 kg
1 tsp	dried thyme	5 mL
1 tbsp	cracked peppercorns	15 mL
2 tbsp	vegetable oil	30 mL
3 tbsp	all-purpose flour	45 mL
¼ cup	liquid honey	50 mL
3 cups	beef stock	750 mL
1	bay leaf	1
3	large carrots	3
1	turnip	1
1	medium rutabaga	1

Preheat oven to 350°F (180°C). Sprinkle roast with thyme and peppercorns.

Heat oil in a large casserole. Add roast and brown on all sides over medium-high heat. Remove roast and set aside.

Stir flour well into pan drippings. Stir in honey, then return roast to casserole. Add beef stock and bay leaf.

Roast, uncovered, in oven for 20 minutes. Meanwhile, peel vegetables and cut into pieces, as shown. Continue cooking in oven another 30 minutes, or until vegetables are tender and meat is done to taste. Serve with a gravy boat of the cooking juices.

COOK'S TIP

This moist oven cooking method is a good way to prepare lean cuts, as it tenderizes the meat without drying it.

1 SERVING		
465 CALORIES	31g CARBOHYDRATE	38g PROTEIN
21g FAT	3.3g FIBER	83mg CHOLESTEROL

VEAL ROLLS WITH CHEESE SAUCE

4 SERVINGS

COOK'S TIP

You can use this same recipe with thin cutlets of chicken, turkey, or pork. If you wish, stir 2 tbsp (30 mL) low-fat mayonnaise into the cheese sauce to add another dimension to the flavor.

1/2 cup	grated Gruyère cheese	125 mL
1/2 cup	grated Parmesan cheese	125 mL
1 cup	skim milk	250 mL
1	garlic clove, finely chopped	1
2 tbsp	white sauce and gravy thickener	30 mL
4	veal cutlets, 5 oz (150 g) each	4
	salt and pepper	

In a bowl, stir together the 2 cheeses with garlic and milk. Cover and refrigerate 4 hours or overnight.

Preheat oven to 350°F (180°C).

Pour chilled cheese mixture into a small saucepan. Heat over medium heat until bubbling. Stir in sauce thickener. Keep warm.

Meanwhile, pound veal cutlets and roll them up. Arrange in a greased baking dish. Bake in preheated oven 18 to 20 minutes.

Pour cheese sauce over veal rolls and bake another 5 minutes. Serve with fried mushrooms and steamed spinach, if desired.

1 SERVING		
386 CALORIES	7g CARBOHYDRATE	49g PROTEIN
18g FAT	0.1g FIBER	166mg CHOLESTEROL

VEAL MEDALLIONS WITH VERMOUTH

4 SERVINGS

4	veal filets, about 5 oz (150 g) each	4
4	slices bacon, chopped	4
I cup	dry red vermouth	250 mL
I cup	chicken stock	250 mL
2 tbsp	whipping cream	30 mL
	grated zest of I lemon	

Cut veal into slices about ½ inch (2 cm) thick. Place veal slices in a skillet with chopped bacon. Brown on both sides over medium-high heat. Pour off excess fat.

Stir in vermouth and lemon zest. Cover and let simmer 5 minutes. Add chicken stock and cook over low heat 7 minutes to reduce sauce. Remove meat from skillet and set aside to keep warm.

Stir whipping cream into sauce. Cook over low heat until slightly thickened. Serve sauce with veal medallions.

~

COOK'S TIP

Thrifty French cooks sometimes stretch meat dishes such as this by serving the meat on top of toasted bread rounds. Use a firm country style bread or English muffin halves, and brown the bread in a little butter or olive oil.

1 SERVING		
308 CALORIES	1g CARBOHYDRATE	40g PROTEIN
16g FAT	0.2g FIBER	155mg CHOLESTEROL

BAKED HAM WITH PEAR AND CRANBERRY SAUCE

~

6 to 8 SERVINGS

COOK'S TIP

This is a good solution for festive occasions when you do not want to spend much time in the kitchen. The sauce can be made ahead and frozen. Boil the ham the day before and leave overnight in the cooking liquid, then finish cooking in the oven an hour before your meal. Serve with a steamed green vegetable and potatoes.

4 cups	cold water	1 liter
4 cups	beer or unsweetened apple juice	1 liter
2	carrots, quartered	2
4	onions, quartered	4
1	garlic clove, finely chopped	1
4	celery stalks	4
1	bay leaf	1
1 tbsp	dry mustard	15 mL
1 tbsp	pickling spice	15 mL
1	smoked ham, 5 to 7 lbs (2.5 to 3 kg)	1

Place all ingredients except ham in a large saucepan (big enough to hold the ham). Cover and let simmer 30 minutes.

Put ham in hot liquid. Cover and simmer over very low heat, without boiling, about 1 hour.

Let ham cool in cooking liquid. Remove ham and remove rind and excess fat layer. Place ham in a baking pan.

Baste with some of the Pear and Cranberry Sauce. Bake in 300°F (160°C) oven 40 to 45 minutes. Baste with pan juices during cooking. Serve hot or cold.

~

1 SERVING		
557 CALORIES	35g CARBOHYDRATE	66g PROTEIN
17g FAT	3.3g FIBER	166mg CHOLESTEROL

PEAR AND CRANBERRY SAUCE

MAKES 2 CUPS (500 mL)

2 cups	cranberries	500 mL
I cup	peeled and grated fresh pears (or chopped canned pears)	250 mL
I	pinch ground cloves	I
I	pinch ground allspice	I
³/4 cup	sugar	175 mL
¹/4 cup	water	50 mL
I tbsp	lemon juice	15 mL
I tbsp	grated orange or lemon zest	15 mL

Combine all ingredients in a large saucepan. Cover and bring to a boil. Turn down heat and let simmer, stirring a few times, just until cranberries burst their skins.

Sieve the sauce or leave chunky, as you prefer. Serve sauce hot or cold with baked ham.

~

1 SERVING (¼ CUP/50 ML)		
96 CALORIES	24g CARBOHYDRATE	0g PROTEIN
0g FAT	2.6g FIBER	0mg CHOLESTEROL

HAM AND VEGETABLE CRÊPES

4 SERVINGS

COOK'S TIP

Use purchased crêpes if you are short of time. These stuffed crêpes are lower in fat than most versions, but still rather rich. Serve with a salad to start and a light fruit dessert.

CRÊPE BATTER

³/4 cup	all-purpose flour	175 mL
¹/2 tsp	salt	2 mL
1	egg	1
1 cup	skim milk	250 mL
1 tbsp	melted butter or margarine	15 mL
	vegetable oil for frying	

FILLING

¹/3 cup	julienned carrots	75 mL
¹/3 cup	julienned celery	75 mL
¹/3 cup	julienned leeks	75 mL
1¹/2 cups	julienned lean cooked ham	375 mL

LIGHT WHITE SAUCE

2 cups	skim milk	500 mL
¹/4 cup	all-purpose flour	50 mL
2 tbsp	melted butter or margarine	30 mL
¹/4 tsp	ground nutmeg	1 mL
1 cup	grated Emmenthal or Swiss cheese	250 mL
	salt and pepper	

Mix all crêpe ingredients except oil in a food processor, or beat together in a bowl until smooth. Brush a nonstick skillet with oil and heat over medium heat. Pour in ¼ cup (50 mL) batter to make a crêpe. When brown on first side, turn and cook second side. Repeat with remaining batter. Set crêpes aside.

Lightly steam carrots, celery and leeks. Drain and combine in a bowl with the ham. Place a few spoonfuls of mixture on each crêpe and roll up. Arrange side by side in a baking dish. Set aside.

To make the white sauce: heat milk in a saucepan until barely bubbling. Stir together flour and melted butter until well combined. Stir flour mixture into milk. Season with nutmeg, salt and pepper. When smooth and thickened, pour over crêpes. Top with grated cheese.

Bake in preheated 400°F (200°C) oven until lightly browned on top.

1 Cook crêpes one by one.

2 Combine julienned ham and vegetables.

3 Stuff and roll crêpes.

4 Cover with white sauce and grated cheese.

1 SERVING		
468 CALORIES	35g CARBOHYDRATE	28g PROTEIN
24g FAT	1.4g FIBER	295mg CHOLESTEROL

PORK FILET WITH ORANGE AND GREEN PEPPERCORN SAUCE

6 SERVINGS

COOK'S TIP

The sweet flavor of braised diced rutabaga plays up the pork flavor nicely. Dice rutabaga and cook slowly in a little butter or oil until lightly browned. Steamed snowpeas add a fresh color note.

2	pork filets, I lb (450 g) each	2
I tbsp	all-purpose flour	15 mL
I tbsp	vegetable oil	15 mL
I	garlic clove, chopped	I
¼ cup	dry white wine	50 mL
2 tbsp	frozen orange juice concentrate	30 mL
2 tsp	green peppercorns	10 mL
½ cup	whipping cream	125 mL
	salt and pepper	
	strips of orange peel	

Preheat oven to 375°F (190°C).

Dust pork with flour. Heat oil in ovenproof skillet over medium heat. Brown pork on all sides. Sprinkle pork with garlic, salt and pepper. Decorate with strips of orange peel.

Roast in oven about 12 minutes, or until meat thermometer reads 160°F (70°C). Interior of pork should be barely rosy. Remove filets from pan, cover with foil and let stand 10 minutes.

Pour off excess fat from skillet. Stir wine into pan drippings to deglaze. Add frozen orange juice and peppercorns. Heat over medium heat until reduced by half, scraping pan well.

Reduce heat and stir in cream. Let simmer about 1 minute, or until sauce is creamy.

Cut each filet into 3 pieces. Serve with peppercorn sauce.

1 SERVING		
329 CALORIES	4g CARBOHYDRATE	22g PROTEIN
25g FAT	0.1g FIBER	83mg CHOLESTEROL

ROAST PORK WITH PRUNES

~

6 SERVINGS

2 lb	boneless rolled pork loin or filet	1 kg
3 tbsp	vegetable oil	45 mL
10 oz	dried pitted prunes	300 g
	crushed peppercorns	

Preheat oven to 425°F (220°C). Roll pork roast on all sides in crushed peppercorns, pressing them well onto the surface. Baste roast on all sides with oil. Place in a roasting pan.

Roast in preheated oven 30 minutes. Turn the roast, reduce heat to 400°F (200°C), and cook another 30 minutes. Turn roast again, reduce heat to 350°F (180°C), and roast 40 minutes more.

While roast is cooking, place prunes in a saucepan and cover with cold water. Bring to a boil, then remove from heat. Set aside to allow prunes to plump up.

Pour off pan juices from roast 10 minutes before roast is cooked to taste. Pour juices into a small nonstick skillet. Drain prunes and add them to skillet. Season to taste with salt and pepper and set aside.

Arrange cooked roast on a serving dish, surrounded with prunes. Serve with steamed broccoli and cauliflower florets, carrots and mashed potatoes, if desired.

~

COOK'S TIP

Whichever pork cut you select, ask the butcher to roll and tie the roast in an even log shape so that the slices will be uniform.

1 SERVING

338 CALORIES	31g CARBOHYDRATE	22g PROTEIN
14g FAT	3.7g FIBER	56mg CHOLESTEROL

BAKED STUFFED LAMB CHOPS

4 SERVINGS

NUTRITION TIP

Sweet potatoes, like other orange-colored vegetables, are a good source of beta-carotene.

8	lamb rib chops, 3/4 inch (2 cm) thick	8
1 tsp	salt	5 mL
1/2 tsp	pepper	2 mL
2 tsp	chopped fresh mint	10 mL
1/4 cup	butter, diced	50 mL
1	onion, chopped	1
1	medium sweet potato, peeled and diced	1
1 cup	dry breadcrumbs	250 mL
1	egg, beaten	1
1 tbsp	finely chopped fresh parsley	15 mL
2 tbsp	dry white wine	30 mL
1/4 cup	chicken stock	50 mL

Preheat oven to 325°F (160°C). Cut a slit in the side of each chop to make a pocket. Sprinkle interior with salt, pepper and mint.

Melt half the butter in a skillet, add onion, and cook over medium heat until soft. Add sweet potato. Cover and cook over medium heat 8 to 10 minutes, stirring occasionally, until sweet potato is tender.

Remove from heat and mash sweet potato and onion together. Stir in breadcrumbs, egg, parsley, white wine and chicken stock. Mix well.

Stuff lamb chops with mixture. Hold slits closed with bamboo skewers. Baste chops with remaining butter. Place in a single layer in a baking dish and bake 30 to 35 minutes, or until done to taste.

Serve with rice and a green vegetable of your choice.

	1 SERVING	
580 CALORIES	35g CARBOHYDRATE	38g PROTEIN
32g FAT	2.7g FIBER	198mg CHOLESTEROL

FILET OF LAMB WITH RHUBARB

4 SERVINGS

2 cups	diced rhubarb, fresh or frozen	500 mL
1 tbsp	vegetable oil	15 mL
4	lamb filets, 4 oz (110 g) each	4
1/3 cup	white vermouth	75 mL
3/4 cup	vegetable stock	175 mL
	juice of 1 orange	

In a saucepan, cook rhubarb together with orange juice over medium heat about 15 minutes or until rhubarb reaches a compote (jam-like) consistency. Set aside.

Slice lamb filets crosswise into medallions about ¾ inch (2 cm) thick. Heat oil over high heat and cook lamb pieces 2 minutes on each side. Remove lamb and keep warm.

Return pan to heat and stir in vermouth. Add vegetable stock and cook 2 minutes to reduce. Serve lamb topped with vermouth sauce, and accompanied with rhubarb compote.

COOK'S TIP

French cooks often serve lamb with tender flageolet or haricot beans. You can substitute canned, drained and rinsed white beans or pea beans, heated with a little olive oil and herbs. All dried beans are a good source of fiber.

1 SERVING		
228 CALORIES	5g CARBOHYDRATE	25g PROTEIN
12g FAT	0.9g FIBER	78mg CHOLESTEROL

ROAST STUFFED LEG OF LAMB

8 SERVINGS

1 tbsp	butter or margarine	15 mL
3	garlic cloves, crushed	3
2	onions, chopped	2
10 oz	package frozen spinach, thawed	300 g
1 cup	15% cream	250 mL
1/2 lb	bulk sausage meat	225 g
1/2 cup	grated Swiss cheese	125 mL
1	boneless leg of lamb	1
3 tbsp	vegetable oil	45 mL
1 tsp	dried thyme	5 mL
1 tsp	dried rosemary	5 mL
1 cup	dry white wine	250 mL
3 cups	chicken stock	750 mL
1 cup	vegetable juice	250 mL
1	bay leaf	1

COOK'S TIP

Boneless leg of lamb usually comes rolled and tied. You will have to untie it to stuff it, and then tie it again with kitchen string to keep the filling inside.

Preheat oven to 450°F (230°C). In a saucepan, melt butter and cook garlic and onions over medium heat about 5 minutes.

Add spinach and cream. Cook 5 minutes more. Transfer to a bowl and let cool. Stir in crumbled sausage meat and grated cheese, mixing well.

Stuff lamb leg with mixture. Tie leg tightly closed and rub surface with oil, thyme and rosemary. Place in a roasting pan in the oven.

When surface is browned, reduce oven heat to 400°F (200°C). Add wine, stock, vegetable juice and bay leaf to pan. Roast, uncovered, another 40 to 50 minutes, until done to taste.

Let stand 10 minutes before carving. Skim fat from pan juices and serve in a gravy boat.

1 SERVING

395 CALORIES	7g CARBOHYDRATE	40g PROTEIN
23g FAT	1.7g FIBER	25mg CHOLESTEROL

INDIAN LAMB CURRY

4 SERVINGS

2	onions, chopped	2
I	garlic clove, chopped	I
2 tbsp	vegetable oil	30 mL
2	tomatoes, diced	2
I	bay leaf	I
2 tbsp	curry powder	30 mL
2 lbs	cubed boneless lamb shoulder	I kg
I cup	water	250 mL
¹/₂ cup	plain nonfat yogurt	125 mL
	cayenne pepper	

COOK'S TIP

This is an infinitely versatile recipe for almost any type of meat. It's also a good way to use up leftover roast turkey or beef, although you won't need to simmer it as long. For added color and nutrition, stir in some frozen peas or leftover green beans during the last few minutes of cooking.

Heat 1 tbsp (15 mL) oil in a casserole and cook onions and garlic until soft over medium heat. Add tomatoes and bay leaf. Cook over low heat a few minutes. Stir in curry powder. Let simmer 2 minutes. Remove from heat and set aside.

Heat remaining oil in large nonstick skillet. Add cubed lamb and cook over high heat until browned on all sides, stirring from time to time.

Add lamb to casserole with onion mixture. Add water. Let simmer over low heat about 1 hour, or until lamb is tender and sauce is thickened. Stir in yogurt at the last minute, and season to taste with cayenne.

Serve with steamed rice and a fruit chutney as an accent.

1 SERVING

313 CALORIES	9g CARBOHYDRATE	31g PROTEIN
17g FAT	1.4g FIBER	92mg CHOLESTEROL

LOBSTER RAGOUT
WITH SPINACH FETTUCINE

~

4 SERVINGS

11 oz	can frozen lobster (or 2 cups fresh shelled lobster meat)	320 g
1/2 cup	lobster juice (drained from lobster) or chicken stock	125 mL
1/4 cup	whipping cream	50 mL
1 1/2 tsp	cornstarch	7 mL
1/4 cup	olive oil	50 mL
1 tsp	mustard seeds	5 mL
1	garlic clove, chopped	1
1	red bell pepper, diced	1
8	large fresh mushrooms, sliced	8
1/2 tsp	salt	2 mL
1/4 cup	chopped fresh parsley	50 mL
1 lb	spinach fettucine, cooked and drained	450 g
	juice of 1 lemon	

Thaw frozen lobster, drain, and reserve juice. Cut meat into pieces, reserving claws for garnish. Set aside.

In a bowl, combine ½ cup (125 mL) lobster juice with whipping cream. Stir in cornstarch until dissolved. Set aside.

Heat olive oil over medium-high in a wok or large skillet equipped with a lid. Add mustard seeds and cover immediately with lid, as seeds will jump. Shake pan 20 to 30 seconds or until seeds stop popping. Reduce heat.

Stir in garlic, red pepper, mushrooms, lemon juice and salt. Cook 2 minutes.

Add lobster meat, parsley, and lobster juice mixture. Cook until lobster is heated through and sauce is slightly thickened.

Arrange cooked fettucine on heated plates and surround with lobster mixture. Garnish with reserved claws and chopped parsley.

~

1 SERVING

602 CALORIES	*83g CARBOHYDRATE*	*27g PROTEIN*
18g FAT	*0.8g FIBER*	*72mg CHOLESTEROL*

CREAMY TARRAGON SCAMPI

4 SERVINGS

COOK'S TIP

This is a good way to prepare frozen scampi, as the cooking procedure will keep them moist and tender, as long as you don't overcook them. Serve with steamed rice or pasta.

12 to 16	scampi	12 to 16
2 tsp	vegetable oil	10 mL
1	onion, chopped	1
6	fresh mushrooms, quartered	6
1 cup	canned stewed tomatoes	250 mL
1 tbsp	chopped fresh parsley	15 mL
1/2	garlic clove, finely chopped	1/2
3 tbsp	whipping cream	45 mL
1 tbsp	butter or margarine	15 mL
1	pinch tarragon	1
2 tbsp	dry sherry or brandy	30 mL
	juice of 1/2 lemon	
	salt and freshly ground pepper	

Using scissors, cut scampi shells open along bottom and peel off shells. Cut scampi in half lengthwise. Toss with lemon juice and set aside.

Heat oil in a skillet and cook onion and mushrooms until softened. Add tomatoes, parsley and garlic. Stir well and simmer a few minutes to thicken slightly.

Pour in cream. Stir and cook over medium heat until slightly thickened. Season to taste and set aside.

Heat butter in a nonstick skillet over medium-high heat. Add scampi and cook, stirring, until pink. Add tarragon and sherry; stir well. Cook over medium-high heat until scampi are tender. Do not overcook.

Stir in reserved tomato sauce and serve immediately.

1 SERVING		
154 CALORIES	7g CARBOHYDRATE	9g PROTEIN
10g FAT	1.3g FIBER	93mg CHOLESTEROL

SMOKED SALMON CRÊPES

4 SERVINGS

I	batch crêpes (see recipe page 168)	I

FILLING

I tbsp	vegetable oil	15 mL
I cup	julienned leeks (white part only)	250 mL
I cup	julienned zucchini	250 mL
I cup	julienned smoked salmon	250 mL
	salt and pepper	

BASIL SAUCE

I tbsp	butter or margarine	15 mL
I tbsp	chopped dry French shallots	15 mL
¹/₂ cup	dry white wine	125 mL
¹/₂ cup	15% cream	125 mL
I cup	light white sauce (see recipe page 168)	250 mL
¹/₂ cup	chopped fresh basil	125 mL
	salt and pepper	

Make crêpes according to recipe on page 168, or use purchased crêpes. Set aside.

To make the basil sauce: melt butter in a saucepan and cook shallots until soft. Add white wine and cook until reduced by ⅓. Stir in cream and white sauce. Simmer a few minutes, then stir in basil and season to taste. Keep sauce hot.

Preheat oven to 400°F (200°C).

Heat oil in a skillet over high heat. Add leeks and zucchini. Stir-fry 2 to 3 minutes. Remove from heat and stir in julienned smoked salmon. Season to taste. Spread mixture on crêpes, and fold in quarters. Arrange crêpes in a greased baking dish.

Bake in oven about 10 minutes. Garnish with basil sauce just before serving.

COOK'S TIP

Crêpes are a great way to stretch expensive ingredients such as smoked salmon. And it's fun to think of interesting fillings using your favorite ingredients; you can try anything from caviar to fresh strawberries with whipped cream!

1 SERVING		
637 CALORIES	40g CARBOHYDRATE	27g PROTEIN
41g FAT	2.4g FIBER	180 mg CHOLESTEROL

SALMON WITH SORREL SAUCE

~

4 SERVINGS

<table>
<tr><td>1 tbsp</td><td>olive oil</td><td>15 mL</td></tr>
<tr><td>1 tbsp</td><td>butter or margarine</td><td>15 mL</td></tr>
<tr><td>4</td><td>thick crosscuts of salmon filet, 7 oz (200 g) each</td><td>4</td></tr>
<tr><td>¼ cup</td><td>chopped fresh sorrel</td><td>50 mL</td></tr>
<tr><td>¼ cup</td><td>dry white wine</td><td>50 mL</td></tr>
<tr><td>¼ cup</td><td>light cream cheese</td><td>50 mL</td></tr>
<tr><td>¼ cup</td><td>skim milk</td><td>50 mL</td></tr>
<tr><td>2 tbsp</td><td>fresh lemon juice</td><td>30 mL</td></tr>
<tr><td></td><td>freshly ground pepper</td><td></td></tr>
</table>

COOK'S TIP

Sorrel is an herb with an acidic taste that adds a wonderful crisp flavor to sauces and salads. If you cannot find sorrel, you can make the sauce using about ½ cup (125 mL) spinach or watercress instead.

Preheat oven to 350°F (180°C). Heat oil and butter in an ovenproof skillet over medium heat. Add salmon and cook 5 minutes on each side. Stir in sorrel and white wine. Cover and bake in oven 10 minutes.

Remove salmon from pan and keep warm. Over low heat, simmer pan juices. Gradually whisk in cream cheese and then milk. Stir in lemon juice and season to taste.

Pour sorrel sauce on heated plates, and arrange salmon on top. Delicious served with sautéed potatoes.

~

1 Cook the salmon on both sides in oil and butter.

2 Add chopped sorrel and white wine. Cover and bake 10 minutes.

3 Remove salmon from pan and keep warm. Stir in cream cheese and milk.

4 Add lemon juice and season sauce to taste.

1 SERVING		
321 CALORIES	2g CARBOHYDRATE	40g PROTEIN
17g FAT	0.1g FIBER	118mg CHOLESTEROL

CAJUN SALMON

~

4 SERVINGS

COOK'S TIP

You can use this same spice mixture and technique to prepare boneless chicken breasts. It is important to use fresh spices and herbs in this and other recipes. Ground spices lose their flavor after 6 months, so throw them away, and replace with small quantities of fresh ones.

I	garlic clove, finely chopped	I
I tsp	dried basil	5 mL
I tsp	dried thyme	5 mL
1/2 tsp	ground nutmeg	2 mL
3 tbsp	paprika	45 mL
3 tbsp	curry powder	45 mL
I tsp	cayenne pepper	5 mL
1/4 tsp	ground cloves	I mL
1/2 tsp	ground cinnamon	2 mL
1/2 tsp	black pepper	2 mL
4	thick crosscuts of salmon filet, 7 oz (200 g) each	4
I tbsp	vegetable oil	15 mL

In a bowl, stir together garlic with herbs and spices. Coat salmon pieces with spice mixture, patting mixture firmly into the salmon.

Preheat oven to 350°F (180°C). Heat oil in a nonstick skillet over high heat. Add salmon and cook 3 minutes on each side. Finish cooking in the oven 15 minutes.

Serve with a spicy tomato sauce and rice or potatoes, if desired.

~

1 SERVING		
260 CALORIES	0g CARBOHYDRATE	38g PROTEIN
12g FAT	0g FIBER	102mg CHOLESTEROL

SOLE AND TROUT
WITH TOMATO BASIL SAUCE

❧

6 SERVINGS

3	sole filets, skin removed	3
6	rainbow trout filets, skin removed	6
I tbsp	soft butter or margarine	15 mL
2 cups	chicken stock or fish stock	500 mL
	salt and pepper	

TOMATO BASIL SAUCE

4	large ripe or canned tomatoes, coarsely chopped	4
I cup	chicken or fish stock	250 mL
3/4 cup	dry white wine	175 mL
1/4 cup	10% cream	50 mL
I tsp	chopped fresh basil	5 mL
I	garlic clove	I

Preheat oven to 400°F (200°C).

Lay out fish filets on work surface and cut into strips lengthwise to make 18 strips. Braid together 2 trout strips with 1 strip of sole. You should have 6 braids in all.

Grease a baking pan. Using a metal spatula, gently arrange fish braids in pan. Pour in chicken stock. Cover pan tightly with foil and bake 6 to 8 minutes, or just until fish flakes easily with a fork. Be careful not to overcook. Serve fish braids on a bed of heated tomato basil sauce.

To make the sauce: blend all ingredients in a food processor or blender until smooth. Strain, if desired. Heat sauce in a saucepan over low heat until hot.

~

1 SERVING		
231 CALORIES	5g CARBOHYDRATE	37g PROTEIN
7g FAT	1.0g FIBER	108mg CHOLESTEROL

SOLE AND CARROT TIMBALES

4 SERVINGS

2 tbsp	butter or margarine	30 mL
I	onion, chopped	I
I	garlic clove, finely chopped	I
1/2 cup	chopped fresh mushrooms	125 ml
1/2 cup	grated carrots	125 mL
1/3 cup	dry breadcrumbs	75 mL
1/4 cup	chopped fresh parsley	50 mL
I tbsp	lemon juice	15 mL
1/4 tsp	dried marjoram	I mL
I	egg, lightly beaten	I
1 1/2 lbs	sole filets	675 g
	salt and pepper	

COOK'S TIP

To make a light béchamel sauce: Heat 1 tbsp (15 mL) vegetable oil in a saucepan. Stir in 1 tbsp (15 mL) all-purpose flour. When blended, gradually whisk in 1 cup (250 mL) heated milk. Simmer over low heat until thickened. Strain out lumps if necessary. Season to taste with salt and chopped fresh parsley.

Preheat oven to 400°F (200°C). Melt butter in a skillet. Add onion and garlic and cook 4 minutes. Add mushrooms and cook 2 minutes.

Remove from heat. Stir in grated carrots, breadcrumbs, parsley, lemon juice, marjoram, salt and pepper. Stir in egg. Set aside.

Grease 4 ramekins. Line them with sole filets, cutting pieces as necessary so that sole is only one layer thick on bottom and sides of ramekins. Fill centers of ramekins with carrot mixture. Cover each with foil.

Place ramekins in a baking dish. Pour boiling water in baking dish to halfway up sides of ramekins. Bake 15 to 20 minutes, or until fish is cooked (it should flake with a fork.) Unmold timbales and serve with a homemade or canned white sauce, if desired, and with vegetable garnish of your choice.

1 SERVING

264 CALORIES	*10g CARBOHYDRATE*	*38g PROTEIN*
8g FAT	*0.9g FIBER*	*184mg CHOLESTEROL*

SOLE FILETS MONACO

4 SERVINGS

8	sole filets, fresh or frozen, about 3¹/₂ oz (100 g) each	8
1 tbsp	olive oil	15 mL
2 tbsp	pickled capers, drained	30 mL
2	lemons, peeled, membranes removed from segments	2
2 tbsp	chopped pitted black olives	30 mL
¹/₄ cup	dry white wine	50 mL
¹/₄ cup	toasted croutons	50 mL
1 tbsp	chopped fresh parsley	15 mL
	all-purpose flour	
	salt and freshly ground pepper	

Season the sole filets and coat them in flour on both sides. Heat oil in a large nonstick skillet and cook sole filets 2 to 3 minutes on each side over medium-high heat. They should be lightly browned. Remove from skillet and set aside.

In the same skillet, heat capers, lemon segments and black olives over medium heat until warmed through. Add white wine. Let simmer 3 to 4 minutes over low heat. Add croutons and parsley.

Return filets briefly to pan to rewarm. Serve sole on a bed of the sauce, and garnished with fruit such as mango slices and kiwi.

COOK'S TIP

Capers are the tiny buds of the caper bush, which grows in the Mediterranean region. When pickled, these buds taste a little like sour gherkins. They complement fish, and are a classic accompaniment to smoked salmon. Heat increases their pungent flavor, so never cook them too long.

1 SERVING		
260 CALORIES	8g CARBOHYDRATE	39g PROTEIN
8g FAT	0.9g FIBER	106mg CHOLESTEROL

NEW ENGLAND BOUILLABAISSE

4 SERVINGS

2 tbsp	olive oil	30 mL
3	green onions, chopped	3
1	garlic clove, chopped	1
28 oz	can tomatoes with herbs	796 mL
1/2 cup	chicken stock	125 mL
1	large potato, diced	1
1 tsp	dried basil	5 mL
1 tsp	Worcestershire sauce	5 mL
1/4 tsp	dried dill weed	1 mL
1/2 lb	fish filets (such as haddock, halibut, cod, turbot, bellyfish, ocean perch), cubed	225 g
1/2 lb	small peeled shrimp, fresh or frozen	225 g
1 lb	cultivated mussels	450 g
	salt and freshly ground pepper	

COOK'S TIP

True bouillabaisse is a complex mixture of fish and shellfish native to the Mediterranean. For a really spectacular version, add a can of thawed frozen lobster meat. Cultivated mussels are sweet and succulent, but unlike the wild version, are really easy to prepare. Just rinse them in cool water, and pop them into the pot.

Heat oil in a large saucepan over medium heat. Add green onions and cook 2 minutes. Add garlic, stir well and cook 1 minute.

Stir in tomatoes, breaking them up with a fork. Add chicken stock, potato, basil, Worcestershire and dill. Cover and let simmer 15 minutes or until potato is tender. Stir from time to time to prevent sticking.

Add cubed fish and shrimp. Let simmer 5 minutes uncovered, or until fish is nearly cooked. Add mussels, cover, and cook until mussels have opened. Discard any unopened mussels. Serve in big soup plates, with lots of crusty bread. Sprinkle servings with grated Swiss cheese, if desired.

1 SERVING

273 CALORIES	19g CARBOHYDRATE	29g PROTEIN
9g FAT	2.4g FIBER	152mg CHOLESTEROL

TAGLIATELLE WITH TWO SAUCES

4 SERVINGS

1 tbsp	olive oil	15 mL
2	garlic cloves, chopped	2
8 oz	canned baby clams, drained	225 g
19 oz	can herb-flavored tomatoes	540 mL
1/2 tsp	dried oregano	2 mL
1 tsp	chopped fresh coriander	5 mL
1	egg, lightly beaten	1
1 cup	light ricotta cheese	250 mL
1/4 cup	grated Parmesan cheese	50 mL
1 tbsp	chopped fresh parsley	15 mL
1 lb	tagliatelle or fettucine, cooked	450 g
	salt and freshly ground pepper	

Heat oil in a saucepan and add garlic and clams. Cook over medium heat 3 to 5 minutes. Stir in tomatoes and herbs. Let simmer over low heat 15 to 20 minutes, stirring from time to time.

In a bowl, stir together egg, ricotta, Parmesan and parsley. Season to taste with salt and pepper.

Arrange piping hot tomato sauce on plates with cooked drained pasta. (If you wish, you can toss the pasta with the sauce.) Make a little "nest" in the pasta and fill with the ricotta cheese mixture.

1 SERVING		
613 CALORIES	89g CARBOHYDRATE	35g PROTEIN
13g FAT	1.3g FIBER	126mg CHOLESTEROL

HOMEMADE PASTA

4 SERVINGS

3 cups	all-purpose flour	750 mL
6	eggs	6
	olive oil	

Make a mound of the flour on a work surface. Make a hollow in the flour with a spoon.

Break 6 eggs into the hollow. Using your hands, gradually work the flour from the edges into the eggs, drawing in more and more flour. When the dough is well combined, add a splash of olive oil and work it in.

If the dough is too stiff to roll out, you may work in up to ½ cup (125 mL) water. When dough is smooth and pliable, roll out on a lightly floured surface. Cut into desired noodle shapes with a sharp knife.

~

1 Make a hollow in the top of mound of flour. Break eggs into the hollow.

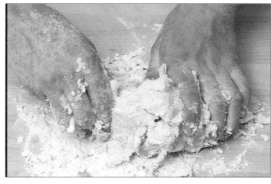

2 Gradually work flour into eggs, drawing flour from the edges with your hands.

3 Add a splash of olive oil. Add enough water to make dough pliable.

4 Roll out dough thinly on lightly floured surface.

1 SERVING		
497 CALORIES	76g CARBOHYDRATE	19g PROTEIN
13g FAT	3.1g FIBER	410mg CHOLESTEROL

INDIVIDUAL LASAGNE

4 SERVINGS

3 tbsp	butter or margarine	45 mL
1/4 cup	all-purpose flour	50 mL
2 cups	skim milk	500 mL
1	pinch nutmeg	1
16	green lasagne noodles, cooked	16
3/4 cup	grated Emmenthal cheese	175 mL
	salt and freshly ground pepper	

TOMATO MEAT SAUCE

1 tbsp	olive oil	15 mL
1/2	onion, chopped	1/2
1	garlic clove, chopped	1
1 lb	ground lean veal or turkey	450 g
2 tbsp	all-purpose flour	30 mL
19 oz	can tomatoes	540 mL
1/4 cup	tomato paste	50 mL
1	bay leaf	1
1 tsp	dried thyme	5 mL
1/2 tsp	dried marjoram	2 mL
1 tsp	sugar	5 mL

Preheat oven to 400°F (200°C).

Melt butter in a saucepan over medium heat and stir in flour well. Gradually add milk, stirring constantly to avoid lumps. Add nutmeg and season to taste. When sauce is smooth and thick, remove from heat. Cover and keep warm.

In a second saucepan, heat oil over medium heat. Stir in onion and garlic. Stir in meat, breaking up lumps with a fork. Cook 5 minutes, or until meat is browned. Sprinkle in flour and stir well.

Stir in tomatoes with their juice, tomato paste, bay leaf, thyme, marjoram and sugar. Simmer over low heat 15 minutes, stirring from time to time. Remove bay leaf and keep sauce warm.

Arrange a layer of lasagne noodles in the bottom of gratin dishes. Cover with tomato sauce, then a layer of white sauce. Repeat layers to use all ingredients. Cover with grated cheese. Bake in oven 15 to 20 minutes.

1 Prepare a white sauce with butter, flour and milk.

2 Sauté onion, garlic and meat until browned. Stir in flour.

3 Stir in tomatoes and seasonings.

4 Layer noodles, tomato sauce and white sauce in small baking dishes.

1 SERVING		
844 CALORIES	103g CARBOHYDRATE	45g PROTEIN
28g FAT	2.3g FIBER	138mg CHOLESTEROL

BARBECUE

Barbecuing has come a long way in the past few decades. A few purists still insist on barbecuing over genuine wood coals, but most of us have opted for the convenience of gas grills, which provide us with hot coals in minutes.

The convenience means that we can barbecue whenever we want, not just on weekends. But too many of us are still cooking up the same old burgers and steaks, instead of adapting to the convenience and health benefits of the many meat, chicken and fish cuts now available.

This chapter is packed with a variety of barbecue meals that are far from traditional, but incredibly easy. The emphasis is on lower-fat cuts of beef and alternatives such as chicken, turkey, and fish. A number of them involve easy marinades that add flavor and tenderness to less-expensive cuts.

You will also find suggestions for vegetable accompaniments that can be cooked right on the grill along with the main course. And for nutritious salads that can be made ahead and refrigerated without danger of wilting. So get out of the kitchen and get the most out of barbecue season!

~

SURPRISE CHICKEN BURGERS

4 SERVINGS

I lb	ground chicken	450 g
I tbsp	water	15 mL
3 tbsp	paprika	45 mL
3 tbsp	curry powder	45 mL
2	pinches cayenne pepper	2
1/2 tsp	ground oregano	2 mL
1/2 tsp	ground thyme	2 mL
4	slices Swiss cheese	4
	freshly ground pepper	

COOK'S TIP

A hinged grill rack allows you to turn low-fat burgers, like those made from chicken or lean beef, without crumbling.

In a bowl, sprinkle chicken with water and mix gently. Shape chicken into 4 patties. (The water will help prevent burgers from crumbling.) Set aside.

In a shallow bowl, mix paprika, curry, cayenne, oregano, thyme and pepper to taste. Coat patties on both sides in spice mixture.

Cook patties on oiled, preheated barbecue grill 6 to 8 minutes on each side.

Serve on toasted hamburger buns with cheese slices and garnishes of your choice.

1 SERVING		
263 CALORIES	I g CARBOHYDRATE	40g PROTEIN
11g FAT	0g FIBER	98 mg CHOLESTEROL

GRILLED CHICKEN WINGS
AND STUFFED ZUCCHINI

~

6 SERVINGS

3	zucchini, cut in $1/2$ lengthwise	3
2	green onions, chopped	2
I	green pepper, finely chopped	I
I	tomato, seeded and finely chopped	I
$1/2$ cup	green lentils, cooked	125 mL
I tsp	chopped fresh basil	5 mL
6	slices cheddar cheese	6
2 tbsp	ground hazelnuts	30 mL
24	chicken wings	24
	BBQ spice	
	salt and freshly ground pepper	

COOK'S TIP

Cook chicken wings over medium heat so that they do not char on the outside before the inside is cooked. Oil the grill before heating to prevent sticking. The wings are cooked when the joints move freely.

Scoop out seed section of zucchini to make boats. Set aside zucchini shells, and put scooped out sections in a bowl. Chop coarsely.

Add green onions, green pepper and tomato. Mix well, then stir in cooked drained lentils and basil. Season to taste.

Arrange each zucchini shell on a square of foil and stuff with lentil mixture. Cover with slice of cheese. Seal each foil package.

Cook foil packages on the barbecue grill 15 to 20 minutes. Zucchini should be fork tender. Unwrap and sprinkle with hazelnuts before serving.

Meanwhile, dust chicken wings in BBQ seasoning. Cook on grill until tender. Serve with stuffed zucchini boats.

~

1 SERVING

562 CALORIES   9g CARBOHYDRATE   46g PROTEIN

38g FAT   2.5g FIBER   146mg CHOLESTEROL

GRILLED CHICKEN BREASTS INDIAN-STYLE

6 SERVINGS

6	skinless, boneless chicken breast halves, about 5 oz (150 g) each	6
1/4 cup	vegetable oil	50 mL
3/4 cup	plain yogurt	175 mL
4	garlic cloves, crushed	4
2 tsp	paprika	10 mL
2 tsp	ground cumin	10 mL
2 tsp	turmeric	10 mL
1/2 tsp	ground ginger	2 mL
2 tsp	liquid beef stock concentrate	10 mL
	juice of 3 lemons	

Slash the surface of the chicken breasts and arrange them in a shallow dish. Set aside.

In a bowl combine all remaining ingredients, stirring well.

Pour mixture over chicken breasts, making sure all surfaces are well coated. Cover and refrigerate 12 hours.

Cook on an oiled, preheated barbecue grill 10 minutes on each side, or until cooked through, basting frequently with marinade.

COOK'S TIP

Traditional tandoori cooking is done in a clay oven heated with coals. The spicy yogurt marinade typical of the tandoori style tenderizes meat and keeps it juicy.

1 SERVING

268 CALORIES	3g CARBOHYDRATE	37g PROTEIN
12g FAT	0g FIBER	99mg CHOLESTEROL

GRILLED CHICKEN WITH HONEY GINGER SAUCE

~

4 SERVINGS

COOK'S TIP

*Chicken tournedos
are thick pieces
of boneless breast
wrapped with bacon,
to resemble the better
known beef tournedos.
If your butcher cannot
supply them, use plain
boneless chicken breast.*

2 tsp	finely chopped fresh ginger	10 mL
3 tbsp	liquid honey	45 mL
2 tbsp	balsamic vinegar	30 mL
1	onion, sliced	1
½ cup	dry white wine	125 mL
½ cup	water	125 mL
4	chicken tournedos or filets	4
2 tbsp	liquid chicken stock concentrate	30 mL
1 tbsp	cornstarch	15 mL

In a shallow dish, stir together ginger, honey, vinegar, onion, wine and water. Arrange chicken in this marinade. Let marinate, covered, 4 hours in refrigerator, turning chicken from time to time.

Drain chicken and cook on an oiled, preheated barbecue grill over low heat for 10 minutes each side, basting with marinade during cooking.

In a small saucepan, heat leftover marinade until boiling. Stir together chicken stock concentrate and cornstarch in a cup. Add to marinade. Bring to a boil and cook until sauce is thick. Serve sauce with chicken.

~

1 SERVING		
291 CALORIES	17g CARBOHYDRATE	31g PROTEIN
11g FAT	0.1g FIBER	94mg CHOLESTEROL

GRILLED TURKEY STEAKS
WITH OLD-FASHIONED BBQ SAUCE

~

4 SERVINGS

1 cup	tomato sauce	250 mL
3 tbsp	liquid chicken stock concentrate	45 mL
3 tbsp	vegetable oil	45 mL
1/4 cup	cider vinegar	50 mL
1 tbsp	dry mustard	15 mL
3 tbsp	brown sugar	45 mL
1/2 tsp	garlic powder	2 mL
2 tbsp	finely chopped onion	30 mL
1	pinch pepper	1
4	turkey steaks, cut from breast	4

In a bowl, combine all ingredients except turkey steaks. Let stand 10 minutes for flavors to blend.

Place turkey in marinade and let marinate 3 to 4 hours, covered, in the refrigerator.

Remove turkey from marinade and cook on an oiled, preheated barbecue grill about 5 minutes on each side, basting frequently with the marinade.
Serve with baked potatoes.

~

COOK'S TIP

Turkey, like chicken, can sometimes carry salmonella bacteria. Be sure to keep raw turkey refrigerated, and discard leftover marinade, or boil it a few minutes if you want to serve it as a sauce.

1 SERVING

215 CALORIES	4g CARBOHYDRATE	34g PROTEIN
7g FAT	0g FIBER	78mg CHOLESTEROL

MARITIME MIXED GRILL

4 SERVINGS

I tbsp	vegetable oil	15 mL
2	garlic cloves, finely chopped	2
¹/₄ cup	dry white wine	50 mL
I tsp	Dijon mustard	5 mL
16	chicken wings	16
2 tbsp	barbecue spice	30 mL
16	large shrimp, peeled except for tails	16
16	large scallops	16
8	slices bread	8
I tbsp	olive oil	15 mL
	freshly ground pepper	

SAUCE

I cup	plain yogurt	250 mL
I	garlic clove, finely chopped	I
¹/₂ cup	diced seeded cucumber	125 mL
	freshly ground pepper	

In a large bowl, combine oil, garlic, wine, mustard, and pepper to taste.

Cut chicken wings into 3 pieces at joints. Reserve tip pieces for stock, or discard. Shake meaty segments of wings in a bag with barbecue spice. Place spiced wings in marinade mixture, along with shrimp and scallops. Stir to coat pieces on all sides. Refrigerate 3 hours, covered.

Soak 8 wooden skewers in water 20 minutes. Thread 2 shrimp and 2 scallops on each skewer. Set aside.

Trim crusts from bread, flatten slices with rolling pin, and cut circles. Brush lightly on both sides with olive oil.

To make sauce: combine yogurt, garlic, cucumber and pepper to taste. You can process mixture in food processor if you prefer a smooth sauce.

Cook marinated wing pieces on grill about 15 minutes, turning from time to time. Add brochettes and cook 3 to 4 minutes each side. Baste wings and seafood frequently with marinade during cooking. At the last minute, toast bread slices on grill, rotating ½ turn to make grill pattern. Serve with yogurt dipping sauce and a couscous or tabouli salad (see page 234).

1 SERVING		
637 CALORIES	28g CARBOHYDRATE	57g PROTEIN
33g FAT	0.9g FIBER	202mg CHOLESTEROL

GRILLED TURKEY KEBABS

4 SERVINGS

COOK'S TIP

A bulgur or couscous salad is a quick solution to serve with barbecued food. It is a good source of fiber and complex carbohydrates, and can be varied to use what you have on hand.

1/4 cup	dry white wine	50 mL
2 tbsp	Worcestershire sauce	30 mL
1 tsp	dried thyme	5 mL
1	garlic clove, finely chopped	1
1/4 cup	chicken stock	50 mL
1 1/2 lbs	boneless turkey breast, in 1 1/2 inch (4 cm) cubes	675 g
12	fresh mushrooms	12
12	cubes fresh pineapple	12
	freshly ground pepper	

In a large bowl, stir together wine, Worcestershire, thyme, garlic and chicken stock.

Place turkey, pineapple cubes and mushrooms in mixture. Season to taste with pepper. Cover and let marinate in refrigerator at least 2 hours.

Soak 8 wooden skewers in water 20 minutes.

Drain marinade and reserve. Thread turkey, mushrooms and pineapple on skewers. Cook on preheated grill 10 to 12 minutes, turning often and basting with marinade.

To make the accompanying salad, follow basic instructions on page 234, and stir in chopped tomatoes and cooked frozen succotash (lima beans with corn.) Season with oil, vinegar and fresh herbs.

1 SERVING		
249 CALORIES	10g CARBOHYDRATE	41g PROTEIN
5g FAT	1.4g FIBER	91mg CHOLESTEROL

ORIENTAL BURGERS

4 SERVINGS

1/2 lb	lean ground beef	225 g
2 tbsp	liquid chicken stock concentrate	30 mL
1/4 cup	grated Parmesan cheese	50 mL
2 tbsp	chopped fresh chives or green onion	30 mL
I	egg, beaten	I
I cup	beansprouts	250 mL
1/2 lb	ground chicken	225 g
I tbsp	sesame oil	15 mL

In a bowl, mix together ground beef, Chicken stock concentrate, cheese, chives, egg and beansprouts. Mix well and shape into 4 patties.

Shape chicken into 4 equal patties. Press a chicken patty together with each beef patty. Brush patties on both sides with sesame oil.

Cook on oiled, preheated barbecue grill 5 minutes on each side. Serve on toasted hamburger buns with tomato slices, lettuce or garnishes of your choice.

COOK'S TIP

Sesame oil has a delicious but rather strong flavor, so don't overdo it. Like other cold-pressed oils, it can turn rancid, so buy it in small quantities, and keep refrigerated once opened.

1 SERVING		
223 CALORIES	2g CARBOHYDRATE	29g PROTEIN
11g FAT	0.3g FIBER	129mg CHOLESTEROL

BARBECUE

BEEF BURGERS MEXICAN-STYLE

∾

4 SERVINGS

1 lb	lean ground beef	450 g
1	egg, beaten	1
1	onion, chopped	1
1	garlic clove, finely chopped	1
1/4 cup	dry breadcrumbs	50 mL
1 tsp	chili powder	5 mL
1 tsp	ground coriander	5 mL
2 tbsp	Worcestershire sauce	30 mL
	salt and freshly ground pepper	

Place beef in a bowl and break it up with a fork. Add egg, onion, garlic, breadcrumbs, spices, and salt and pepper. Mix well.

Shape into 4 equal patties. Baste with Worcestershire.

Cook patties on oiled, preheated barbecue grill until done to taste. Serve on grilled hamburger buns with condiments of your choice.

∾

ALL-PURPOSE BARBECUE SAUCE AND DIP

∾

MAKES ABOUT 1 CUP (250 mL)

6 tbsp	tomato catsup	90 mL
2 tbsp	tomato paste	30 mL
2 tbsp	vegetable oil	30 mL
1	pinch curry powder	1
2 tbsp	brandy or cognac	30 mL
1	dash hot pepper sauce (or more to taste)	1
1	onion, chopped	1
1	garlic clove, chopped	1
2 tbsp	chopped fresh parsley	30 mL
1 tbsp	chopped fresh chives	15 mL
	freshly ground pepper	

In a bowl, stir together catsup, tomato paste and oil. Whisk together until smooth.

Dissolve curry powder in brandy and add hot pepper sauce. Stir into catsup mixture.

Stir in onion, garlic, parsley, chives and pepper to taste. Mix well.

∾

COOK'S TIP

This all-purpose sauce can be used like steak sauce for steaks, chops and burgers. It also makes a delicious dip for raw or cooked vegetables, or for tortilla chips.

1 SERVING		
200 CALORIES	6g CARBOHYDRATE	26g PROTEIN
8g FAT	0.4g FIBER	110mg CHOLESTEROL

1 SERVING (1/4 CUP/50 ML)		
90 CALORIES	8g CARBOHYDRATE	1g PROTEIN
6g FAT	0.9g FIBER	0mg CHOLESTEROL

BISTRO BEEFSTEAK SANDWICHES

4 SERVINGS

I cup	beef stock	250 mL
I tsp	cornstarch, dissolved in a little water	5 mL
4	club or minute steaks, about 7 oz (200 g) each	4
3 tbsp	Dijon mustard	45 mL
I	red onion, sliced crosswise	I
I tbsp	vegetable oil	15 mL
4	small baguettes or submarine loaves	4
I cup	shredded lettuce	250 mL
2	tomatoes, thinly sliced	2

COOK'S TIP

You can use this same procedure to make sandwiches using turkey breast steaks or chicken filet.

In a small saucepan, bring beef stock to a boil. Stir in cornstarch mixture to thicken slightly. Remove from heat and keep warm.

Brush steaks on both sides with mustard. Cook on preheated barbecue grill 2 to 3 minutes each side, or broil under preheated broiler.

Brush onion slices with oil. Cook on grill until hot through.

Grill bread lightly. Layer steaks, onion, lettuce and tomatoes on bread. Pour a little sauce over each steak, or serve heated sauce on the side as a dipping sauce.

1 Heat beef stock and thicken with dissolved cornstarch.

2 Baste steaks with mustard, and grill on barbecue.

3 Grill onion slices brushed with oil.

4 Toast bread and arrange steak and garnishes on top.

1 SERVING		
570 CALORIES	61g CARBOHYDRATE	50g PROTEIN
14g FAT	2.9g FIBER	94mg CHOLESTEROL

MEDITERRANEAN PITA BURGERS
~

12 BURGERS

COOK'S TIP

Pita bread pockets make a nice change from ordinary burger buns. They are sturdy enough to cram full of delicious garnishes without falling apart. Keep a package on hand in the freezer.

2	eggs	2
1 tsp	curry powder	5 mL
1 tsp	ground cumin	5 mL
1/4 tsp	cayenne pepper	1 mL
2	garlic cloves, finely chopped	2
2 lbs	ground lean beef	1 kg
2 cups	fine dry breadcrumbs	500 mL
8	pitted green olives, finely chopped	8
6	pita breads, cut in 1/2	6

GARNISH

lettuce leaves
sliced green olives
plain low-fat yogurt

In a bowl, beat the eggs, then stir in spices and garlic.

Add ground beef, breadcrumbs and olives. Mix well.

Shape into 12 patties and cook on an oiled, preheated grill to the desired degree of doneness.

Meanwhile, wrap pita breads in foil and heat on the grill for a few minutes. Place a cooked patty in each pita half, along with some lettuce, olives, and yogurt.

~

1 BURGER		
266 CALORIES	31g CARBOHYDRATE	22g PROTEIN
6g FAT	0.5g FIBER	74mg CHOLESTEROL

GRILLED MARINATED FLANK STEAK

4 SERVINGS

1	thick flank steak, about 2 lbs (1 kg)	1
10 oz	can beef gravy	284 mL
	MARINADE	
1¹/₂ cups	dry red wine	375 mL
¹/₄ cup	red wine vinegar	50 mL
2 tbsp	vegetable oil	30 mL
3	garlic cloves, finely chopped	3
1	onion, sliced	1
¹/₂ tsp	dried basil	2 mL
¹/₂ tsp	dried thyme	2 mL
	freshly ground pepper	

Combine all marinade ingredients in a shallow dish. Place meat in marinade, cover and refrigerate at least 5 hours, turning meat from time to time.

Drain beef and cook on preheated barbecue grill about 15 minutes on each side, basting with marinade often during the last few minutes of cooking. Let meat stand a few minutes before slicing.

Bring remaining marinade to a boil over high heat and let reduce by ¹/₄. Stir in beef gravy. Simmer 5 to 8 minutes. Serve gravy mixture with flank steak sliced thinly on the diagonal.

COOK'S TIP

Even if you like your meat salted, do not put salt in the marinade, or on the steak, until it is nearly cooked. Salt brings the juices to the surface, drying out the meat.

1 SERVING		
430 CALORIES	6g CARBOHYDRATE	52g PROTEIN
22g FAT	0.3g FIBER	85mg CHOLESTEROL

BARBECUED VEAL
OR LAMB CHOPS WITH HERBS

4 SERVINGS

COOK'S TIP

*Place a few sprigs
of fresh rosemary on
the hot coals while
cooking the chops.
They will release a
wonderful aroma
and add flavor.*

12	veal or lamb chops	12
	MARINADE	
2 tbsp	chopped fresh thyme	30 mL
2	bay leaves	2
2 tbsp	chopped fresh rosemary	30 mL
1 tbsp	chopped fresh sage	15 mL
1 tbsp	chopped fresh savory	15 mL
2 tbsp	chopped fresh basil	30 mL
2 tbsp	chopped fresh mint	30 mL
1 tsp	fennel seeds	5 mL
1/2 tsp	aniseed	2 mL
1 tsp	ground pepper	5 mL
1 tsp	dry mustard	5 mL
2	garlic cloves, finely chopped	2
1/2 cup	canola oil	125 mL

Combine all marinade ingredients well
in a large bowl. Add veal or lamb chops,
and stir to coat all surfaces well.
Let marinate at least 3 hours in
refrigerator, covered.

Drain chops and cook on preheated
barbecue grill 5 to 8 minutes on each side,
or to taste. Baste with marinade towards
end of cooking time.

Serve with small potatoes cut in half,
basted with marinade, and cooked
on the grill, if desired.

~

1 SERVING		
679 CALORIES	0g CARBOHYDRATE	73g PROTEIN
43g FAT	0g FIBER	282mg CHOLESTEROL

LAST-MINUTE MIXED GRILL

4 SERVINGS

2	chicken wieners, cut in ¹/₂ lengthwise	2
4	slices of beef filet, about 3 oz (90 g) each	4
4	slices of pork filet, about 3 oz (90 g) each	4
1	red bell pepper, seeded and quartered	1
1	yellow bell pepper, seeded and quartered	1
8	new red potatoes, parboiled and quartered	8
8	large mushrooms (optional)	8

BASTING SAUCE

¹/₄ cup	liquid beef stock concentrate	50 mL
2 tsp	Worcestershire sauce	10 mL
¹/₄ cup	dry white wine	50 mL
1 tsp	dry mustard	5 mL
1	garlic clove, finely chopped	1
1 tbsp	chopped fresh parsley	15 mL

Combine all basting sauce ingredients in a bowl. Baste wieners and meat slices with sauce. Place wieners and meat on oiled, preheated barbecue grill and cook 4 to 5 minutes each side.

Meanwhile, thread vegetables on skewers (soaked in water if you use wooden skewers). Brush with the same basting sauce and cook on grill until tender.

~

COOK'S TIP

This is the perfect barbecue recipe when you don't have time for marinating. Keep thinly sliced meat in the freezer, separated by waxed paper. It thaws in almost no time!

1 SERVING		
465 CALORIES	55g CARBOHYDRATE	32g PROTEIN
13g FAT	5.9g FIBER	82mg CHOLESTEROL

MAPLE-MARINATED PORK CHOPS

4 SERVINGS

COOK'S TIP

Chops have a tendency to curl on the grill. To help prevent this, trim off excess fat, and slash the edges with a sharp knife before cooking.

4	pork chops, 1 inch (2.5 cm) thick	4

MARINADE

4	green onions, finely chopped	4
2	garlic cloves, finely chopped	2
¼ cup	maple syrup	50 mL
4 tsp	catsup	20 mL
1 cup	unsweetened apple juice	250 mL
1	pinch chili powder	1
2	pinches ground cinnamon	2
	freshly ground pepper	

Combine all marinade ingredients in a shallow dish.

Arrange pork chops in marinade, making sure all surfaces are coated. Cover and refrigerate at least 2 hours, turning the chops from time to time.

Cook on an oiled, preheated barbecue grill about 15 to 20 minutes, or until cooked through. Baste with marinade from time to time.

Serve with baked potatoes and sliced vegetables dotted with butter, wrapped in foil, and cooked about 25 minutes on the grill.

	1 SERVING	
167 CALORIES	5g CARBOHYDRATE	21g PROTEIN
7g FAT	0g FIBER	56mg CHOLESTEROL

GRILLED BUTTERFLIED PORK

4 SERVINGS

4	slices of pork loin, 1 to 1½ inches (2.5 to 4 cm) thick, totaling about 1½ lbs	4

	MARINADE	
¾ cup	dry white wine	175 mL
¼ cup	fresh lemon juice	50 mL
1 tsp	dry mustard	5 mL
1 tbsp	chopped fresh rosemary	15 mL
1 tbsp	olive oil	15 mL
	freshly ground pepper	

To make the marinade, stir together the wine, lemon juice, mustard, rosemary, olive oil and pepper.

Trim as much fat as possible from pork slices. To butterfly the pork, cut slices almost entirely through to make them half as thick. Open up the two sides as if opening a book. With the flat side of a large knife, pound pork lightly to flatten a bit.

Place pork pieces in marinade, cover, and refrigerate at least 3 hours.

Drain butterflied pork and cook on preheated barbecue grill 8 to 9 minutes on each side, basting with leftover marinade towards the end of cooking time.

1 SERVING		
277 CALORIES	1g CARBOHYDRATE	30g PROTEIN
17g FAT	0g FIBER	69mg CHOLESTEROL

CHINESE BARBECUED PORK

4 SERVINGS

COOK'S TIP

Wooden skewers are cheap and attractive, but must be soaked before using or they will burn.

1½ lbs	lean boneless pork loin or filet	675 g
½ cup	light soy sauce	125 mL
¼ cup	sherry	50 mL
1 tbsp	corn syrup	15 mL
2	garlic cloves, finely chopped	2
2	green onions, chopped	2
2 tbsp	vegetable oil for basting	30 mL

Cut pork into strips about 5 inches (12.5 cm) long, 2 inches (5 cm) wide and ½ inch (1 cm) thick.

In a bowl, combine soy sauce, sherry, corn syrup, garlic and green onions. Stir in pork strips and let marinate 3 to 4 hours in the refrigerator, covered.

Soak wooden skewers in water 10 to 15 minutes. Drain pork strips and thread them onto skewers lengthwise.

Place skewers on a plate and baste them on both sides with oil. Barbecue 5 to 8 minutes on a preheated grill, or place under a preheated broiler 5 to 8 minutes. Baste with marinade during cooking. Serve with steamed rice, and vegetables of your choice.

1 SERVING		
337 CALORIES	5g CARBOHYDRATE	32g PROTEIN
21g FAT	0g FIBER	69mg CHOLESTEROL

CALIFORNIA PORK AND PINEAPPLE KEBABS

4 SERVINGS

I lb	pork filet, cut in I inch (2.5 cm) cubes	450 g
4	mushrooms	4
I	red or green bell pepper, cubed	I
I	red onion, cut in wedges	I
2	fresh pineapple slices, cubed	2

MARINADE

2 tbsp	vegetable oil	30 mL
1/2 cup	unsweetened apple juice	125 mL
1/3 cup	molasses	75 mL
1/4 cup	light soy sauce	50 mL
2	garlic cloves	2

SAUCE

3/4 cup	plain yogurt	175 mL
3	garlic cloves, finely chopped	3
5	mint sprigs, chopped	5
1/2 cup	diced cucumber	125 mL

Combine all marinade ingredients in a bowl. Add cubed pork. Cover and let marinate in refrigerator 2 to 3 hours, turning meat from time to time.

Combine sauce ingredients in a small bowl and refrigerate until serving time.

Thread marinated meat on skewers alternating with vegetables and pineapple chunks.

Cook on oiled, preheated barbecue grill until done to taste, basting from time to time with the marinade. Serve with cucumber sauce and a rice or pasta salad.

1 SERVING		
287 CALORIES	24g CARBOHYDRATE	23g PROTEIN
11g FAT	1.5g FIBER	45mg CHOLESTEROL

LAMB BURGERS WITH GOAT'S CHEESE FILLING

4 SERVINGS

1½ lbs	ground lamb	675 g
6 tbsp	Dijon mustard	90 mL
1 tbsp	chopped fresh thyme	15 mL
1 tbsp	chopped fresh mint	15 mL
1 tbsp	chopped fresh parsley	15 mL
1	garlic clove, finely chopped	1
½	small onion, finely chopped	½
4	slices goat's cheese	4
	freshly ground pepper	
	vegetable oil	

COOK'S TIP

For an interesting flavor combination, garnish burgers with lettuce and peach or nectarine slices.

In a bowl, combine lamb with mustard, thyme, mint, parsley, garlic, onion and pepper to taste.

Shape into 8 thin patties. Place a slice of goat's cheese on 4 of the patties and cover with 4 remaining patties. Seal edges well.

Brush patties with vegetable oil and cook on preheated barbecue grill 3 to 4 minutes on each side. Serve burgers on toasted hamburger buns with garnishes of your choice.

1 Combine lamb with all ingredients except cheese and oil.

2 Shape into 8 patties.

3 Lay a cheese slice on 4 patties. Cover with remaining patties.

4 Seal edges and brush with oil before grilling.

1 SERVING		
412 CALORIES	3g CARBOHYDRATE	46g PROTEIN
24g FAT	0.8g FIBER	144mg CHOLESTEROL

ORANGE AND GINGER-MARINATED LAMB CHOPS

4 SERVINGS

1 tbsp	butter or margarine	15 mL
1	onion, finely chopped	1
2 tbsp	liquid vegetable stock concentrate	30 mL
2 tbsp	tomato paste	30 mL
1 inch	piece fresh ginger, grated	2.5 cm
2 tsp	brown sugar	10 mL
2 tsp	olive oil	10 mL
8	lamb rib chops	8
	juice and grated zest of 1 orange	
	orange segments for garnish	

Melt butter in a saucepan and cook onion until soft. Add vegetable stock concentrate, tomato paste, grated ginger, brown sugar, oil, orange juice and zest.

Simmer mixture uncovered 7 to 8 minutes or until reduced by ¼. Let cool and pour into a shallow dish.

Place chops in marinade, coating all sides well. Cover and refrigerate 6 to 12 hours.

Cook chops on an oiled, preheated barbecue grill 15 to 20 minutes, or until done to taste, basting from time to time with marinade. If you run out of marinade, use a little tomato paste diluted with vegetable stock concentrate. Serve garnished with orange segments.

~

1 SERVING		
327 CALORIES	11g CARBOHYDRATE	28g PROTEIN
19g FAT	0.9g FIBER	96mg CHOLESTEROL

SHASHLIK

4 SERVINGS

1 lb	boneless lamb cubes, 1/2 inch (1 cm) square	450 g
	MARINADE	
2 tbsp	vegetable oil	30 mL
2 tbsp	red wine vinegar	30 mL
1/2 tsp	freshly ground pepper	2 mL
1	garlic clove, chopped	1
1 tbsp	chopped fresh parsley	15 mL
1/2 tsp	dried tarragon	2 mL
1/2 tsp	dried thyme	2 mL

Combine all marinade ingredients in a bowl. Marinate lamb cubes at least 12 hours in refrigerator, covered.

Thread lamb on 3 inch (8 cm) wooden skewers that have been soaked 20 minutes in water.

Cook kebabs on preheated barbecue grill 2 to 3 minutes on each side, basting with marinade towards the end of cooking time.

Couscous flavored with almonds and raisins makes a nice accompaniment. For color, grill some bell pepper strips alongside the shashlik.

COOK'S TIP

These shashlik make an excellent starter course for an outdoor barbecue, in which case the recipe will serve 8.

1 SERVING		
209 CALORIES	0g CARBOHYDRATE	23g PROTEIN
13g FAT	0g FIBER	73mg CHOLESTEROL

MIXED SEAFOOD GRILL

4 SERVINGS

COOK'S TIP

To make this recipe indoors, arrange drained, marinated seafood on a broiler pan and cook under preheated broiler about 3 minutes on each side.

8	large scallops	8
8	large shrimp, peeled	8
1/2 lb	salmon filet, cut in strips	225 g
1/2 lb	halibut filet, cut in strips	225 g

MARINADE

1 tbsp	canola oil	15 mL
1/4 cup	dry white wine	50 mL
1/4 cup	fresh lemon juice	50 mL
2 tbsp	chopped green onions	30 mL
2 tbsp	chopped fresh chives	30 mL
1 tbsp	chopped fresh parsley	15 mL
1 tbsp	chopped fresh dill	15 mL
1 tbsp	chopped fresh rosemary	15 mL
2 tsp	chopped fresh thyme	10 mL
1 tsp	freshly ground pepper	5 mL

Combine all marinade ingredients in a shallow dish.

Arrange scallops, shrimp, salmon and halibut in marinade, and spoon marinade over to coat all sides. Cover and refrigerate 2 hours.

Remove seafood from marinade and thread onto wooden skewers which have been soaked 20 minutes in water.

Cook on preheated barbecue grill 5 to 7 minutes on each side, basting with marinade towards the end of cooking time.

Bring leftover marinade to a boil in a saucepan and simmer a minute or 2 to use as a sauce, if desired. Serve seafood with rice and vegetables.

1 Combine marinade ingredients in a shallow dish.

2 Arrange scallops, shrimp, salmon and halibut in marinade.

3 Drain ingredients before threading on skewers.

1 SERVING		
217 CALORIES	3g CARBOHYDRATE	31g PROTEIN
9g FAT	0.3g FIBER	92mg CHOLESTEROL

GRILLED RED MULLET
WITH SUNDRIED TOMATO SAUCE

4 SERVINGS

COOK'S TIP

*Sun-dried tomatoes can
be bought in two forms.
The oil-packed ones
need only to be drained.
The dry-packed ones
must be rehydrated; pour
boiling water over them
and let soak about
30 minutes, then drain.*

4	bay leaves	4
2 tsp	dried thyme	10 mL
2 tbsp	dry white wine	30 mL
4	red mullet, about 7 oz (200 g) each	4
2 tbsp	olive oil	30 mL

SUNDRIED TOMATO SAUCE

1 tbsp	olive oil	15 mL
2 cups	peeled, seeded and chopped fresh tomatoes	500 mL
1/3 cup	chopped sundried tomatoes, soaked if necessary (see Cook's Tip)	75 mL
1/3 cup	chopped green onions	75 mL
2	garlic cloves, finely chopped	2
1/2 tsp	dried basil	2 mL
1/2 cup	dry white wine	125 mL
	freshly ground pepper	
	juice of 2 lemons	

To make the sauce: heat oil in a saucepan and add tomatoes, drained sundried tomatoes, onions, garlic and basil. Cook over medium heat 5 minutes.

Season to taste, and stir in wine and lemon juice. Simmer over low heat 8 to 10 minutes.

Divide bay leaves, thyme and white wine between cavities of mullet. Brush mullet with olive oil and cook on oiled, preheated barbecue grill 5 to 8 minutes on each side. If you prefer, you can wrap the fish in foil before grilling; they will be less likely to char and will cook more uniformly.

Serve cooked mullet on a bed of the hot tomato sauce, and garnish with fresh herbs. Rice complements the fish nicely.

~

1 SERVING		
290 CALORIES	10g CARBOHYDRATE	22g PROTEIN
18g FAT	1.5g FIBER	53mg CHOLESTEROL

GRILLED HALIBUT WITH CARDAMOM

4 SERVINGS

¹/₂ cup	dry white wine	125 mL
1 tbsp	vegetable oil	15 mL
1 tbsp	ground cardamom	15 mL
¹/₄ cup	unsweetened orange juice	50 mL
4	halibut steaks, about 7 oz (200 g) each	4
	freshly ground pepper	

In a shallow dish, combine wine, oil, cardamom, orange juice and pepper to taste.

Arrange halibut in marinade, cover, and let marinate 3 hours in refrigerator.

Grill halibut steaks on oiled, preheated barbecue grill about 6 to 8 minutes on each side, or until fish flakes with a fork. Baste with marinade towards end of cooking time.

If you wish, wrap parboiled potatoes and leeks in foil and finish cooking them on the barbecue along with the steak. You can grill thick slices of firm tomatoes, dusted with seasoned crumbs, on a foil tray alongside.

COOK'S TIP

Instead of halibut, you can use salmon, fresh tuna, or swordfish steaks.

1 SERVING		
248 CALORIES	4g CARBOHYDRATE	40g PROTEIN
8g FAT	0g FIBER	60mg CHOLESTEROL

CITRUS-MARINATED GRILLED SALMON STEAKS

4 SERVINGS

NUTRITION TIP

Salmon is a fatty fish, but instead of the saturated fat found in meat, it contains "good" omega-3 fatty acids, known to help prevent heart disease.

4	salmon steaks, 1 inch (2.5 cm) thick	4
¼ cup	fresh orange juice	50 mL
1 tsp	grated orange zest	5 mL
¼ cup	fresh lemon juice	50 mL
1 tsp	grated lemon zest	5 mL
¼ cup	fresh lime juice	50 mL
1 tsp	grated lime zest	5 mL
1	onion, grated	1
1 tsp	liquid honey	5 mL
3 tbsp	vegetable oil	45 mL
	a few drops Tabasco sauce	
	freshly ground pepper	

Arrange salmon in a single layer in a shallow dish.

In a bowl, combine all remaining ingredients and pour over salmon. Cover with a sheet of plastic wrap and let marinate in refrigerator at least 1 hour, turning steaks once.

Cook on an oiled, preheated barbecue grill 5 to 7 minutes on each side. Baste with marinade during cooking.

1 SERVING		
363 CALORIES	9g CARBOHYDRATE	39g PROTEIN
19g FAT	0.5g FIBER	26mg CHOLESTEROL

BARBECUED STUFFED SALMON WITH BEURRE BLANC

4 SERVINGS

COOK'S TIP

*This beurre blanc sauce
is one recipe in which you
must have the flavor
of real butter. If you
don't want to use it, skip
the sauce, and serve
stuffed salmon with
vegetables of your choice.*

I cup	finely chopped fresh fennel bulb	250 mL
I tbsp	butter or margarine	15 mL
1/4 cup	15% cream	50 mL
2 tbsp	fresh lemon juice	30 mL
4	thick crosscuts of salmon filet	4
	freshly ground pepper	
	vegetable oil	

VEGETABLE GARNISH

2	carrots, cut in long julienne strips	2
2	celery stalks, cut in long julienne strips	2
2	zucchini, cut in long julienne strips	2

BEURRE BLANC SAUCE

1/2 cup	butter	125 mL
3	dry French shallots, chopped	3
1/2 cup	dry white wine	125 mL
2 tbsp	15 % cream	30 mL
2 tbsp	plain yogurt	30 mL

Cook fennel in butter, in a covered saucepan, until very soft. Purée in food processor or blender. Add cream, lemon juice and pepper to taste. Process until smooth.

Cook julienne of vegetables 2 minutes in boiling salted water. Drain and keep warm.

To make the sauce: melt 1 tbsp (15 mL) butter in a small saucepan over medium-low heat. Add shallots and cook very lightly. Add wine, bring to a boil, and let reduce by ¾. Stir in cream and remove from heat. Using a whisk, stir in remaining butter bit by bit to make a smooth sauce. Stir in yogurt and set aside to keep warm.

Slit salmon pieces through their thickness to make deep pockets. Stuff with fennel mixture. Brush salmon well with oil. Cook on oiled, preheated barbecue grill 6 to 8 minutes on each side.

Pour beurre blanc sauce on 4 plates, and arrange vegetable julienne on top. Place a salmon piece on each plate.

1 SERVING		
603 CALORIES	13g CARBOHYDRATE	41g PROTEIN
43g FAT	2.9g FIBER	187mg CHOLESTEROL

TURBOT IN CITRUS SAUCE

4 SERVINGS

4	turbot filets, about 7 oz (200 g) each	4
2	chopped dry French shallots or green onions	2
¹/₂ cup	dry white wine	125 mL
1	lime, in segments	1
1	lemon, in segments	1
1	grapefruit, in segments	1
2 tbsp	chopped fresh parsley	30 mL
	butter or margarine	
	freshly ground pepper	

Cut 4 pieces of foil big enough to wrap turbot filets. Rub foil with butter and arrange turbot on top.

In a bowl, combine all remaining ingredients. Divide mixture among turbot filets. Seal packages firmly. Place packages on preheated grill and cook 12 to 15 minutes, turning once.

Serve at once with green vegetable of your choice, and rice if desired.

1 SERVING		
249 CALORIES	9g CARBOHYDRATE	33g PROTEIN
9g FAT	1.7g FIBER	96mg CHOLESTEROL

THAI-STYLE SEA BASS IN COCONUT MILK

4 SERVINGS

COOK'S TIP

Lemongrass is a flavor characteristic of Thai cooking that can be found in Oriental groceries and gourmet sections of supermarkets. If you cannot find it, substitute grated lemon zest.

I	hot red pepper, finely chopped	I
³/₄ cup	canned coconut milk	175 mL
2	garlic cloves, finely chopped	2
2 tbsp	fresh lime juice	30 mL
I tsp	chopped fresh ginger	5 mL
I tbsp	chopped fresh lemongrass	15 mL
8	sea bass filets, about 3 oz (90 g) each	8
2 tbsp	vegetable oil	30 mL
I	small can water chestnuts (optional)	I
I	small can bamboo shoots (optional)	I

In a shallow dish, combine hot pepper, coconut milk, garlic, lime juice, ginger and lemongrass.

Arrange sea bass in marinade, cover, and let marinate 2 hours in refrigerator.

Drain fish and cooked on an oiled, preheated barbecue grill 3 to 5 minutes on each side, turning carefully.

Heat remaining marinade in a small saucepan. Add drained water chestnuts and bamboo shoots, if desired. Cook about 2 minutes or until thickened slightly.

Serve fish with sauce, and with steamed rice and snowpeas, if desired.

1 SERVING		
352 CALORIES	9g CARBOHYDRATE	34g PROTEIN
20g FAT	1.7g FIBER	144mg CHOLESTEROL

FISH KEBABS WITH ORANGE SAUCE

4 SERVINGS

2	dry French shallots, finely chopped	2
2 tbsp	vegetable oil	30 mL
I tbsp	chopped fresh chives	15 mL
4	pike filets, about 7 oz (200 g) each	4
8	orange slices, with rind	8
I tbsp	cornstarch, dissolved in a little water	15 mL
	juice of 2 oranges	

In a bowl, stir together orange juice, shallots, oil and chives.

Cut pike steaks into cubes about 1 inch (2.5 cm) square. Marinate in orange juice mixture several hours, refrigerated.

Thread fish cubes on wooden skewers that have been soaked 20 minutes in water. Cook kebabs on oiled, preheated grill about 4 minutes each side.

Meanwhile, heat remaining marinade in a small saucepan and stir in dissolved cornstarch. Heat until thickened. Pour sauce over pike kebabs to serve. Accompany with rice, and with vegetables such as sliced zucchini or carrots cooked in foil packages on the grill.

	1 SERVING	
284 CALORIES	13g CARBOHYDRATE	40g PROTEIN
8g FAT	0.7g FIBER	78mg CHOLESTEROL

WILD RICE SALAD

4 SERVINGS

COOK'S TIP

The price of wild rice is quite high. But when cooked, it increases in volume far more than ordinary rice, making a small amount go a long way.

1 cup	wild rice	250 mL
8 cups	boiling water	2 liters
1 tsp	salt	5 mL
1	orange	1
1½ cups	diced red, yellow and green bell peppers	375 mL
1	large apple, cored and diced	1
½ cup	chopped green onions	125 mL
½ cup	chopped fresh parsley	125 mL
1 tbsp	lemon juice	15 mL

DRESSING

1	egg	1
⅓ cup	unsweetened orange juice	75 mL
2 tbsp	wine vinegar	30 mL
1 tsp	Dijon mustard	5 mL
1 tsp	grated orange zest	5 mL
½ tsp	dried tarragon	2 mL
½ tsp	salt	2 mL
1	pinch pepper	1
3 tbsp	water	45 mL
3 tbsp	vegetable oil	45 mL

Rinse raw rice in plenty of cold water. Drain and pour it into the boiling water with the salt. Cover, reduce heat, and let simmer about 45 minutes. Grains should be soft but a little chewy. Drain rice and let cool to room temperature.

Place all dressing ingredients except oil in the bowl of a food processor or blender. Process a few seconds. With motor still running, pour in oil in a very thin stream. Set dressing aside.

Cut zest of the orange into thin strips and set aside for garnish. Peel orange and cut off white pith. Remove membranes from segments. Set aside.

Place drained rice in a large bowl. Stir in diced peppers, apple, green onions, parsley and lemon juice. Pour on dressing and toss gently. Decorate with orange segments and zest. Serve at room temperature or chilled.

1 Cook wild rice in salted boiling water.

2 In food processor, mix all dressing ingredients except the oil. Add oil in a thin stream.

3 Peel oranges and cut membranes from segments.

4 Combine cooked rice, bell peppers, apple, green onions, parsley and lemon juice. Toss with dressing.

1 SERVING		
328 CALORIES	46g CARBOHYDRATE	9g PROTEIN
12g FAT	5.1g FIBER	68mg CHOLESTEROL

TABOULI SALAD

~

4 SERVINGS

COOK'S TIP

You can use couscous instead of bulgur, following package directions to prepare it. The lime juice and zest can be replaced with lemon juice and zest, if you prefer.

2 cups	water	500 mL
1 cup	quick-cooking bulgur	250 mL
1	red onion, chopped	1
1/2 cup	packed chopped fresh parsley	125 mL
1/2 cup	chopped fresh mint	125 mL
3	tomatoes, seeded and finely chopped	3
1/2	seedless cucumber, finely chopped	1/2

DRESSING

1/4 cup	olive oil	50 mL
2	garlic cloves, chopped	2
1/2 cup	fresh lime juice	125 mL
1 tbsp	Dijon mustard	15 mL
2 tbsp	liquid honey	30 mL
1	pinch cayenne pepper	1
	grated zest of 1 lime	

Bring water to a boil in a saucepan. Stir in bulgur and remove from heat. Cover and let stand until cool and liquid is completely absorbed.

Place onion, parsley and mint in food processor or blender. Process until finely chopped, but not puréed.

Stir together dressing ingredients in a bowl. Pour into food processor and pulse motor on and of until mixed.

Place cooled bulgur in a salad bowl. Stir in chopped tomatoes and cucumber well. Pour parsley and dressing mixtures over and stir well. Chill 4 hours in refrigerator, covered, before serving.

~

1 SERVING		
313 CALORIES	43g CARBOHYDRATE	6g PROTEIN
13g FAT	3.4g FIBER	0mg CHOLESTEROL

CHILLED PASTA SALAD WITH BASIL

~

4 SERVINGS

I lb	spiral pasta, cooked and drained	450 g
1/2	red bell pepper, chopped	1/2
1/4 cup	chopped pitted black olives	50 mL
2 tbsp	chopped fresh parsley	30 mL
2	fresh tomatoes, peeled, seeded and chopped	2

DRESSING

2 tbsp	red wine vinegar	30 mL
I tbsp	olive oil	15 mL
I tbsp	water	15 mL
2 tbsp	finely chopped fresh basil	30 mL
2 tsp	Dijon mustard	10 mL

In a large salad bowl, toss cooked pasta together with red pepper, olives, parsley and tomatoes. Set aside.

Combine dressing ingredients in a small bowl.

Pour dressing over pasta and toss well. Cover and refrigerate about 2 hours to allow flavors to blend. Serve cold.

COOK'S TIP

You can easily turn this pasta salad into a complete salad meal by adding a source of protein such as cubed cooked chicken, canned salmon or tuna, chopped hardboiled eggs, or diced cheese.

1 SERVING		
426 CALORIES	81g CARBOHYDRATE	12g PROTEIN
6g FAT	1.1g FIBER	0mg CHOLESTEROL

FRUITY COLESLAW

4 TO 6 SERVINGS

NUTRITION TIP

Yogurt is a good way to provide a creamy texture to salad dressings, while eliminating the fat and calories of mayonnaise and other thick salad dressings.

I tbsp	lemon juice	15 mL
I	red apple, cored and diced	I
2 cups	grated cabbage	500 mL
2	celery stalks, finely chopped	2
1/2 cup	red or green grapes	125 mL
1/2 cup	diced Cheddar cheese	125 mL
I tbsp	vegetable oil	15 mL
3 tbsp	plain yogurt	45 mL
I tsp	liquid honey	5 mL

Pour the lemon juice over the diced apple to keep it from turning brown.

Drain apple before combining with other ingredients, reserving lemon juice.

In a bowl, combine drained apple, cabbage, celery, grapes and cheese. Set aside.

In another bowl, stir together reserved lemon juice, oil, yogurt and honey.

Pour dressing over other ingredients and toss well before serving.

1 SERVING		
114 CALORIES	12g CARBOHYDRATE	3g PROTEIN
6g FAT	1.2g FIBER	11mg CHOLESTEROL

BARBECUE BAKED APPLES

4 SERVINGS

1/2 cup	chopped dried apricots	125 mL
I tbsp	raisins	15 mL
I	pinch ground cloves	I
I	pinch ground allspice	I
1/3 cup	brown sugar	75 mL
2 tbsp	soft butter	30 mL
4	apples, washed and cored	4
	whipping cream (optional)	

In a bowl, stir together chopped apricots with raisins, spices, brown sugar and butter.

Fill apples with apricot mixture. Wrap each apple in a double thickness of heavy foil.

Cook on the barbecue grill 45 to 50 minutes, or until the apples are tender to a fork. Be sure to turn apples frequently during cooking so all sides are cooked.

Whip the cream until stiff. Unwrap the apples and serve with whipped cream, if desired.

1 Combine filling ingredients.

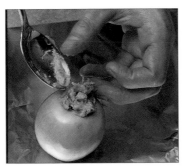

2 Spoon into cored apples. Wrap in double thickness of foil.

1 SERVING		
202 CALORIES	36g CARBOHYDRATE	1g PROTEIN
6g FAT	3.2g FIBER	16mg CHOLESTEROL

BRUNCHES, LUNCHES AND SNACKS

~

The hectic lifestyles most of us lead today means
that we often don't have the time to sit down
and enjoy a full-course meal together with the
family — much less find the time to prepare it!

Often, we grab a snack on the run,
or eat at non-traditional times because
our schedules are fast-paced. It's a lifestyle that
can easily lead to an over-reliance on junk foods
and fast food outlets, which may not meet
our nutritional requirements.

On the other hand, you may be looking
for some new and different totable lunch foods,
or recipes that are interesting and quick
to make on a lazy weekend morning.

This chapter contains a selection of quick
meal ideas for all those non-traditional
mealtimes. Some are perfect for Sunday brunch,
and others are ideal for a quick late night snack.
There are even some easy-to-make afterschool
snacks for kids with sweet tooths.

All are fast and easy, and some are simple
enough that your children can learn
to prepare them themselves!

~

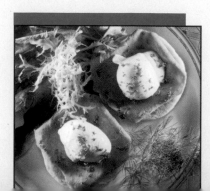

GOURMET SCRAMBLED EGGS

4 SERVINGS

I tbsp	butter or margarine	15 mL
I cup	grated zucchini	250 mL
1/2 cup	grated carrot	125 mL
1/4 cup	chopped onion	50 mL
5	eggs, lightly beaten	5
1/4 tsp	pepper	I mL
1/2 cup	cream-style cottage cheese	125 mL
	chopped fresh parsley	

COOK'S TIP

Salt tends to toughen eggs. Never add salt while they are cooking, only once they are cooked.

Melt butter in a large nonstick skillet over medium heat. Stir in zucchini, carrot and onion. Cover and cook 2 minutes. Remove cover and cook another 1 or 2 minutes.

Stir in eggs and reduce heat to low. Season with pepper. Cook until eggs are set but still moist, stirring from time to time from the edges of the pan towards the center.

Gently stir in cottage cheese. Serve garnished with chopped parsley.

1 Cook vegetables 2 minutes, covered. Remove cover and cook 1 to 2 minutes.

2 Stir in eggs and pepper. Reduce heat to low.

3 Continue cooking, stirring occasionally, until eggs are set but still moist.

4 Stir in cottage cheese and parsley.

1 SERVING		
172 CALORIES	4g CARBOHYDRATE	12g PROTEIN
12g FAT	1.1g FIBER	354mg CHOLESTEROL

EGG AND AVOCADO SCRAMBLE

4 SERVINGS

1/2	red bell pepper, diced	1/2
4	avocados	4
1 tbsp	butter or oil	15 mL
6	eggs, lightly beaten	6
1/2 cup	plain yogurt	125 mL
2 tbsp	chopped fresh chives	30 mL

Bring a saucepan of salted water to a boil. Add red pepper cubes and blanch 5 seconds only. Drain, rinse under cold water, and set aside.

Cut avocados in half and discard pits. Spoon out flesh and chop coarsely. Cover and refrigerate.

Heat butter or oil in a skillet over medium heat. Add beaten eggs and cook, stirring constantly, until barely set.

Stir in reserved avocado flesh, yogurt and diced red pepper. Cook just until heated through. Garnish with chives and serve hot.

1 SERVING		
276 CALORIES	18g CARBOHYDRATE	15g PROTEIN
16g FAT	5.2g FIBER	421mg CHOLESTEROL

SPANISH-STYLE
SCRAMBLED EGGS AND HAM

4 TO 6 SERVINGS

8	eggs	8
1/4 cup	skim milk	50 mL
1	pinch thyme	1
1	pinch pepper	1
2 tbsp	butter or margarine	30 mL
4	green onions, chopped	4
3/4 cup	chopped red or green bell pepper	175 mL
1	small zucchini, chopped	1
1	tomato, diced	1
1 cup	diced cooked ham	250 mL
3/4 cup	grated cheese or processed cheese spread	175 mL

Beat eggs together with milk. Season with thyme and pepper. Set aside.

Heat 1 tbsp (15 mL) butter in a large nonstick skillet. Add vegetables and ham and cook over medium heat until vegetables are soft. Remove from pan and set aside.

Melt remaining butter in the same skillet. Pour in egg mixture. Cook over medium heat until eggs are set but still moist, stirring from time to time from the edges of the pan towards the center.

Arrange eggs on ovenproof plates and surround with vegetable and ham mixture. Top eggs with cheese. Place under hot broiler a few seconds to melt cheese before serving.

1 SERVING		
237 CALORIES	4g CARBOHYDRATE	17g PROTEIN
17g FAT	1.0g FIBER	400mg CHOLESTEROL

POTATO CAKES

4 SERVINGS

1 tbsp	butter or margarine	15 mL
2 tbsp	chopped onion	30 mL
¼ cup	chopped red bell pepper	50 mL
½ cup	diced cooked ham	125 mL
1	garlic clove, finely chopped	1
3	potatoes, peeled and parboiled	3
¼ cup	chopped fresh parsley	50 mL
2 tbsp	vegetable oil	30 mL
	salt and pepper	

COOK'S TIP

You may find it more convenient to cook this as a single potato cake, as shown in the photo. Cook one side on the stovetop, then finish by baking in a 400°F (200°C) oven until top is browned.

Melt butter in a nonstick skillet over medium heat. Cook onion, red pepper, ham and garlic until onion is soft. Set aside.

Grate potatoes with the grater blade of a food processor or with a hand grater.

In a bowl, stir together grated potatoes with reserved ham mixture. Stir in parsley and season to taste with salt and pepper.

Shape mixture into 4 equal pancakes. Cook in oil over medium heat in a nonstick skillet about 3 minutes on each side, or until cooked through and nicely browned.

1 Cook onion, red pepper, ham and garlic until onion is soft.

2 Grate potatoes by hand or with food processor.

3 Combine potatoes with ham mixture.

4 Shape into 4 equal potato cakes before frying.

1 SERVING		
207 CALORIES	22g CARBOHYDRATE	5g PROTEIN
11g FAT	2.1g FIBER	16mg CHOLESTEROL

CHEESY BRUNCH MUFFINS

3 TO 6 SERVINGS

1 cup	grated Emmenthal or Swiss cheese	250 mL
1 tbsp	butter or margarine	15 mL
¹/₂ tsp	dry mustard	2 mL
2 tbsp	beer	30 mL
3	English muffins, split and toasted	3
6	eggs	6
6	slices cooked ham	6
	salt and pepper	
	chopped fresh parsley	

In a saucepan, stir together the cheese, butter, mustard and beer. Heat gently over medium heat, stirring constantly, until smooth and creamy. Season to taste. Remove sauce from heat and let cool a bit.

Preheat oven broiler. Pour sauce mixture over toasted muffin halves. Brown under broiler until lightly browned.

Meanwhile, poach eggs in simmering water until done to taste. Drain.

Place a ham slice and poached egg on each muffin half. Serve immediately, sprinkled with parsley, if desired.

1 SERVING		
259 CALORIES	14g CARBOHYDRATE	17g PROTEIN
15g FAT	0.3g FIBER	305mg CHOLESTEROL

QUICK SAUSAGE ROLLS

~

4 SERVINGS

4	pork and beef link sausages, cooked	4
2	eggs	2
1/2	bag fresh spinach, steamed and drained	1/2
4	squares ready-made puff pastry, about 4 inches (10 cm) square	4
1	egg, beaten	1
	salt and pepper	

Preheat oven to 400°F (200°C).

Place cooked sausages in food processor with 2 eggs and drained cooked spinach. Season with salt and pepper. Process to make a fairly coarse paste.

Spread mixture over squares of puff pastry. Fold each square in half.

Place pastry packages on a baking sheet. Bake about 15 minutes, or until browned. Serve with tomato sauce, if desired, and a salad.

~

COOK'S TIP

These sausage rolls are a good way to use leftover breakfast sausage. They are also good eaten cold, or can be made smaller to serve with cocktails.

GRILLED HAM
WITH RASPBERRY VINEGAR
❧

4 SERVINGS

COOK'S TIP

This makes a very elegant Sunday brunch dish or quick luncheon recipe, especially if served with steamed fresh asparagus, and followed with the fruit salad opposite.

1/2 cup	red wine vinegar	125 mL
2	raspberry tea sachets	2
8	slices smoked ham, 2 oz (60 g) each	8
1 cup	beef stock	250 mL
4	English muffins	4

Heat vinegar in a small saucepan and add tea bags. Remove from heat and let stand until partly cooled.

Grill ham slices in a ridged grill pan or skillet until slightly browned and heated through. Keep warm.

Remove tea bags from vinegar and pour mixture into grill pan. Heat over medium-high heat, scraping the bottom to remove any browned bits. Cook until reduced by half.

Split English muffins and toast halves. Arrange ham slice over each half. Place 2 muffin halves on each plate, and top with raspberry-flavored sauce.

~

1 SERVING		
316 CALORIES	31g CARBOHYDRATE	30g PROTEIN
8g FAT	0.5g FIBER	64mg CHOLESTEROL

FRUIT SALAD WITH GRENADINE

4 SERVINGS

I	orange	I
I	pink grapefruit	I
I	mango, peeled and pitted	I
I	papaya, peeled and pitted	I
I	green apple, cored	I
I	pear, cored	I
I cup	seedless red grapes, halved	250 mL
I cup	passionfruit juice	250 mL
¹/₄ cup	grenadine syrup	50 mL
2 tbsp	chopped fresh mint	30 mL

Peel the orange and grapefruit, and cut the segments from the membranes enclosing them with a sharp knife. Place segments with their juice in a salad bowl.

Dice mango and papaya. Cut apple and pear in slices. Toss fruit together in a large salad bowl. Stir in passionfruit juice, grenadine, and chopped mint.

Cover and refrigerate about 2 hours to allow flavors to combine. Serve in small bowls garnished with fresh mint.

1 SERVING		
233 CALORIES	54g CARBOHYDRATE	2g PROTEIN
1g FAT	6.2 g FIBER	0mg CHOLESTEROL

HOT TUNA CROISSANTS

8 SERVINGS

1/4 cup	light mayonnaise	50 mL
2 tbsp	chopped sweet gherkins	30 mL
1 tbsp	Dijon mustard	15 mL
1/4 cup	finely chopped onion	50 mL
7 oz	can waterpacked tuna, drained and flaked	200 g
2	hardboiled eggs, chopped	2
8	croissants	8
1 cup	grated Emmenthal or Swiss cheese	250 mL
1 tbsp	sesame seeds	15 mL

COOK'S TIP

There is no real substitute for the flaky rich quality of croissants, but if your bakery does not supply them, bake up some refrigerator crescent rolls.

Preheat oven to 375°F (190°C).

Stir together mayonnaise, chopped gherkins, mustard, and onion. Stir in flaked tuna and chopped eggs.

Split croissants open and fill with tuna mixture. Sprinkle tuna with grated cheese and sesame seeds. Close croissants.

Place stuffed croissants on a baking sheet and heat in oven 3 to 4 minutes. Serve hot or cold.

1 SERVING

372 CALORIES	29g CARBOHYDRATE	19g PROTEIN
20g FAT	0.3g FIBER	100mg CHOLESTEROL

PUFFED CHEESE
AND SEAFOOD SANDWICH

2 SERVINGS

2	English muffins	2
3 oz	leftover cooked fish (turbot, halibut, sole or haddock), flaked	90 g
1/4 cup	cooked baby shrimp	50 mL
1 tbsp	mayonnaise	15 mL
1 tsp	relish	5 mL
4	tomato slices	4
4	slices cheese, your choice	4
	lettuce leaves	
	salt and pepper	

Toast muffin halves and set aside.

Stir together fish, shrimp, mayonnaise, and relish. Season to taste with salt and pepper. Spread over muffin halves.

Top each muffin half with a tomato slice and a cheese slice.

Heat under a preheated broiler a few seconds until cheese melts. Serve on lettuce leaves.

COOK'S TIP

Canned shrimp is perfect for this recipe. If you do not have leftover fish, substitute canned crabmeat.

1 SERVING		
240 CALORIES	16g CARBOHYDRATE	17g PROTEIN
12g FAT	0.5g FIBER	57mg CHOLESTEROL

GREEK-STYLE TUNA SANDWICHES

2 SERVINGS

COOK'S TIP

You may trim crusts from bread or cut it into circles, as shown, if you want the sandwiches to look a little fancier.

1 tbsp	light mayonnaise	15 mL
1 tsp	lemon juice	5 mL
1/4 tsp	dried oregano	1 mL
3 1/2 oz	can waterpacked tuna, drained	100 g
2 tbsp	light cottage cheese	30 mL
1 tbsp	chopped green onion	15 mL
4	slices wholewheat bread, toasted	4
1	tomato, sliced	1
2 tbsp	crumbled feta cheese	30 mL
	pepper	

Preheat oven to 400°F (200°C).

In a bowl, mix together mayonnaise, lemon juice and oregano. Stir in tuna, cottage cheese and green onion.

Spread an equal amount of tuna mixture on 4 bread slices.

Cover each piece with a slice or 2 of tomato, some feta cheese, and pepper.

Wrap slices separately in foil. Heat in oven 4 to 5 minutes.

1 SERVING		
282 CALORIES	33g CARBOHYDRATE	24g PROTEIN
6g FAT	0.9g FIBER	19mg CHOLESTEROL

SALMON SUBMARINE SANDWICHES

4 SERVINGS

2 cups	flaked cooked fresh salmon	500 mL
1/4 cup	light mayonnaise	50 mL
2 tbsp	plain yogurt	30 mL
1 tbsp	fresh lemon juice	15 mL
2 tbsp	chopped fresh chives	30 mL
2 tbsp	chopped fresh parsley	30 mL
1 tbsp	chopped fresh tarragon	15 mL
2 tsp	Dijon mustard	10 mL
1/2 tsp	pepper	2 mL
4	submarine rolls	4
	shredded lettuce leaves	

Flake salmon into a bowl and remove any bones; set aside.

In a second bowl, combine mayonnaise, yogurt, lemon juice, chives, parsley, tarragon, mustard and pepper.

Add salmon and stir gently to combine. Split bread and spread salmon mixture over bottom halves. Top salmon with lettuce and cover with top half of bread.

COOK'S TIP

Instead of fresh salmon, use 2 cans of drained waterpacked salmon. If you use salmon packed in oil, drain it well and rinse before using. Substitute 1/2 tsp (2 mL) dried tarragon for the fresh, if necessary.

1 SERVING		
427 CALORIES	58g CARBOHYDRATE	24g PROTEIN
11g FAT	1.9g FIBER	40mg CHOLESTEROL

PROVENÇALE SANDWICH

4 SERVINGS

2 tbsp	olive oil	30 mL
2 tbsp	fresh lemon juice	30 mL
2	garlic cloves, finely chopped	2
4	kaiser rolls	4
4	lettuce leaves	4
4	anchovy filets (optional)	4
12	pitted black olives, sliced	12

FILLING

½ cup	thinly sliced English cucumber	125 mL
2	tomatoes, cut in thin wedges	2
½ cup	chopped green bell pepper	125 mL
2	green onions, chopped	2
2	7 oz (200 g) cans waterpacked tuna, drained and flaked	2
2 tbsp	chopped fresh parsley	30 mL
	salt and pepper	

In a small bowl, stir together oil, lemon juice and garlic.

Cut off the top ⅓ of each kaiser roll and set aside. Hollow out the lower section of each kaiser (reserve crumbs for another use). Brush hollows with oil mixture.

In a bowl, gently toss together all filling ingredients.

Arrange a lettuce leaf in the hollow of each kaiser bottom. Stuff with filling mixture. Garnish filling with anchovies and olive slices, if desired. Cover with top of kaiser roll. Serve with sliced tomatoes and wedges of hardboiled egg, if desired.

1 Combine oil, lemon juice and garlic.

2 Slice off top ⅓ of kaiser rolls and reserve. Brush kaiser bottoms with oil mixture.

3 Combine filling ingredients.

4 Fill kaisers with lettuce and filling, and garnish with anchovies and olives.

1 SERVING		
452 CALORIES	39g CARBOHYDRATE	38g PROTEIN
16g FAT	3.5g FIBER	26mg CHOLESTEROL

CRAB SALAD IN PITA BREAD

4 SERVINGS

COOK'S TIP

Try your favorite sandwich filling such as egg, tuna or chicken salad, packed into pita pockets. Fill up the pockets with sprouts or grated vegetables for added vitamins and fiber.

7 oz	can crabmeat, drained and flaked	200 g
1/2 cup	diced tofu	125 mL
1/4 cup	light mayonnaise	50 mL
1 tbsp	chopped fresh chervil or parsley	15 mL
1 tbsp	chopped fresh chives	15 mL
1 tbsp	drained capers	15 mL
4	wholewheat pita breads	4
2	hardboiled eggs, sliced	2
1/2 cup	alfalfa or radish sprouts	125 mL
	salt and pepper	

In a bowl, stir together crabmeat, tofu, mayonnaise, chervil, chives and capers. Season with salt and pepper.

Cut pita breads in half and stuff pockets with crab mixture. Garnish with egg slices and sprouts.

1 SERVING		
339 CALORIES	37g CARBOHYDRATE	23g PROTEIN
11g FAT	4.7g FIBER	163mg CHOLESTEROL

HOT TWO-MEAT CROISSANTS

4 SERVINGS

4	croissants or crescent rolls	4
2	skinless, boneless chicken breast halves, cooked and thinly sliced	2
4 oz	cold cooked ham, cut in strips	110 g
12	spinach leaves, blanched	12
1 cup	light white sauce (see recipe page 168)	250 mL
1 cup	grated Emmenthal or Swiss cheese	250 mL

Cut croissants in half lengthwise. Cover bottom halves with sliced chicken and ham and blanched spinach.

Preheat oven to broil. Place croissant bottoms in baking pan. Top with some white sauce and grated cheese. Heat under broiler until cheese melts. Add croissant tops for the last few seconds to warm.

~

COOK'S TIP

Use the white sauce recipe on page 168, your own favorite recipe, or canned white sauce. But beware! This is a high fat sandwich, so serve it with something low-fat.

1 SERVING		
578 CALORIES	34g CARBOHYDRATE	43g PROTEIN
30g FAT	0.6g FIBER	123mg CHOLESTEROL

GREEK-STYLE
PITA SANDWICHES WITH PORK

4 SERVINGS

4 tbsp	olive oil	60 mL
4 tbsp	fresh lemon juice	60 mL
1 tbsp	prepared mustard	15 mL
2	garlic cloves, peeled	2
1 lb	lean pork, cut in thin strips	450 g
1 tsp	dried oregano	5 mL
1 cup	plain yogurt	250 mL
1 cup	chopped peeled cucumber	250 mL
1 tbsp	chopped garlic	15 mL
1 tsp	fennel seed (optional)	5 mL
2	pita breads	2
	shredded lettuce	
	red onion rings	

COOK'S TIP

Be careful not to overcook the pork. Thinly cut and marinated, it will cook very quickly. Overcooking will toughen it.

Stir together olive oil, lemon juice, mustard, whole garlic cloves and oregano. Pour over pork. Cover and refrigerate 2 to 3 hours, or overnight if you wish.

Stir together yogurt, cucumber and chopped garlic, or blend in blender or processor until smooth.

Remove pork from marinade and drain. Cook pork in a nonstick skillet until browned and tender, stirring from time to time.

Stuff pork into pita halves with shredded lettuce. Pour in a little yogurt sauce and decorate with onion rings.

$\sim$

1 SERVING

421 CALORIES	23g CARBOHYDRATE	26g PROTEIN
25g FAT	0.5g FIBER	50mg CHOLESTEROL

HAM BURGERS

∽

4 SERVINGS

1 lb	ground cooked ham	450 g
1/4 cup	chopped sweet gherkins	50 mL
1/4 cup	skim milk	50 mL
1 1/2 cups	fresh breadcrumbs	375 mL
1	egg	1
1 tbsp	oil	15 mL
2	pita breads	2
1	tomato, sliced	1
1/2	English cucumber, sliced	1/2
	lettuce leaves	

In a bowl, combine ground ham, chopped pickles, milk, breadcrumbs and egg.

Shape into 4 patties (or make 12 to 16 little meatballs, if you prefer).

Heat oil in a nonstick skillet over medium-high heat. Cook ham patties on both sides until golden and crisp on exterior.

Cut pita breads in half. Stuff each pocket with a ham patty, and garnish with tomato, cucumber and lettuce.

∽

COOK'S TIP

This is a good way to use up leftover baked ham. It is easy to grind in a food processor or even a blender.

	1 SERVING	
485 CALORIES	*58g CARBOHYDRATE*	*34g PROTEIN*
13g FAT	*1.5g FIBER*	*129mg CHOLESTEROL*

MIDDLE-EASTERN SANDWICHES

6 SERVINGS

I lb	ground lamb	450 g
I	garlic clove, finely chopped	I
I tsp	chopped fresh coriander	5 mL
2 tbsp	olive oil	30 mL
2	green peppers, cut in strips	2
2	onions, chopped	2
3	pita breads	3

CUCUMBER SAUCE

I	cucumber, peeled, seeded and finely chopped	I
I tbsp	salt	15 mL
I cup	plain yogurt	250 mL
2	small green onions, chopped	2
I tsp	ground cumin	5 mL

To make cucumber sauce: sprinkle chopped cucumber with salt and let stand 15 minutes in a strainer.

In a bowl, stir together yogurt, green onions and cumin. Rinse cucumber and squeeze out excess liquid. Stir into yogurt mixture. Set sauce aside.

Preheat oven to 400°F (200°C). Combine lamb, garlic and coriander. Shape mixture into 1 inch (2.5 cm) meatballs.

Heat oil in a large nonstick skillet over medium-high heat. Add meatballs and cook about 5 minutes, turning from time to time. Add green peppers and onions. Cook another 5 minutes or until vegetables are soft.

Cut pitas in half. Wrap in foil and warm a few minutes in oven or toaster oven.

Stuff pita pockets with lamb and vegetable mixture. Serve with cucumber sauce.

1 SERVING		
274 CALORIES	25g CARBOHYDRATE	21g PROTEIN
10g FAT	1.5g FIBER	53mg CHOLESTEROL

GARLICKY CHEESE AND HAM LOAF

4 SERVINGS

COOK'S TIP

This recipe makes a delicious treat cooked over an open fire outdoors. Prepare foil packages at home, and keep chilled in a cooler until ready to heat.

I	French-style loaf or baguette	I
¹/₃ cup	butter or margarine	75 mL
I or 2	garlic cloves, chopped	I or 2
I tbsp	chopped fresh herbs (chives, parsley, etc)	15 mL
I tsp	lemon juice	5 mL
¹/₂ cup	processed cheese spread	125 mL
4	slices cooked ham, cut in 4	4

Preheat oven to 375°F (190°C). Cut loaf into 4 equal section. Cut each section in 4 crosswise slices, but do not cut all the way through. The slices should be attached at the bottom. Set aside.

In a bowl, combine butter, garlic, herbs, lemon juice and processed cheese. Spread cheese mixture between slits in each section of bread, reserving a little for the tops. Place a slice of ham in each one.

Place each bread section on a piece of foil, spread remaining cheese mixture over tops, and wrap tightly. Heat in oven 15 minutes. Serve hot.

1 SERVING		
424 CALORIES	38g CARBOHYDRATE	14g PROTEIN
24g FAT	0.9g FIBER	67mg CHOLESTEROL

GARDEN SANDWICHES

4 SERVINGS

I cup	grated **Swiss cheese**	250 mL
I cup	grated **carrots**	250 mL
I	**tomato, seeded and chopped**	I
¹/₂ cup	**cauliflower in small florets**	125 mL
2 tbsp	**light mayonnaise**	30 mL
4	**English muffins, split and toasted**	4
	salt and pepper	

Preheat oven to 350°F (180°C).

In a bowl, stir together grated cheese, carrots, tomato, cauliflower and mayonnaise. Season to taste.

Spread mixture on 4 muffin halves. Top with remaining halves.

Place on baking sheet and heat in oven about 6 minutes. Serve hot with salad greens, if desired.

~

COOK'S TIP

You can make these sandwiches even faster in the microwave oven at maximum power for 3 minutes.

1 SERVING		
300 CALORIES	34g CARBOHYDRATE	14g PROTEIN
12g FAT	1.8g FIBER	28mg CHOLESTEROL

MUSHROOM SANDWICHES

4 SERVINGS

COOK'S TIP

If your children are fussy about eating wholewheat bread, try making sandwiches with a slice of white and one of wholewheat, as shown.

2 tbsp	butter or margarine	30 mL
1½ cups	sliced fresh mushrooms	375 mL
1 tsp	lemon juice	5 mL
3	eggs, beaten	3
1	pinch cayenne pepper	1
¼ cup	grated Parmesan cheese	50 mL
8	slices bread	8
	salt and pepper	

Melt butter in a nonstick skillet over medium-high heat. Add mushrooms and cook, stirring from time to time, until lightly browned. Stir in lemon juice.

Add beaten eggs, cayenne, cheese, and salt and pepper to taste. Cook until mixture is the same consistency as scrambled eggs.

Spread between bread slices and cut into wedges to serve. Accompany with salad.

1 SERVING		
294 CALORIES	30g CARBOHYDRATE	12g PROTEIN
14g FAT	1.4g FIBER	224mg CHOLESTEROL

VEGETABLE SUBMARINE SANDWICHES

~

4 SERVINGS

10 oz	can cream of mushroom soup	284 mL
1/4 cup	finely chopped onion	50 mL
1	celery stalk, diced	1
1/2	green pepper, diced	1/2
1/2 cup	broccoli, in small florets	125 mL
1/2 cup	drained canned kernel corn	125 mL
4	submarine rolls	4
	salt and pepper	

In a bowl, stir together all ingredients except submarine rolls.

Cut rolls in half lengthwise. Stuff with vegetable mixture.

Serve cold, or heat in the microwave at maximum power for 2 minutes.

~

NUTRITION TIP

This is a good way to pack fiber and vitamins into your lunch sandwich. You can substitute your own choice of vegetables, and use another cream-style soup.

1 SERVING		
405 CALORIES	69g CARBOHYDRATE	12g PROTEIN
9g FAT	3.3g FIBER	1 mg CHOLESTEROL

ROAST PEPPER
TORTILLA SANDWICHES
~

4 SERVINGS

I	green bell pepper	I
I	red bell pepper	I
I	bunch watercress	I
I cup	light cream cheese	250 mL
4	pitted black olives	4
$1/4$ tsp	Tabasco sauce	I mL
$1/2$ tsp	dried basil	2 mL
4	large flour tortillas	4
I cup	alfalfa sprouts	250 mL
	salt and pepper	

COOK'S TIP

*These tortilla rolls
make a nice lunch box
replacement for an
ordinary sandwich.
Wrap each roll tightly
in foil or plastic wrap.*

Grill the bell peppers under the broiler or over an open
flame until charred and black on all sides. Place them
in a paper bag until cool, then rub off charred skin.
Remove seeds and membranes and set aside.

Tear off stems from watercress and discard. Pour boiling
salted water over watercress leaves and let stand 5 minutes
to soften. Let cool and drain.

In the bowl of a food processor, place cream cheese,
roasted peppers, watercress, olives, Tabasco and basil.
Add salt and pepper to taste. Process until smooth.

Spread cream cheese mixture evenly over tortillas,
top with alfalfa sprouts, and roll tortillas tightly.

~

1 SERVING

215 CALORIES	20g CARBOHYDRATE	9g PROTEIN
11g FAT	2.2g FIBER	32mg CHOLESTEROL

HOMEMADE SOFT
WHOLEWHEAT TORTILLAS

MAKES 12 TORTILLAS

2 ²/₃ cups	wholewheat flour	650 mL
1 tsp	salt	5 mL
3 tbsp	vegetable shortening, diced	45 mL
1 ¹/₄ cups	warm water	300 mL

1 Combine flour and salt in a large bowl. Work in vegetable shortening with your fingertips until evenly distributed and grainy.

2 Add enough of the water to make a workable dough. Knead 3 minutes, then cover with a damp cloth. Let stand 10 minutes.

3 Divide dough into 12 equal pieces. Shape one at a time into a ball, and roll out as thinly as possible on a lightly floured surface.

4 Oil a nonstick skillet, wiping out excess oil with a paper towel. Heat skillet over medium-high heat. Cook first tortilla about 30 seconds, or until lightly browned in patches. Turn and cook second side about 10 seconds. Repeat with remaining tortillas.

1 SERVING		
220 CALORIES	39g CARBOHYDRATE	7g PROTEIN
4g FAT	6.8g FIBER	0mg CHOLESTEROL

BEEF AND POTATO STUFFED TACOS

~

4 servings

2 tbsp	vegetable oil	30 mL
1 cup	diced raw potato	250 mL
1	small red onion, chopped	1
1	red or green bell pepper, diced	1
12 oz	can kernel corn, drained	341 mL
2	garlic cloves, finely chopped	2
1 lb	lean ground beef	450 g
8	taco shells	8
	salt and pepper	
	Mexican-style hot sauce (optional)	

COOK'S TIP

You can make this same recipe with ground turkey or chicken. Stir in some ground cumin and fresh chopped cilantro for a more authentic Mexican flavor.

Heat oil in a nonstick skillet over medium-high heat and add diced potatoes, onion, bell pepper, corn and garlic.

Stir in ground beef. Cook, stirring from time to time, until beef is browned and potatoes are tender. Season to taste.

Pour off excess fat. Fill taco shells with beef mixture and season with hot sauce, if desired. Serve hot with a crisp salad.

~

1 SERVING		
421 CALORIES	39g CARBOHYDRATE	28g PROTEIN
17g FAT	3.0g FIBER	42mg CHOLESTEROL

FISHERMAN-STYLE STUFFED POTATOES

4 SERVINGS

4	large potatoes, baked	4
7 oz	can waterpacked salmon or tuna	200 g
5 cups	coarsely chopped broccoli, lightly steamed	1.25 liters
¼ cup	diced celery	50 mL
¼ cup	chopped green onion	50 mL
½ cup	light mayonnaise	125 mL
2 tsp	Dijon mustard	10 mL
½ cup	plain low-fat yogurt	125 mL
	salt and pepper	
	paprika	

Preheat oven to 350°F (180°C). Slice off the top of each baked potato. Spoon out potato flesh, being careful not to break skin. Place potato flesh in a bowl and mash.

Stir the drained salmon or tuna into mashed potato. Add steamed drained broccoli, celery, green onion, mayonnaise, mustard, and yogurt. Season to taste.

Stuff hollowed-out potatoes with broccoli mixture. Place in baking pan. Sprinkle with paprika.

Bake in preheated oven 10 to 12 minutes. Serve hot, with a dab of yogurt, if desired.

1 SERVING

466 CALORIES 64g CARBOHYDRATE 21g PROTEIN

14g FAT 9.7g FIBER 13mg CHOLESTEROL

QUICK SHRIMP AND RICE

2 SERVINGS

2 tbsp	vegetable oil	30 mL
1/2 cup	chopped onion	125 mL
2 cups	cooked white rice	500 mL
1	pinch salt	1
1	egg, beaten	1
7 oz	can baby shrimp	200 g
1/4 cup	canned peas	50 mL

Heat oil in a nonstick skillet over medium heat. Add onion and cook, stirring occasionally, until onion is soft.

Add rice and salt and cook, stirring, about 2 minutes.

Pour beaten egg into rice and stir rapidly until egg is set. Remove skillet from heat.

Immediately stir in drained shrimp and peas. Reheat if necessary. Season to taste with pepper. Serve hot, with a grated carrot salad, if desired.

COOK'S TIP

If you do not have leftover cooked rice on hand, this recipe can still be made almost as fast if you use instant rice prepared according to package directions.

1 SERVING		
550 CALORIES	66g CARBOHYDRATE	31g PROTEIN
18g FAT	2.4g FIBER	332mg CHOLESTEROL

EASY RATATOUILLE

4 SERVINGS

COOK'S TIP

Leftover ratatouille can be served chilled as an appetizer or salad. Sprinkle with a little red wine vinegar to enhance the flavors.

2 tbsp	olive oil	30 mL
1	onion, diced	1
1	eggplant, diced	1
1	red bell pepper, seeded and diced	1
1	green bell pepper, seeded and diced	1
1	garlic clove, finely chopped	1
1	bay leaf	1
1	zucchini, diced	1
2 tbsp	tomato paste	30 mL
3	tomatoes, diced	3
	salt and pepper	

Heat oil over medium heat in a large nonstick skillet. Add onion and eggplant. Stir-fry 5 minutes.

Add diced peppers, garlic, bay leaf and zucchini. Cook, stirring, another 5 minutes.

Stir in tomato paste and mix well. Add diced tomatoes, turn heat to low, and cook about 10 minutes. Remove bay leaf and season to taste. Serve with rice.

1 SERVING		
135 CALORIES	15g CARBOHYDRATE	3g PROTEIN
7g FAT	5.8g FIBER	0mg CHOLESTEROL

EGGPLANT SANDWICHES

4 SERVINGS

I	large eggplant	I
¹/₄ cup	salt	50 mL
I cup	dry breadcrumbs	250 mL
¹/₃ cup	grated Parmesan cheese	75 mL
¹/₃ cup	chopped fresh parsley	75 mL
8	thin slices cooked lean ham	8
4	thin slices Emmenthal cheese	4
2	eggs, lightly beaten	2
3 tbsp	vegetable oil	45 mL
	salt and pepper	

Leave skin on eggplant. Cut lengthwise to make 8 slices about ½ inch (1 cm) thick.

Arrange on a large plate and sprinkle with salt. Let stand 30 minutes. Rinse eggplant slices and pat dry with paper towels.

In a small bowl, combine breadcrumbs, Parmesan and parsley. Season to taste and set aside.

Place 2 ham slices and 1 cheese slice between 2 eggplant slices. Repeat to make 4 sandwiches. Dip each sandwich into beaten egg, then in breadcrumb mixture.

Heat oil in a large nonstick skillet and fry eggplant sandwiches about 8 minutes on each side. The exterior should be brown and crispy.

COOK'S TIP

If you cannot fit all sandwiches in the skillet at the same time, keep cooked ones in a warm oven on paper towels to absorb excess grease.

1 SERVING		
386 CALORIES	26g CARBOHYDRATE	21g PROTEIN
22g FAT	2.0g FIBER	172mg CHOLESTEROL

COTTAGE CHEESE PIZZA

~

4 SERVINGS

NUTRITION TIP

Pizza can be a nutritious and low-fat meal as long as you avoid loading it with high-fat cheeses and meats. Instead, pile it with fresh vegetables and herbs for flavor.

1 cup	cottage cheese	250 mL
1	garlic clove, finely chopped	1
3 tbsp	dry white wine	45 mL
2	pinches dried basil or oregano	2
1	Italian-style flatbread or cooked plain pizza shell	1
1 cup	cold meat of your choice (ham, salami, etc), cut in thin strips	250 mL
2	tomatoes, sliced	2
	pepper	
	freshly chopped parsley	

Preheat oven to 350°F (180°C).

In a bowl, stir together cottage cheese, garlic, wine, basil, and pepper to taste. Spread mixture over flatbread.

Garnish with strips of cold meat and tomatoes. Sprinkle with parsley. Bake 8 to 10 minutes.

~

1 SERVING

295 CALORIES	43g CARBOHYDRATE	15g PROTEIN
7g FAT	3.2g FIBER	25mg CHOLESTEROL

CALIFORNIA SALAD PIZZA

4 SERVINGS

COOK'S TIP

Sun-dried tomatoes can be bought in two forms. The oil-packed ones need only to be drained. The dry-packed ones must be rehydrated; pour boiling water over them and let soak about 30 minutes, then drain.

I	Italian-style flatbread or cooked plain pizza shell	I
1/2	head lettuce, shredded	1/2
I cup	grated Cheddar cheese	250 mL
I cup	canned mandarin segments	250 mL
3/4 cup	sundried tomatoes, drained and chopped	175 mL
3 tbsp	sesame seeds	45 mL
1/4 cup	raisins	50 mL
	herb-flavored oil and vinegar dressing	

Cover flatbread with a layer of shredded lettuce.

Spread grated cheese evenly over lettuce. Top with drained mandarin segments, sundried tomatoes, sesame seeds and raisins.

Sprinkle with oil and vinegar dressing just before serving.

1 SERVING		
420 CALORIES	51 g CARBOHYDRATE	18 g PROTEIN
16 g FAT	4.8 g FIBER	31 mg CHOLESTEROL

PIZZA EXPRESS

1 SERVING

1	English muffin, halved	1
2 tbsp	canned tomato sauce	30 mL
2	slices cooked salami or bologna	2
2	slices tomato	2
2	slices Gruyère, Emmenthal or mozzarella cheese	2
4	chopped pitted black olives	4

Toast English muffin halves. Spread tomato sauce on muffin halves.

Top each half with a slice of meat, then a tomato slice, and finally a slice of cheese. Garnish with chopped olives.

Place under the broiler until cheese melts. Served with some carrot and celery sticks and a glass of low-fat milk or juice, this makes a nutritious and fast lunch.

COOK'S TIP

An open can of tomato sauce will keep up to a week if you transfer it into a lidded glass jar and store it in the refrigerator.

1 SERVING

482 CALORIES	35g CARBOHYDRATE	27g PROTEIN
26g FAT	1.7g FIBER	74mg CHOLESTEROL

CHOCOLATE GRANOLA BARS

MAKES 8 BARS

¹/₂ cup	packed brown sugar	125 mL
¹/₂ cup	corn syrup	125 mL
¹/₂ cup	peanut butter	125 mL
1 cup	oatmeal	250 mL
1 cup	puffed rice cereal	250 mL
¹/₂ cup	unsalted peanuts	125 mL
¹/₄ cup	unsalted sunflower seeds	50 mL
¹/₂ cup	semi-sweet chocolate chips	125 mL

Combine brown sugar, corn syrup and peanut butter in a saucepan. Heat over medium-low heat until mixture is smooth.

In a large bowl, stir together oatmeal, puffed rice, peanuts, sunflower seeds and chocolate chips.

Pour warm peanut butter mixture over oatmeal mixture. Mix well. Press mixture into an oiled pan. Let cool before cutting into bars or squares.

1 SERVING		
419 CALORIES	52g CARBOHYDRATE	10g PROTEIN
19g FAT	3.5g FIBER	0mg CHOLESTEROL

PEANUT BUTTER AND MOLASSES CANDIES

MAKES ABOUT 2 DOZEN

1/2 cup	crunchy-style peanut butter	125 mL
1/3 cup	molasses	75 mL
1 tsp	vanilla extract	5 mL
1	pinch salt	1
3/4 cup	powdered skim milk	175 mL
2 tbsp	icing sugar	30 mL
1	egg white, lightly beaten	1
1 cup	chopped peanuts	250 mL

In a bowl, stir together the peanut butter, molasses and vanilla with a wooden spoon.

Add salt, milk powder and icing sugar. Stir well to mix. Shape into 1 inch (2.5 cm) balls.

Dip each candy in beaten egg white, then in chopped peanuts to coat all sides.

NUTRITION TIP

These delicious treats make a great lunch box addition; the peanut butter and milk powder supply protein.

1 CANDY		
102 CALORIES	8g CARBOHYDRATE	4g PROTEIN
6g FAT	0.9g FIBER	1 mg CHOLESTEROL

EVERYDAY BAKING

~

Nothing makes a kitchen smell like home
as much as fresh-baked bread, muffins
or cookies hot from the oven.
But where to find the time?

We think you will be surprised to find
how easy it is to make the baked goods in this
cookbook. Fiber-rich muffins, cakes that taste
great even without icing, and fabulously
easy-to-make homemade croissants.

There are recipes for some cookies and squares
that are better than anything you can buy.
And even a couple of bread recipes that you can
make even if you have never tried your hand
at homemade bread in your life!

So get out your mixing bowl and wooden
spoon, and impress your friends and family
with good old-fashioned home baking
that will have them cheering for more.

~

ITALIAN-STYLE BREAD

MAKES 2 LOAVES

1¾ cups	warm water	425 mL
2 tbsp	dry yeast	30 mL
2 tsp	salt	10 mL
5 cups	all-purpose flour	1.2 liters

Pour ½ cup (125 mL) warm water into a large bowl. Sprinkle yeast on top and let stand 10 minutes, then stir. Add remaining water, salt, and 2 cups (500 mL) flour. Stir well.

Add enough flour, about 2 cups (500 mL), to make a stiff dough. Dust a work surface heavily with flour and place dough on it. Knead dough by stretching it with the palms of your hands and folding it over. Continue kneading about 10 minutes. If the dough sticks to your fingers, sprinkle on a little more flour and knead it in. The dough should feel smooth and elastic.

Place dough in a clean oiled bowl and cover with a clean cloth. Let sit at room temperature about 30 minutes, or until doubled in volume.

Punch down dough with your fist, then place on a floured surface. Cut dough into 2 equal pieces. Roll out each with a rolling pin to about 12 inches (30 cm) square. Roll up each square. Pinch seams to seal. Roll each loaf on the surface a few times to make layers stick together.

Place seam side down on a greased baking pan. Cover with a clean cloth and let stand in a warm place 30 minutes or until doubled in volume.

Preheat oven to 400°F (200°C). Dust a little flour over tops and slash in 3 or 4 places. Bake about 25 minutes.

1 Dissolve yeast in water, then add remaining ingredients.

2 Knead, then cover and let rise.

3 Roll out dough, then roll up to make loaves. Let rise again.

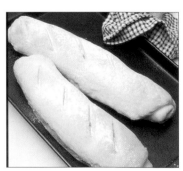

4 Dust with flour and slash tops before baking.

1 LOAF		
1203 CALORIES	256g CARBOHYDRATE	38g PROTEIN
3g FAT	12.7g FIBER	0mg CHOLESTEROL

SUPER-SIMPLE HOMEMADE BREAD

MAKES 1 LOAF

1 tsp	dry yeast	5 mL
1/2 cup	warm water	125 mL
2 cups	all-purpose flour	500 mL
1/2 tsp	salt	2 mL

Sprinkle yeast over water in a small bowl. Let sit about 10 minutes until mixture looks frothy. Stir well.

Mix flour and salt in a large bowl. Make a well in the middle. Pour in water and yeast mixture. With a wooden spoon, pull flour from edges until flour and liquid are mixed.

Lightly flour a work surface and place dough on it. Knead dough by stretching it with the palms of your hands and folding it over. Continue kneading about 10 minutes.

If the dough sticks to your fingers, sprinkle on a little more flour and knead it in. The dough should feel smooth and elastic.

Place dough in a clean oiled bowl and cover with a clean cloth. Let sit at room temperature about 1 hour, until doubled in volume.

Lightly pat out dough into rectangle shape about 10 inches (25 cm) long. Fold under long sides of rectangle to make a loaf shape. Place on oiled baking pan, seams down. Let stand 30 minutes, covered with a clean cloth. Meanwhile, preheat oven to 400°F (200°C).

Slash top of loaf diagonally 2 or 3 times. Bake about 30 minutes, until golden brown.

1 LOAF		
975 CALORIES	206g CARBOHYDRATE	31g PROTEIN
3g FAT	10.6g FIBER	0mg CHOLESTEROL

WHOLEWHEAT RAISIN BREAD

MAKES 2 SMALL LOAVES

5¹/₂ cups	wholewheat flour	1.4 liters
1 tbsp	salt	15 mL
1 tbsp	dry yeast	15 mL
1 tbsp	honey	15 mL
1³/₄ cups	warm water	425 mL
2 tbsp	soy flour	30 mL
¹/₂ cup	raisins	125 mL

In a large bowl, stir together flour and salt. Set aside.

In a second bowl, combine yeast and honey. Stir in ¾ cup (175 mL) of the warm water. Stir in soy flour, then let stand 5 minutes in a warm place (such as on top of the refrigerator).

Combine yeast mixture with the flour mixture, raisins and remaining water. Knead dough as described on previous page until it is smooth and elastic. Place in a clean bowl, cover with a cloth, and let rise 30 minutes in a warm place.

Knead dough another 5 minutes and cut in two. Shape each portion into a round loaf. Place on nonstick baking pans. Cover and let rise another 30 minutes, or until doubled in bulk.

Meanwhile, preheat oven to 350°F (180°C). Bake loaves about 25 to 30 minutes. Let cool on a rack.

~

1 LOAF		
1487 CALORIES	301g CARBOHYDRATE	55g PROTEIN
7g FAT	47.4g FIBER	0mg CHOLESTEROL

CINNAMON DANISH

MAKES 2 DOZEN

4 cups	all-purpose flour	1 liter
1½ cups	sugar	375 mL
2 tbsp	quick dry yeast	30 mL
1 tsp	salt	5 mL
½ cup	water	125 mL
½ cup	2% milk	125 mL
¾ cup	butter or margarine	175 mL
2	eggs	2
2 tbsp	ground cinnamon	30 mL

GLAZE

1 cup	apricot jelly, melted	250 mL

In a large bowl, combine 2 cups (500 mL) flour, ½ cup (125 mL) sugar, yeast and salt. Set aside.

Heat together water, milk and ½ cup (125 mL) butter until hot. Pour mixture over flour mixture. Stir in eggs and about 2 cups (500 mL) flour, or enough to make a dough than forms into a ball.

Sprinkle work surface with flour. Knead dough about 6 minutes, until smooth and elastic. Cover and let rest 10 minutes.

Roll out dough with rolling pin to make a rectangle about 18 x 22 inches (45 x 55 cm). Melt remaining butter and spread over dough. Sprinkle on remaining sugar and cinnamon. Roll up dough like a jelly roll, pinching ends to seal.

Cut into 24 equal slices with a sharp knife. Arrange on greased baking trays. Cover and let rise at room temperature until doubled in volume.

Preheat oven to 350°F (180°C). Bake danishes 20 minutes or until golden brown. Let cool slightly and brush with melted apricot jelly.

~

1 Combine dry ingredients.

2 Heat water, milk and butter. Stir into dry ingredients with eggs.

3 Knead in flour to make a stiff dough. Roll out. Spread with butter, sugar and cinnamon.

4 Roll and cut into slices crosswise.

1 SERVING		
211 CALORIES	34g CARBOHYDRATE	3g PROTEIN
7g FAT	0.7g FIBER	38mg CHOLESTEROL

SWISS CHEESE BISCUITS

MAKES ABOUT 2 DOZEN

1¹/₂ cups	all-purpose flour	375 mL
¹/₄ tsp	dry mustard	1 mL
1	pinch cayenne pepper	1
³/₄ cup	butter or margarine, diced	175 mL
1 cup	grated **Gruyère** cheese	250 mL
1 cup	grated **Emmenthal** cheese	250 mL
1	egg, lightly beaten	1

Combine flour, mustard and cayenne in food processor. Add butter and process until mixture is grainy.

Add cheeses and process until mixed. Wrap dough in plastic wrap and refrigerate 30 minutes.

Preheat oven to 375°F (190°C). Lightly flour a work surface and roll out dough ¼ inch (5 mm) thick. With a cookie cutter or upside-down glass, cut out 2 ½ inch (5 cm) circles. Place on ungreased baking sheet. Brush tops with beaten egg.

Bake 10 to 15 minutes, until golden brown.

1 SERVING		
103 CALORIES	6g CARBOHYDRATE	4g PROTEIN
9g FAT	0.3g FIBER	37mg CHOLESTEROL

CHEESE TREATS

8 SERVINGS

1 cup	light sour cream or plain yogurt	250 mL
4 oz	light cream cheese	110 g
¹/₂ cup	grated Parmesan cheese	125 mL
¹/₃ cup	puffed rice cereal or corn flakes	75 mL
2	eggs	2
1	garlic clove	1
1 tsp	chopped fresh chives	5 mL
1 tsp	chopped fresh basil	5 mL

Preheat oven to 350°F (180°C). Grease an 8 inch (20 cm) square baking pan.

Place all ingredients in food processor and process until very well mixed. (If you want to make this recipe by hand, mince garlic very finely and crush cereal before mixing.)

Pour mixture into prepared pan. Bake about 34 minutes, or until lightly golden.

1 SERVING		
111 CALORIES	5 g CARBOHYDRATE	7 g PROTEIN
7 g FAT	0 g FIBER	83 mg CHOLESTEROL

BAKING POWDER BISCUITS

MAKES 12 TO 14 BISCUITS

2 cups	all-purpose flour	500 mL
3 tsp	baking powder	15 mL
1/2 tsp	salt	2 mL
1/2 cup	vegetable shortening	125 mL
3/4 to 1 cup	2% milk	175 to 250 mL

Preheat oven to 450°F (230°C).

In a large bowl, stir together flour, baking powder and salt. Using a fork or pastry cutter, cut in the shortening until lumps of shortening are the size of small peas.

Add ¾ cup (175) milk and stir gently and rapidly with fork to make a grainy mixture. Add extra milk only if there remains some flour that will not adhere to mixture.

Lightly flour work surface. Pat dough into a ball, and knead a few seconds. Roll out dough ½ inch (1.2 cm) thick. Cut into 2 inch (4 cm) circles with a cookie cutter or upside-down glass. Place on ungreased baking sheet.

Bake 8 to 12 minutes, until golden brown. Serve warm.

1 Combine flour, baking powder and salt. Cut in shortening.

2 Stir in milk with a fork to make a grainy dough.

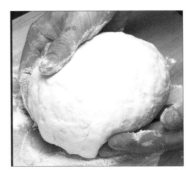

3 Knead dough a few seconds on a floured surface.

4 Roll out dough ½ inch (1.2 cm) thick. Cut out circles.

	1 SERVING	
144 CALORIES	15g CARBOHYDRATE	3g PROTEIN
8g FAT	0.6g FIBER	1 mg CHOLESTEROL

CHEESE AND CARROT MUFFINS

MAKES 16 MUFFINS

2 cups	all-purpose flour	500 mL
4 tsp	baking powder	20 mL
1/2 tsp	salt	2 mL
1	pinch ground cinnamon	1
1 cup	skim milk	250 mL
1	egg	1
2 tbsp	canola oil	30 mL
1/2 cup	honey	125 mL
2 cups	finely grated raw carrots	500 mL
1/4 cup	raisins	50 mL
8 oz	light cream cheese	225 g

Preheat oven to 400°F (200°C). Grease and lightly flour 16 large muffin molds, or line them with paper molds.

Combine flour, baking powder, salt and cinnamon. Place mixture in food processor.

Add milk, egg and oil. Process just until combined.

Add honey, carrots, and raisins. Process just until combined.

Divide batter among prepared muffin molds. Cut cream cheese into 16 cubes. Place a cheese cube on top of each muffin.

Bake about 20 minutes, or until tops spring back when lightly pressed with a finger.

~

1 Combine flour, baking powder, salt and cinnamon.

2 Add milk, egg and oil. Mix lightly.

3 Add honey, carrots, and raisins. Mix lightly.

4 Divide batter among muffin tins. Top with cheese cube.

1 SERVING		
169 CALORIES	27g CARBOHYDRATE	4g PROTEIN
5g FAT	1.0g FIBER	25mg CHOLESTEROL

CORN AND BELL PEPPER MUFFINS

~

MAKES 20 MUFFINS

COOK'S TIP

These make a delicious accompaniment for chili or Mexican scrambled eggs.

2 cups	all-purpose flour	500 mL
1 cup	cornmeal	250 mL
1/4 cup	sugar	50 mL
2 tsp	baking powder	10 mL
1 tsp	salt	5 mL
1 1/2 cups	frozen or canned drained corn kernels	375 mL
1/4 cup	finely chopped green pepper	50 mL
1/4 cup	finely chopped red pepper	50 mL
1/4 cup	finely chopped chives	50 mL
2 cups	evaporated skim milk	500 mL
2	eggs, beaten	2
1/4 cup	melted butter or margarine	50 mL

Preheat oven to 350°F (180°C). Grease 20 muffin molds.

Stir together flour, cornmeal, sugar, baking powder and salt in a large bowl.

Stir in corn kernels, chopped peppers and chives.

Make a well in center of mixture and add milk and eggs. Stir just until all ingredients are moistened. Stir in melted butter gently.

Divide mixture into muffin molds. Bake 20 to 25 minutes, or until golden brown. Let cool before serving.

~

1 SERVING		
143 CALORIES	24g CARBOHYDRATE	5g PROTEIN
3g FAT	1.1g FIBER	34mg CHOLESTEROL

HAM AND VEGETABLE MUFFINS

MAKES 12 MUFFINS

1¹/₂ cups	chopped cooked broccoli or cauliflower	375 mL
1¹/₂ cups	finely chopped cooked ham	375 mL
1	medium onion, chopped	1
¹/₂ cup	diced **Cheddar** cheese	125 mL
2 tbsp	grated **Parmesan** cheese	30 mL
3	eggs	3
¹/₂ cup	canola oil	125 mL
1 cup	skim milk	250 mL
1¹/₄ cups	all-purpose flour	300 mL
3 tsp	baking powder	15 mL
1 tsp	dried parsley	5 mL
¹/₄ tsp	dried thyme	1 mL
¹/₄ tsp	garlic powder	1 mL

Preheat oven to 375°F (190°C). Grease and lightly flour 12 large muffin molds.

Stir together chopped broccoli, ham, onion and cheeses. Set aside.

In a second bowl, beat eggs until frothy. Stir in oil and milk.

Combine dry ingredients in a third bowl. Stir dry ingredients into egg mixture until smooth. Pour mixture over broccoli and ham. Mix well.

Divide batter among prepared muffin molds. Bake 20 to 25 minutes, or until golden brown. Serve hot or cold.

COOK'S TIP

Served with a salad, these muffins are hearty enough to make a complete lunch.

1 SERVING		
218 CALORIES	14g CARBOHYDRATE	9g PROTEIN
14g FAT	1.1g FIBER	81mg CHOLESTEROL

OAT BRAN AND RAISIN MUFFINS

MAKES 12 MUFFINS

COOK'S TIP

Pour the batter into a greased loaf pan and bake until center tests cooked with a toothpick.

2 cups	oat bran	500 mL
1/4 cup	packed brown sugar	50 mL
2 tsp	baking powder	10 mL
1/2 cup	raisins	50 mL
1 cup	plain low-fat yogurt	250 mL
2	egg whites, lightly beaten	2
1/4 cup	2% milk	50 mL
1/4 cup	maple syrup	50 mL
2 tbsp	canola oil	30 mL
1 tsp	grated orange or lemon zest	

Preheat oven to 400°F (200°C). Grease and lightly flour 12 muffin molds, or line with paper liners.

In a food processor or by hand, mix together oat bran, brown sugar, baking powder and raisins.

Add yogurt, egg whites, milk, maple syrup, oil and orange zest. Mix just until dry ingredients are moistened.

Divide batter among prepared molds. Bake about 20 minutes, or until a toothpick inserted in the center of a muffin comes out clean.

1 SERVING		
139 CALORIES	23g CARBOHYDRATE	5g PROTEIN
3g FAT	2.4g FIBER	1 mg CHOLESTEROL

BLUEBERRY MUFFINS

MAKES 12 MUFFINS

I cup	packed light brown sugar	250 mL
3/4 cup	quick-cooking oatmeal	175 mL
2/3 cup	sifted wholewheat flour	150 mL
1/2 cup	all-purpose flour	125 mL
3 tsp	baking powder	15 mL
1/2 tsp	salt	2 mL
1/4 tsp	ground cinnamon	1 mL
I cup	2% milk	250 mL
1/4 cup	canola oil	50 mL
I	egg	I
I cup	fresh or frozen blueberries	250 mL
	grated zest of I orange or lemon	

Preheat oven to 400°F (200°C). Grease 12 muffin molds.

In a food processor or by hand, mix together brown sugar, oatmeal, wholewheat flour, all-purpose flour, baking powder, salt, cinnamon and orange zest.

Add milk, oil and egg. Mix just until dry ingredients are moistened. Fold in blueberries gently with a rubber spatula.

Divide mixture into prepared muffin molds, filling them ¾ full. Bake 20 to 25 minutes, or until muffins are firm to the touch.

COOK'S TIP

Stir quick bread and muffin batters just enough to moisten dry ingredients. Over-beating makes a tough texture with big air bubbles.

1 SERVING		
185 CALORIES	32g CARBOHYDRATE	3g PROTEIN
5g FAT	1.0g FIBER	24mg CHOLESTEROL

CURRANT AND WHEAT GERM MUFFINS

MAKES 2 DOZEN MUFFINS

2 cups	all-purpose flour	500 mL
1½ cups	wholewheat flour	375 mL
1½ cups	wheat germ	375 mL
4 tsp	baking powder	20 mL
2 tsp	ground cinnamon	10 mL
I tsp	baking soda	5 mL
I tsp	ground nutmeg	5 mL
I cup	sugar	250 mL
I tsp	salt	5 mL
I cup	melted margarine or canola oil	250 mL
2	eggs	2
2 cups	skim milk	500 mL
½ cup	molasses	125 mL
2 cups	dried currants	500 mL

Preheat oven to 375°F (190°C). Grease and lightly flour 24 muffin molds, or line with paper liners.

In a large bowl, stir together flour, wholewheat flour, wheat germ, baking powder, cinnamon, baking soda, nutmeg, sugar and salt.

Stir in melted margarine. Stir in eggs one by one, alternating with the milk. When smooth, stir in molasses and currants.

Divide batter among muffin tins, filling ¾ full. Bake about 25 minutes, or until golden.

1 SERVING		
246 CALORIES	42g CARBOHYDRATE	6g PROTEIN
6g FAT	5.6g FIBER	23 mg CHOLESTEROL

PEANUT BUTTER MUFFINS

MAKES 12 MUFFINS

¹/₂ cup	wholewheat flour	125 mL
1 cup	all-purpose flour	250 mL
¹/₄ cup	packed brown sugar	50 mL
1 cup	natural wheat bran	250 mL
3 tsp	baking powder	15 mL
1	pinch salt	1
2	eggs	2
1 cup	skim milk	250 mL
¹/₂ cup	peanut butter	125 mL
¹/₄ cup	canola oil	50 mL
¹/₄ cup	unsweetened apple juice	50 mL

Preheat oven to 350°F (180°C). Grease and lightly flour 12 muffin molds or line with paper liners.

In a large bowl mix both flours, brown sugar, bran, baking powder, and salt. Set aside.

In another bowl, mix together eggs, milk, peanut butter, oil and apple juice until mixture is smooth. Pour liquid mixture into dry ingredients, and stir just until dry ingredients are moistened.

Fill muffin molds ¾ full. Bake about 30 minutes, or until firm to the touch.

1 SERVING		
219 CALORIES	23g CARBOHYDRATE	7g PROTEIN
11g FAT	4.0g FIBER	46mg CHOLESTEROL

EASY HOMEMADE CROISSANTS

MAKES 8 CROISSANTS

1 Buy a package of good-quality frozen puff pastry. Let thaw overnight in refrigerator, or 2 hours at room temperature. Roll out pastry in a rectangle $1/8$ inch (3 mm) thick. Cut pastry into triangles.

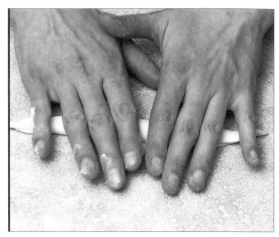

2 Roll up each triangle starting at the wide end and rolling towards the point.

3 Brush a pastry sheet with water. Place rolls on pastry sheet, and pull ends into crescent shape. Let stand 1 hour in refrigerator. At this point, the croissants should be slightly expanded. Brush tops of croissants with an egg beaten together with a splash of milk.

4 Preheat oven to 375°F (190°C). Bake 15 to 20 minutes, or until golden brown. Remove from pan and let cool slightly on a rack before serving.

1 SERVING		
178 CALORIES	19g CARBOHYDRATE	3g PROTEIN
10g FAT	0.1g FIBER	24mg CHOLESTEROL

MAPLE AND WALNUT COFFEE ROLLS

MAKES 10 ROLLS

SYRUP

1¹/₂ cups	maple syrup	375 mL
1¹/₂ cups	water	375 mL

DOUGH

1 cup	all-purpose flour	250 mL
1 cup	wholewheat flour	250 mL
4 tsp	baking powder	20 mL
¹/₄ tsp	salt	1 mL
¹/₃ cup	soft butter or margarine	75 mL
1	egg	1
¹/₂ cup	skim milk	125 mL

FILLING

2 tbsp	soft butter or margarine	30 mL
¹/₂ cup	packed brown sugar	125 mL
¹/₂ cup	chopped walnuts	125 mL

Preheat oven to 400°F (200°C). Grease a 9 x 13 inch (23 x 33 cm) baking pan.

In a saucepan, heat maple syrup and water over medium heat a few minutes. Pour mixture into baking pan.

Place all-purpose and wholewheat flours in a food processor with baking powder and salt. Process a few seconds. Add butter and egg. Process to mix. Add milk and process until mixture pulls away from sides of bowl into a ball.

Sprinkle a work surface with flour. Roll out pastry into a 14 x 16 inch (35 x 40 cm) rectangle. Spread surface with soft butter, and sprinkle with brown sugar and nuts.

Roll up dough to make a long tube and cut crosswise to make 10 slices. Arrange in syrup in baking pan. Bake 30 minutes or until golden brown.

~

1 SERVING

| 393 CALORIES | 64g CARBOHYDRATE | 5g PROTEIN |
| 13g FAT | 2.3g FIBER | 50mg CHOLESTEROL |

PUMPKIN CAKE

8 SERVINGS

1/2 cup	chopped pecans	125 mL
2 tbsp	all-purpose flour	30 mL
1/4 cup	butter or margarine	50 mL
1 cup	brown sugar	250 mL
2/3 cup	canned or homemade pumpkin purée	150 mL
2	eggs (or 4 egg whites)	2
1/2 cup	all-purpose or wholewheat flour	125 mL
1/2 tsp	baking powder	2 mL
1/2 tsp	cinnamon	2 mL
1/2 tsp	ground nutmeg	2 mL
1/4 tsp	ground ginger	1 mL
1/4 tsp	baking soda	1 mL

Preheat oven to 350°F (180°C). Grease a 9 inch (23 cm) square baking pan.

In a small bowl, stir together pecans with 2 tbsp (30 mL) flour. Set aside.

Melt butter together with brown sugar in a saucepan. Remove from heat and stir in pumpkin purée. Mix well and set aside.

In a clean bowl, beat eggs until foamy. Stir eggs well into pumpkin mixture. Set aside.

In a clean bowl, stir together all dry ingredients. Stir this mixture into pumpkin mixture. Stir in pecans. Pour batter into prepared pan.

Bake 30 to 45 minutes. Cake is done when a toothpick inserted in the center comes out clean. Let cool 5 minutes before unmolding. Dust with icing sugar, if desired, before serving.

1 SERVING

267 CALORIES | *39g CARBOHYDRATE* | *3g PROTEIN*
11g FAT | *1.2 g FIBER* | *82mg CHOLESTEROL*

GINGERBREAD LOAF

10 SERVINGS

1/4 cup	canola oil	50 mL
3/4 cup	sugar	175 mL
2	eggs	2
1/2 cup	skim milk	125 mL
1/2 cup	plain nonfat yogurt	125 mL
1 cup	wholewheat flour	250 mL
1 cup	all-purpose flour	250 mL
1 cup	chopped pecans	250 mL
1 tsp	ground ginger	5 mL
1 tsp	baking powder	5 mL
1/2 tsp	baking soda	2 mL
1/2 tsp	salt	2 mL

LEMON NUT ICING (OPTIONAL)

2 cups	icing sugar	500 mL
1/3 cup	fresh lemon juice	75 mL
2 tbsp	very finely chopped pecans	30 mL

Preheat oven to 350°F (180°C). Grease and lightly flour 2 loaf pans 8 x 4 x 2 inches (20 x 10 x 5 cm).

Beat together the oil and sugar until creamy. Beat in eggs. Add milk and yogurt and beat until smooth. Set aside.

In a large bowl, combine all remaining ingredients (except icing ingredients). Add egg mixture and stir just until dry ingredients are moistened.

Divide mixture between loaf pans. Bake 40 to 45 minutes, or until toothpick inserted in center comes out clean. Let cool about 15 minutes before unmolding.

To make the icing: place icing sugar in a bowl, and gradually stir in lemon juice until desired icing consistency. Stir in chopped nuts and spread over loaves.

1 SERVING		
293 CALORIES	38g CARBOHYDRATE	6g PROTEIN
13g FAT	2.8g FIBER	55mg CHOLESTEROL

OLD-FASHIONED CHERRY NUT LOAF

8 TO 10 SERVINGS

2 cups	all-purpose flour	500 mL
1 tsp	baking powder	5 mL
1/2 tsp	baking soda	2 mL
1/4 tsp	salt	1 mL
3/4 cup	chopped pecans	175 mL
3/4 cup	halved maraschino cherries	175 mL
1/2 cup	sugar	125 mL
1/2 cup	soft butter or margarine	125 mL
3	eggs	3
1/2 cup	fresh lemon juice	125 mL
1/2 cup	skim milk	125 mL

LEMON GLAZE

1/3 cup	sugar	75 mL
1/4 cup	fresh lemon juice	50 mL

Preheat oven to 350°F (180°C). Grease a loaf pan.

In a large bowl, stir together flour, baking powder, baking soda, and salt. Fold in pecans and cherries. Set aside.

In a second bowl or a food processor, beat together sugar and butter until creamy. Add eggs one by one, mixing well between each addition. Mix in lemon juice, then milk. Stir in dry ingredients, mixing well.

Pour batter into loaf pan. Bake 55 to 60 minutes, or until a toothpick inserted in center comes out clean.

To make glaze, stir ingredients together well. Prick holes in top of baked loaf with a skewer or fork. Pour 1/2 of glaze over loaf while it is still hot. Let stand 10 minutes, then unmold. Pour remaining glaze over. Serve warm or cold.

1 SERVING

311 CALORIES	56g CARBOHYDRATE	6g PROTEIN
7g FAT	1.6g FIBER	108mg CHOLESTEROL

BANANA BREAD

MAKES 1 LOAF

1/3 cup	canola oil	75 mL
1/4 cup	corn syrup	50 mL
1 1/2 cups	mashed very ripe bananas	375 mL
2	eggs	2
1 cup	wholewheat flour	250 mL
1/2 cup	all-purpose flour	125 mL
1/2 cup	sugar	125 mL
2 tsp	baking powder	10 mL
1 tsp	salt	5 mL
1/2 tsp	baking soda	2 mL

ICING

2 tbsp	milk	30 mL
2 tbsp	lemon juice	30 mL
1 1/2 cups	icing sugar	375 mL
	chocolate chips (optional)	

COOK'S TIP

Stir quick bread and muffin batters just enough to moisten dry ingredients. Over-beating makes a tough bread with big air bubbles.

Preheat oven to 350°F (180°C). Grease a loaf pan.

Beat together oil, corn syrup, bananas and eggs until smooth. Set aside.

Measure wholewheat and white flour into a large bowl. Stir in sugar, baking powder, salt and baking soda.

Gradually stir banana mixture into dry ingredients with a wooden spoon. Stir just until dry ingredients are moistened.

Pour mixture into loaf pan. Bake about 50 minutes, or until a toothpick inserted in the center comes out clean.

To make the icing: heat milk and lemon juice in a saucepan until hot. Place icing sugar in a bowl. Pour hot milk mixture into sugar, stirring. Add just enough liquid to make an icing that will stick to the cake. If you wish, sprinkle top with chocolate chips while icing is still wet.

1 LOAF		
3140 CALORIES	555g CARBOHYDRATE	41g PROTEIN
84g FAT	24.0g FIBER	560mg CHOLESTEROL

QUICK LIGHT CARROT CAKE

10 TO 12 SERVINGS

1¼ cups	plain nonfat yogurt	300 mL
1	package white or golden cake mix	1
2	eggs	2
¼ cup	cold water or evaporated milk	50 mL
½ tsp	cinnamon	2 mL
2 cups	finely grated carrots	500 mL
¼ cup	chopped walnuts	50 mL
2 tbsp	icing sugar	30 mL

Preheat oven to 350°F (180°C). Grease a 9 inch (23 cm) square cake pan.

Beat together yogurt, cake mix, eggs, water, and cinnamon until smooth, using a food processor or electric mixer.

Stir in carrots and nuts. Pour into greased pan. Bake 25 to 30 minutes, or until a toothpick inserted in the center comes out clean.

Let cool completely. Place icing sugar in a sieve and shake over top of cake before serving.

1 SERVING		
247 CALORIES	41g CARBOHYDRATE	5g PROTEIN
7g FAT	0.6g FIBER	47mg CHOLESTEROL

EASY CHOCOLATE CAKE

10 SERVINGS

1½ cups	all-purpose flour	375 mL
1 cup	brown sugar	250 mL
¼ cup	cocoa powder	50 mL
1 tsp	baking soda	5 mL
½ tsp	salt	2 mL
1 cup	2% milk	250 mL
¼ cup	canola oil	50 mL
1 tsp	vanilla extract	5 mL
	icing sugar	

Preheat oven to 350°F (180°C). Grease and lightly flour an 8 inch (20 cm) round cake pan.

In a large bowl, stir together flour, brown sugar, cocoa, baking soda and salt.

Make a well in the center of the dry mixture. Pour in milk, oil, and vanilla. Beat with a wooden spoon or electric mixer until well mixed and smooth.

Pour mixture into prepared cake pan. Bake 30 minutes or until a toothpick inserted in center comes out clean. Let cool a few minutes before unmolding. If you wish, sprinkle with icing sugar, using a sieve to shake sugar evenly over top of cake.

1 SERVING		
190 CALORIES	31 g CARBOHYDRATE	3 g PROTEIN
6 g FAT	1.3 g FIBER	2 mg CHOLESTEROL

ALMOND CAKE

~

6 SERVINGS

2/3 cup	powdered almonds	150 mL
3/4 cup	sugar	175 mL
2	large eggs	2
1/4 cup	all-purpose flour	50 mL
1/4 cup	melted butter, lukewarm	50 mL

COOK'S TIP

This cake is delicious plain, and wonderful with fresh fruit and custard sauce (which you can prepare from a mix, if you like).

Preheat oven to 400°F (200°C). Grease a quiche pan or pie plate.

Beat together almonds and sugar by hand or with food processor. Add eggs one by one, and beat 3 to 5 minutes until mixture is light and foamy.

Add flour and mix well. Add melted butter. Mix gently, just until smooth. Pour mixture into prepared pan. Bake about 15 minutes. The cake should be relatively firm to the touch.

Let stand a few minutes before unmolding. Sprinkle with a little icing sugar, if desired.

~

	1 SERVING	
284 CALORIES	30g CARBOHYDRATE	5g PROTEIN
16g FAT	1.6g FIBER	109mg CHOLESTEROL

COOK'S TIP

*The amount of chocolate
and coffee in this cake
makes for lots of
caffeine, so reserve it
for adults only!*

RICH MOKA CAKE

6 SERVINGS

3	eggs, separated	3
1/2 cup	icing sugar	125 mL
4 oz	bittersweet chocolate	110 g
1 tbsp	strong brewed coffee	15 mL
2 tbsp	all-purpose flour	30 mL
3 tbsp	ground almonds	45 mL
1/3 cup	melted butter	75 mL

Preheat oven to 400°F (200°C). Grease a round cake pan.

In a bowl, stir together egg yolks with icing sugar, beating until glossy and smooth. Set aside.

Melt chocolate in the top of a double boiler over hot water. Stir in coffee. Pour chocolate mixture over egg yolks. Add flour, almonds and butter, and mix well.

Beat egg whites to stiff peaks and fold gently into chocolate mixture. Scrape batter into prepared pan. Bake 20 minutes. Let cool before serving. Sprinkle with icing sugar and with a dollop of vanilla yogurt, if desired.

~

1 SERVING		
321 CALORIES	18 g CARBOHYDRATE	6 g PROTEIN
25 g FAT	7.2 g FIBER	163 mg CHOLESTEROL

COOK'S TIP

The carrots keep this cake moist for a long time, so do not be put off by the number of servings.

SWISS-STYLE CARROT AND ALMOND CAKE

~

10 TO 12 SERVINGS

5	egg yolks	5
³/4 cup	sugar	175 mL
2 cups	grated carrots	500 mL
2 cups	ground almonds	500 mL
³/4 cup	cornstarch	175 mL
1	pinch cinnamon	1
1	pinch ground cloves	1
1 tsp	baking powder	5 mL
1	pinch salt	1
3 tbsp	kirsch	45 mL
5	egg whites, stiffly beaten	5
1 tbsp	apricot jelly, melted	15 mL
	juice of 1 lemon	
	grated zest of 2 lemons	

Preheat oven to 350°F (180°C). Grease and lightly flour a 9 inch (23 cm) round quiche pan or pie plate.

In a bowl, using an electric beater, beat egg yolks together with sugar, lemon juice and grated lemon peel until light and foamy. Beat in grated carrots and ground almonds.

Beat in cornstarch, cinnamon, cloves, baking powder and salt. Add kirsch.

When mixture is smooth, gently fold in stiffly beaten egg whites. Pour into prepared pan.

Bake about 50 minutes, or until toothpick inserted in center comes out clean. Brush with melted jelly while still warm. Garnish with marzipan carrots, if desired.

~

1 SERVING		
271 CALORIES	27g CARBOHYDRATE	7g PROTEIN
15g FAT	3.1g FIBER	114mg CHOLESTEROL

SOFT OATMEAL AND RAISIN COOKIES

MAKES ABOUT 5 DOZEN

3 cups	oatmeal	750 mL
1¹/₂ cups	all-purpose flour	375 mL
1 cup	wheat germ	250 mL
1 tsp	baking powder	5 mL
¹/₂ tsp	salt	2 mL
¹/₂ cup	packed brown suar	125 mL
1 cup	soft butter or margarine	250 mL
¹/₂ cup	honey	125 mL
1¹/₂ tsp	vanilla extract	7 mL
2	eggs	2
¹/₂ cup	raisins	125 mL
¹/₂ cup	chopped almonds	125 mL
¹/₄ cup	sesame seeds	50 mL

Preheat oven to 375°F (190°C). Lightly grease a cookie sheet.

In a large bowl, mix together first 5 ingredients well. Set aside.

In another large bowl, beat together brown sugar, butter and honey until smooth. Beat in vanilla and eggs.

Stir in oatmeal mixture. Add remaining ingredients and mix well.

Drop by small spoonfuls onto cookie sheet. Bake 7 to 8 minutes or until golden brown.

1 COOKIE		
101 CALORIES	12g CARBOHYDRATE	2g PROTEIN
5g FAT	0.9g FIBER	18mg CHOLESTEROL

LIGHT AND CHEWY BROWNIES

MAKES 16 BROWNIES

1/3 cup	soft margarine	75 mL
3/4 cup	sugar	175 mL
1/2 cup	all-purpose flour	125 mL
1/2 cup	cocoa powder	125 mL
1 tsp	baking powder	5 mL
1/2 cup	chopped nuts (optional)	125 mL
1 tsp	vanilla extract	5 mL
4	egg whites	4

Preheat oven to 325°F (160°C). Grease and lightly flour an 8 inch (20 cm) square cake pan.

Beat together margarine and sugar until creamy.

Beat in flour, cocoa, baking powder, nuts and vanilla. Set aside.

In a second bowl, beat egg whites until stiff. Fold egg whites gently into cocoa mixture until smooth.

Pour into prepared pan. Bake 20 to 25 minutes, or until top springs back when pressed lightly with a finger. Let cool completely before cutting. Serve with yogurt, if desired.

1 SERVING		
100 CALORIES	14g CARBOHYDRATE	2g PROTEIN
4g FAT	1.0g FIBER	0mg CHOLESTEROL

OLD-FASHIONED PEANUT BUTTER COOKIES
~

MAKES ABOUT 3½ DOZEN

¹/₃ cup	soft butter or margarine	75 mL
¹/₄ cup	sugar	50 mL
¹/₂ cup	packed brown sugar	125 mL
¹/₂ cup	peanut butter, smooth or crunchy	125 mL
2 tbsp	skim milk	30 mL
1 tsp	vanilla extract	5 mL
1	egg, beaten	1
1³/₄ cups	all-purpose flour	425 mL
1 tsp	baking soda	5 mL
¹/₂ tsp	salt	2 mL

Preheat oven to 375°F (190°C).

Beat together butter, sugar and brown sugar until creamy, using food processor or electric beater. Add peanut butter, milk, vanilla and egg. Mix well.

Stir in flour, baking soda, and salt. Mix well. Let dough stand a few minutes.

Shape dough into 1 inch (2.5 cm) balls. Arrange on an ungreased baking sheet far enough apart so that when you flatten each with a fork, cookies will not touch. Press just enough to flatten slightly and make a fork imprint.

Bake 10 to 12 minutes or until golden brown.

~

1 COOKIE		
67 CALORIES	8g CARBOHYDRATE	2g PROTEIN
3g FAT	0.4g FIBER	10mg CHOLESTEROL

ALMOND CRISPS

MAKES 8

1/2 cup	slivered almonds	125 mL
1/2 cup	sugar	125 mL
2 tbsp	all-purpose flour	30 mL
2	egg whites	2
1 1/2 tbsp	melted butter, lukewarm	22 mL

In a bowl, stir together almonds, sugar and flour. Add egg whites, mixing well with a fork. Stir in melted butter.

Cover and refrigerate mixture 12 hours.

Preheat oven to 300°F (150°C). Use a wet spoon to spoon the mixture onto a nonstick cookie sheet, spreading out each spoonful with the back of the spoon as thinly as possible.

Bake cookies 10 minutes. While cookies are still hot, roll them over a rolling pin to give a curved shape. They will keep this shape when cooled. Let cool completely before serving.

COOK'S TIP

These extra-crisp cookies are elegant served with fruit salad.

1 SERVING		
139 CALORIES	16g CARBOHYDRATE	3g PROTEIN
7g FAT	0.6g FIBER	8mg CHOLESTEROL

CHOCOLATE CHIP AND ALMOND COOKIES

~

MAKES 2 DOZEN

1/3 cup	canola oil	75 mL
1	egg	1
1 tsp	almond extract	5 mL
1 cup	all-purpose or wholewheat flour	250 mL
1/2 cup	packed brown sugar	125 mL
1/2 cup	chopped almonds	125 mL
1/2 tsp	baking soda	2 mL
1/2 tsp	salt	2 mL
1/2 cup	semi-sweet chocolate chips	125 mL

Preheat oven to 350°F (180°C). Lightly grease a cookie sheet.

In a bowl, stir together all the ingredients except the chocolate chips, using a fork or wooden spoon to mix well.

Gently stir in chocolate chips.

Using a tablespoon, drop spoonfuls of cookie dough on cookie sheet, leaving a 1 inch (2.5 cm) space between the cookies. Bake 8 to 10 minutes, or until golden brown.

~

1 COOKIE		
110 CALORIES	12g CARBOHYDRATE	2g PROTEIN
6g FAT	0.6g FIBER	11mg CHOLESTEROL

CHINESE ALMOND COOKIES

MAKES 2½ DOZEN

½ cup	vegetable shortening	125 mL
⅓ cup	sugar	75 mL
⅓ cup	corn syrup	75 mL
1	egg	1
1 tbsp	almond extract	15 mL
1½ cups	all-purpose flour	375 mL
¼ cup	ground almonds	50 mL
1 tsp	baking powder	5 mL
1	pinch salt	1
30	whole almonds	30
1	egg white	1

Preheat oven to 350°F (180°C). Grease 2 cookie sheets.

Beat shortening in a food processor or with an electric mixer until creamy. Beat in sugar, corn syrup, egg and almond extract. Mix well and set aside.

In a large bowl, stir together flour, ground almonds, baking powder and salt. Stir dry ingredients into reserved sugar mixture, mixing until dough pulls together into a ball.

Shape dough into 30 small balls and arrange on cookie sheets, leaving 1 inch (2.5 cm) between each. Press an almond lightly into the top of each. Brush cookies with egg white.

Bake 10 to 12 minutes, or until cookies are golden brown.

COOK'S TIP

You can make your own ground almonds in the food processor or blender, using blanched almonds.

	1 COOKIE	
93 CALORIES	10g CARBOHYDRATE	2g PROTEIN
5g FAT	0.4g FIBER	9mg CHOLESTEROL

COOK'S TIP

Why not add some chocolate chips to half the cookie dough to make 2 kinds of cookies at the same time?

GRANDMA'S CRISPY OATMEAL COOKIES

MAKES 5 DOZEN

2 cups	packed brown sugar	500 mL
1 cup	vegetable shortening	250 mL
3 tbsp	unsweetened orange juice	45 mL
1 tbsp	grated orange zest	15 mL
2	eggs	2
1 cup	all-purpose flour	250 mL
1 cup	wholewheat flour	250 mL
1 tsp	baking soda	5 mL
3/4 tsp	salt	3 mL
2 cups	quick-cooking oatmeal	500 mL
1 cup	chopped walnuts	250 mL
1/3 cup	unsweetened coconut	75 mL

Preheat oven to 350°F (180°C). Grease and lightly flour several cookie sheets.

Beat together first 5 ingredients in a food processor or with an electric mixer until creamy.

Add flour, wholewheat flour, baking soda and salt. Mix well. Add oatmeal, nuts and coconut and mix at slow speed until well blended.

Drop by spoonfuls onto prepared cookie sheets, leaving 2 inches (5 cm) between each. Bake 10 to 12 minutes, or until golden brown. Let stand 1 minute before removing cookies from pan.

1 COOKIE		
98 CALORIES	9g CARBOHYDRATE	2g PROTEIN
6g FAT	0.7g FIBER	9mg CHOLESTEROL

PERFECT CHOCOLATE CHIP COOKIES

MAKES 3 DOZEN

1 cup	wholewheat flour	250 mL
1 cup	oat flour	250 mL
1 tsp	baking soda	5 mL
1/2 tsp	salt	2 mL
1/2 cup	chocolate chips	125 mL
3/4 cup	butter or margarine	175 mL
1/2 cup	sugar	125 mL
1/4 cup	corn syrup	50 mL
1 tsp	vanilla extract	5 mL

Preheat oven to 350°F (180°C). Grease a cookie sheet.

In a bowl, stir together wholewheat and oat flours, baking soda, salt and chocolate chips. Set aside.

In a clean bowl or in food processor, beat together butter, sugar, corn syrup and vanilla until light and creamy.

Gently stir in reserved dry ingredients until well mixed. Drop by spoonfuls onto cookie sheet, leaving 2 inches (5 cm) between each. Bake about 15 minutes, or until golden brown. Let cool 5 minutes before removing from cookie sheet.

~

1 COOKIE		
93 CALORIES	11g CARBOHYDRATE	1g PROTEIN
5g FAT	1.2g FIBER	10 mg CHOLESTEROL

DELIGHTFUL DESSERTS

~

Somehow, a good meal does not seem
quite complete unless it is followed by a taste
of something sweet. But since most of us
are short of time, and are also watching
our waistlines or our fat intake,
we often feel guilty about indulging.

Most of the recipes in this section have been
selected to provide an easy and healthy route
for satisfying that sweet tooth craving. You will
find a number of elegant and interesting ways
to dress up fresh fruit, which should play
a major role in our diets anyway.

But because even the healthiest diets
should have room for the occasional indulgence,
you will also find recipes for some deliciously
decadent cheesecakes and pies that only
appear to be ridiculously rich.
So enjoy!

~

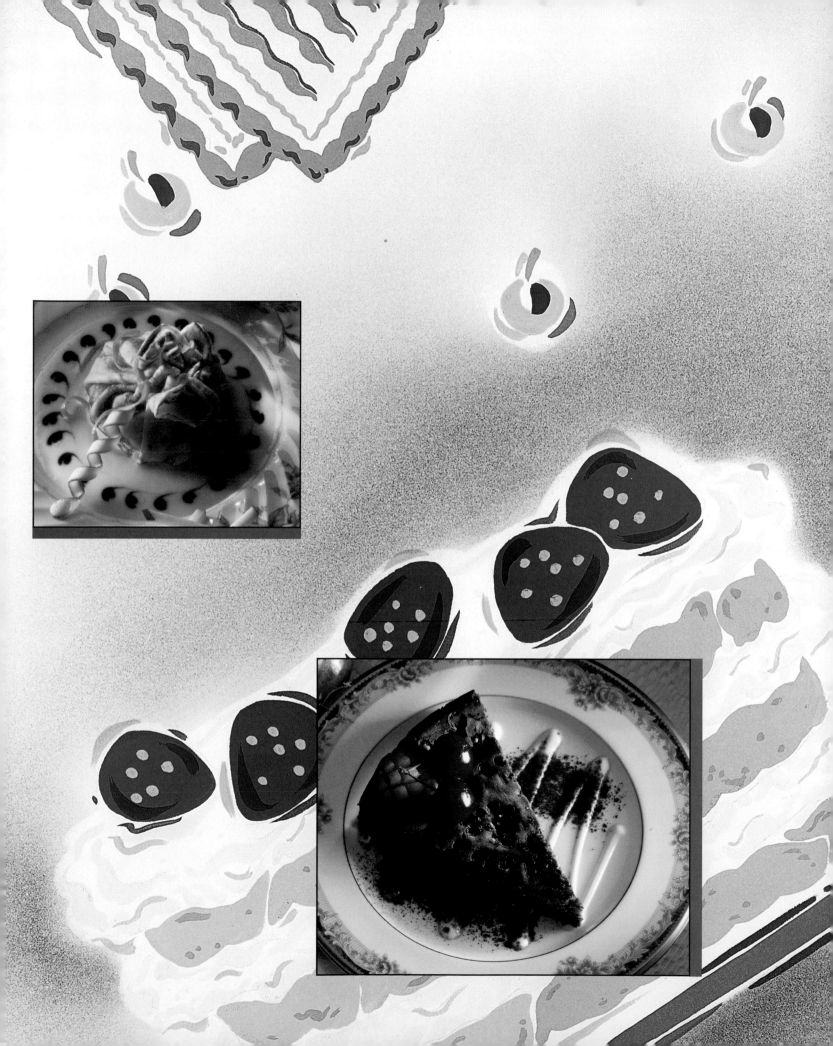

BANANA AND COCONUT CREAM PIE

8 SERVINGS

CRUST

1³/4 cups	sifted all-purpose flour	425 mL
1	pinch salt	1
4 tbsp	cold butter	60 mL
3 tbsp	cold water	45 mL

FILLING

¹/2 cup	skim milk	125 mL
3 oz	shredded unsweetened coconut	90 g
3 tbsp	sugar	45 mL
2	eggs, beaten	2
1 tbsp	light rum	15 mL
2	bananas, sliced and sprinkled with lemon juice	2

SYRUP

4 tbsp	sugar	60 mL
1 tbsp	light rum	15 mL

Place flour and salt in food processor. Dice butter and add. Mix on low speed until mixture is grainy. Add water a little at a time until dough forms a ball that pulls away from edges of food processor. Remove dough, cover it, and let stand 30 minutes.

To make the filling: bring milk to a boil in a saucepan, then let it cool.

In a bowl, combine coconut with sugar. Stir in eggs and cooled milk. Return mixture to saucepan and cook over low heat, stirring constantly, until mixture thickens. Stir in rum and let cool.

Preheat oven to 400°F (200°C). Roll out pastry dough and line a 9 inch (23 cm) pie plate. Prick bottom lightly with a fork. Cover pastry with foil and place some dried beans on top of foil. Bake 10 minutes, then remove beans and foil. Bake another 10 minutes.

When pie crust is cooled, pour in coconut mixture. Drain banana slices, reserving lemon juice, and arrange decoratively over filling.

To make the syrup: heat reserved lemon juice in a saucepan over low heat with sugar and rum. When hot, pour mixture over banana slices. Let cool before serving, garnished with whipped cream if desired.

1 SERVING

405 CALORIES	43g CARBOHYDRATE	6g PROTEIN
16g FAT	2.1g FIBER	84mg CHOLESTEROL

LIGHT PIE CRUST

MAKES 3 PIE SHELLS

3 cups	sifted pastry flour	750 mL
1/2 tsp	salt	2 mL
1/2 cup	light-flavored vegetable oil such as canola	125 mL
1/2 cup	cold water	125 mL
1	egg, beaten	1

NUTRITION TIP

This pastry will not be quite as flaky as one made with butter, lard or vegetable shortening. But butter and lard contain cholesterol; shortening is hydrogenated, which is also implicated in heart disease.

Combine flour and salt in a large bowl. Make a well in the middle.

In another bowl, beat together oil, water and egg.

Pour liquid into flour. Gradually work flour into liquid to make a dough. Shape into a ball and knead 1 minute.

Cut into 3 pieces and roll out each piece on a lightly floured surface.

Place dough carefully in pie plate, and fold edges under to make a double thickness. Trim and flute edges.

1 PIE SHELL		
846 CALORIES	101g CARBOHYDRATE	16g PROTEIN
42g FAT	4.1g FIBER	91mg CHOLESTEROL

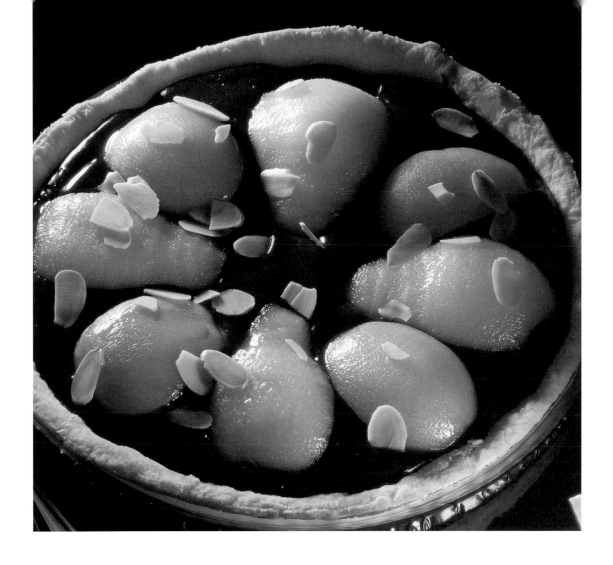

QUICK CHOCOLATE, PEACH AND PEAR PIE

~

8 SERVINGS

1	9 inch (23 cm) pie shell, baked and cooled	1
4 oz	package instant chocolate pudding mix	113 g
1 tsp	liqueur of your choice	5 mL
8	drained canned peach and/or pear halves	8
2 tbsp	toasted slivered almonds	30 mL

Prepare chocolate pudding according to package directions. Stir in liqueur.

Pour pudding mixture into prepared pie shell. Chill until firm.

Arrange peach and pear halves over top. (If you prefer, cut the fruit into thin strips to make serving easier.) Sprinkle with toasted almonds and serve chilled.

~

1 SERVING		
310 CALORIES	38g CARBOHYDRATE	5g PROTEIN
14g FAT	1.4g FIBER	14mg CHOLESTEROL

DELIGHTFUL DESSERTS

AMAGING MAPLE PIE

8 SERVINGS

1	9 inch (23 cm) pie shell, baked	1
4 tbsp	butter	60 mL
4 tbsp	all-purpose flour	60 mL
¹/₂ cup	brown sugar	125 mL
¹/₂ cup	maple syrup	125 mL
¹/₂ cup	hot water	125 mL
4 tbsp	cornstarch, dissolved in a little cold water	60 mL
4 tbsp	chopped walnuts	60 mL

COOK'S TIP

This Canadian specialty is for those with a real sweet tooth! Be sure to use real maple syrup, not a maple-flavored breakfast syrup.

Melt butter in a saucepan. Stir in flour with a wooden spoon.

Add brown sugar, maple syrup, hot water and dissolved cornstarch. Cook over medium heat, stirring constantly, until smooth and slightly thickened.

Pour mixture into pie shell. Garnish with chopped walnuts and let cool. Serve chilled with whipped cream, if desired.

1 Melt butter and stir in flour.

2 Add brown sugar, maple syrup, water and dissolved cornstarch.

3 Pour into baked pie shell.

4 Garnish with nuts and let cool.

1 SERVING		
388 CALORIES	48g CARBOHYDRATE	4g PROTEIN
20g FAT	1.3g FIBER	23mg CHOLESTEROL

DATE AND CREAM CHEESE PIE

8 SERVINGS

1/3 cup	melted butter or margarine	75 mL
2 cups	vanilla wafer crumbs	500 mL
1/2 tsp	ground nutmeg	2 mL
2	egg whites	2
1	pinch salt	1
1/2 cup	sugar	125 mL
1 cup	whipping cream	250 mL
8 oz	light cream cheese	225 g
19 oz	can date pie filling	540 mL
1/4 cup	slivered almonds	50 mL

Preheat oven to 350°F (180°C).

In a bowl, combine melted butter with crumbs and nutmeg. Press mixture into bottom and sides of a 9 inch (23 cm) pie plate. Bake 10 minutes. Let cool.

Place egg whites in food processor. Add salt and process until soft peaks form. Gradually add sugar and mix until stiff. Place mixture in a bowl and set aside.

Place whipping cream in food processor and process until stiff peaks form. Dice cream cheese and add to cream. Process until smooth. Stir this mixture into egg white mixture.

Spoon egg white and cream cheese mixture into pie shell, smoothing the surface. Spread date filling over top. Decorate top with almonds, and with thinned cream cheese, if desired. Refrigerate at least 4 hours before serving.

1 SERVING		
543 CALORIES	59g CARBOHYDRATE	7g PROTEIN
31g FAT	0.8g FIBER	94mg CHOLESTEROL

PARISIAN PEACH TARTS

8 SERVINGS

12 oz	shortcrust pastry (purchased, or double recipe on page 324)	350 g
8	canned, drained peach halves, sliced	8
1/4 cup	apricot or apple jelly	50 mL

PASTRY CREAM FILLING

1	egg	1
1/4 cup	sugar	50 mL
1/4 cup	all-purpose flour	50 mL
2 cups	2% milk, heated	500 mL
1/2 tsp	vanilla extract	2 mL

Preheat oven to 350°F (180°C).

To prepare the pastry cream: in the top of a double boiler, stir together egg with sugar and flour.

Stir in hot milk and vanilla and cook over hot water on medium heat about 5 minutes, stirring from time to time, until thickened.

Place a circle of waxed paper, cut to size, directly over mixture and let cool in refrigerator.

Roll out pastry and line 8 tart molds about 3 inches (8 cm) in diameter. Prick bottoms of shells with a fork. Bake 10 minutes, then let cool.

Spoon cream filling into pastry shells. Arrange sliced peach half over each tart shell. Brush with melted apricot jelly to glaze. Serve chilled, garnished with fresh fruit, if desired.

COOK'S TIP

The pastry cream filling can be used as the base for fresh strawberries, raspberries or blueberries in season.

	1 SERVING	
434 CALORIES	67g CARBOHYDRATE	10g PROTEIN
14g FAT	2.4g FIBER	71mg CHOLESTEROL

GREEK BAKLAVA

10 SERVINGS

COOK'S TIP

Frozen filo will keep several months if tightly wrapped. Rewrap unused portions promptly. See the next page for another easy way to use filo.

1/2 cup	chopped walnuts	125 mL
1/2 cup	chopped almonds	125 mL
1/4 cup	sugar	50 mL
1/2 tsp	ground cinnamon	2 mL
1	pinch ground cloves	1
1 lb	frozen commercial filo pastry, thawed	450 g

SYRUP

1 cup	sugar	250 mL
1/2 cup	liquid honey	125 mL
1 cup	water	250 mL
	grated zest of 1 lemon	

Preheat oven to 350°F (180°C). Lightly oil a 9 x 13 (23 x 33 cm) baking pan.

In a bowl, combine walnuts, almonds, sugar and spices.

Unroll filo and lay out 8 filo sheets on top of each other, brushing the border of each sheet lightly with a little water as you stack them. Lay the stack flat in the baking pan.

Spread 1/2 nut mixture over pastry. Cover with another stack of 8 sheets brushed with water. Spread remaining nut mixture over. Cover with a final stack of filo sheets brushed with water.

With a sharp knife, cut the filo into rectangular or triangular serving pieces. Bake 45 to 60 minutes, until pastry is golden. Remove from oven and let cool.

Meanwhile, combine syrup ingredients in a saucepan and bring to a boil. Lower heat and let simmer 10 minutes. Remove from heat and let cool to lukewarm. Pour evenly over baked filo. Let filo soak up syrup at least 2 hours before serving.

1 SERVING		
378 CALORIES	66g CARBOHYDRATE	6g PROTEIN
10g FAT	1.8g FIBER	0mg CHOLESTEROL

BLUEBERRY PAVLOVA

~

4 SERVINGS

4	filo pastry sheets	4
1¹/₂ cups	canned blueberry pie filling	375 mL
2 tbsp	melted butter or margarine	30 mL
2 tbsp	liquid honey	30 mL
¹/₂ tsp	water	2 mL
2	star anise seeds	2

Preheat oven to 350°F (180°C). Cut filo into 5 inch (12.5 cm) wide strips. Stack strips to make 4 thicker strips.

Place blueberry filling in the middle of one end of each strip. Fold filo to make a triangle, then continue folding to the end of pastry. Brush ends with melted butter to seal.

Place triangles on baking sheet and brush tops with butter. Bake about 10 minutes, until barely golden.

Meanwhile, heat honey, water and star anise in a saucepan about 10 minutes over medium heat. Remove star anise and let liquid cool to lukewarm. Brush liquid over cooked pastries, and use the rest as a sauce, if desired.

~

1 Stack filo strips. Place filling at one end. Fold to make a triangle. Continue folding to end of strip.

2 Baste tops of finished triangles with melted butter before baking.

1 SERVING		
259 CALORIES	47g CARBOHYDRATE	2g PROTEIN
7g FAT	0.8g FIBER	16mg CHOLESTEROL

BANANA TOFU CHEESECAKE

8 SERVINGS

CRUST

I cup	vanilla wafer crumbs	250 mL
1/4 cup	soft (non-hydrogenated) margarine, melted	50 mL

CHEESE FILLING

12 oz	tofu, cut in 1/2 inch (1 cm) cubes	350 g
11/2 cups	cream-style cottage cheese	375 mL
2	ripe bananas, mashed	2
I tbsp	liquid honey	15 mL
I tbsp	all-purpose flour	15 mL
	juice and grated zest of 1 lime	

TOPPING

2	bananas, sliced	2
1/4 cup	apricot jelly	50 mL
I tbsp	lemon juice	15 mL

NUTRITION TIP

Tofu is a good source of protein, low in fat and cholesterol-free. And it absorbs the other flavors like a sponge, so its own flavor is unnoticeable.

Preheat oven to 350°F (180°C). Grease an 8 inch (20 cm) springform pan.

To make the crust, stir together wafer crumbs with melted margarine. Press mixture into bottom of greased pan. Set aside.

To make the filling: place tofu, cottage cheese, mashed bananas, honey, flour and lime juice and zest in food processor. Process until smooth and creamy. Spoon mixture over crumb crust. Bake 45 minutes, or until tofu mixture is firm.

To make the topping: arrange banana slices over top of cooled cake. Heat apricot jelly and lemon juice over low heat until jelly is liquified. Brush mixture over top of bananas and cheesecake.

1 SERVING

292 CALORIES	35g CARBOHYDRATE	11g PROTEIN
12g FAT	1.7g FIBER	15mg CHOLESTEROL

APPLE CHEESECAKE

12 SERVINGS

CRUST

1 cup	all-purpose flour	250 mL
1/4 cup	brown sugar	50 mL
1/3 cup	butter or margarine	75 mL

FILLING

8 oz	light cream cheese, softened	225 g
1/4 cup	sugar	50 mL
1 tsp	grated lemon zest	5 mL
1	egg	1
6	medium apples, cored, peeled and sliced	6
1 tbsp	lemon juice	15 mL
2 tbsp	sugar	30 mL

GLAZE

1/4 cup	apple jelly	50 mL

Preheat oven to 400°F (200°C).

In a bowl, using a fork, stir together flour, brown sugar and butter until mixture is grainy. Press mixture into the bottom of a 9 inch (23 cm) springform pan. Bake 10 minutes.

Remove pan from oven and set aside. Reduce oven temperature to 350°F (180°C).

In another bowl, stir together cream cheese, sugar and lemon zest until mixture is smooth and light. Add egg and beat well. Pour mixture onto baked crust.

Combine apple slices, lemon juice and sugar. Arrange over cream cheese filling, pressing lightly into cheese mixture. Bake 35 minutes.

In a small saucepan, melt apple jelly over medium heat. Brush over top of cooked cake while still warm. Refrigerate cake immediately. Serve cold.

1 SERVING		
245 CALORIES	30g CARBOHYDRATE	2g PROTEIN
13g FAT	1.6g FIBER	50mg CHOLESTEROL

GRAPEFRUIT CHEESECAKE

8 SERVINGS

1½ cups	graham cracker crumbs	375 mL
½ cup	soft (non-hydrogenated) margarine, melted	125 mL
2	pink or white grapefruit	2
2 tbsp	plain gelatin	30 mL
1 cup	light cream cheese, softened	250 mL
⅔ cup	plain yogurt	150 mL
2 tbsp	liquid honey	30 mL
4	egg whites, stiffly beaten	4
	juice and grated zest of 1 lemon	

Combine graham crumbs and margarine. Press ⅔ of this mixture into the bottom of a 9 inch (23 cm) springform pan. Let cool.

Peel grapefruit and cut off white pith. With a sharp knife, and working over a bowl, slice on both side of grapefruit membranes to remove the segments. Reserve juice in bowl. Set aside segments.

Sprinkle gelatin over reserved juice. Let stand 2 to 3 minutes to soften gelatin. Place bowl with gelatin over a saucepan of hot water. Heat until gelatin is melted. Set aside.

In another bowl, beat cream cheese together with yogurt and honey. Stir in gelatin mixture, lemon zest and lemon juice. Mix well. Stir in stiffly beaten egg whites. Pour mixture over crust. Refrigerate until serving time.

To serve, unmold cheesecake and press reserved crumb mixture around sides. Decorate top with grapefruit segments.

1 SERVING		
327 CALORIES	29g CARBOHYDRATE	10g PROTEIN
19g FAT	1.5g FIBER	18mg CHOLESTEROL

CHOCOLATE CHEESECAKE

8 SERVINGS

COOK'S TIP

*Use this same procedure
to make an easy fruit
cheesecake; replace the
melted chocolate with
puréed fruit and the
chocolate chips with
chopped fruit or berries.*

I cup	graham cracker crumbs	250 mL
I tbsp	cocoa powder	15 mL
¹/₄ cup	melted butter or margarine	50 mL
	grated zest of I lemon	

FILLING

2 oz	semi-sweet baking chocolate	60 g
16 oz	light cream cheese	450 g
³/₄ cup	packed brown sugar	175 mL
4	eggs	4
I	pinch salt	I
I cup	chocolate chips	250 mL

Preheat oven to 350°F (180°C).

Stir together graham crumbs, cocoa, butter and lemon zest. Press into a 10 inch (25 cm) springform pan. Bake 10 minutes. Set aside.

To make the filling: melt baking chocolate in top of a double boiler over hot water. Let cool slightly and reserve.

In a large bowl, beat cream cheese together with sugar until creamy. Beat in eggs one at a time. Beat in salt and melted chocolate. Stir in ½ of chocolate chips.

Pour mixture over crust and sprinkle remaining chocolate chips on top. Bake 55 to 60 minutes, or until filling is set. Let cool completely before unmolding.

1 SERVING		
706 CALORIES	48g CARBOHYDRATE	7g PROTEIN
54g FAT	2.7g FIBER	231mg CHOLESTEROL

EASY APPLE CAKE

6 SERVINGS

²/₃ cup	all-purpose flour	150 mL
6 tbsp	sugar	90 mL
4 tbsp	vegetable oil	60 mL
¹/₂ cup	2% milk	125 mL
1	egg	1
1 tbsp	baking powder	15 mL
1	pinch salt	1
3	apples, peeled, cored, and cut in thin wedges	3

Preheat oven to 375°F (190°C). Grease and lightly flour a 9 inch (23 cm) round cake pan.

In a bowl, beat together all ingredients, except apple wedges, with a wooden spoon until smooth. Pour batter into prepared pan.

Arrange apple wedges over batter. Bake 30 to 40 minutes until a toothpick inserted in center comes out clean.

Let cool slightly before unmolding. Serve warm or cold, garnished with plain or vanilla yogurt, whipped cream or ice cream.

~

COOK'S TIP

Instead of apples, use canned drained peaches or pears to make this easy recipe.

1 SERVING		
247 CALORIES	34g CARBOHYDRATE	3g PROTEIN
11g FAT	1.6g FIBER	47mg CHOLESTEROL

TIRAMISU

8 SERVINGS

COOK'S TIP

You can also layer the tiramisu in individual molds. For our photo, foil collars were placed inside the molds when the molds were half filled; the collars were removed carefully after chilling.

4	egg yolks	4
1/2 cup	sugar	125 mL
1/4 cup	coffee-flavored liqueur (eg. Kahlua)	50 mL
1 lb	mascarpone cheese	450 g
4	egg whites	4
1/2 cup	sugar	125 mL
1 1/2 cups	very strong coffee	375 mL
24	ladyfingers	24
2 tbsp	cocoa powder	30 mL

Beat together egg yolks and ½ cup (125 mL) sugar until pale and foamy. Beat in liqueur and mascarpone. Set aside.

In another bowl, beat egg whites with a clean beater until stiff peaks form. Fold whites gently into yolk mixture with a rubber spatula until smooth. Set aside.

Dissolve remaining sugar in the coffee. Dip 12 ladyfingers in coffee mixture and arrange them in the bottom of a 9 inch (23 cm) dish.

Spread half of mascarpone mixture over ladyfingers. Dip remaining ladyfingers in coffee, arrange over cheese mixture, and spread remaining cheese mixture on top.

Sift cocoa over top of tiramisu and refrigerate 24 hours before serving.

1 Beat egg yolks and sugar until pale and foamy. Stir in liqueur and mascarpone cheese.

2 Beat egg whites until stiff, then fold into cheese mixture.

3 Dissolve sugar in strong coffee and dip ladyfingers in it. Arrange in dish.

4 Spread cheese mixture over ladyfingers. Repeat layers.

1 SERVING		
473 CALORIES	44g CARBOHYDRATE	8g PROTEIN
28g FAT	0.5g FIBER	202mg CHOLESTEROL

OLD-FASHIONED JAM ROLL

~

6 SERVINGS

$^1/_2$ cup	icing sugar	125 mL
3	eggs	3
$^1/_3$ cup	all-purpose flour	75 mL
2 tbsp	sugar	30 mL
$^1/_2$ cup	strawberry jam	125 mL

Preheat oven to 375°F (190°C). Grease and lightly flour a 9 x 13 inch (23 x 33 cm) pan.

Beat together icing sugar and eggs with an electric beater or food processor until pale and frothy.

Gradually stir in flour with a rubber spatula. Spread batter on prepared pan and bake 10 minutes.

Meanwhile, cut a piece of waxed paper the same size as the pan and sprinkle sugar evenly over it. Carefully turn the cake upside-down on the waxed paper to unmold. Let cool a few minutes.

Spread jam evenly over cake. Roll cake gently, starting at one of the short ends. Do not slice cake until it has cooled completely.

~

1 SERVING		
195 CALORIES	38g CARBOHYDRATE	4g PROTEIN
3g FAT	0.5g FIBER	137mg CHOLESTEROL

EASY CHOCOLATE MOUSSE CAKE

4 SERVINGS

I	envelope plain gelatin	I
2 tbsp	cold water	30 mL
1/2 cup	hot water	125 mL
I cup	whipping cream	250 mL
6 oz	semi-sweet chocolate, melted	180 g
2	egg whites, stiffly beaten	2
I	small sponge cake, about 6 inches (15 cm) across	I

In a small bowl, sprinkle gelatin over cold water. Let gelatin soak a few minutes, then add hot water and stir until gelatin dissolves completely. Let cool.

Beat whipping cream until stiff. Stir in slightly cooled melted chocolate. Stir in gelatin mixture and egg whites. Set aside.

Dice sponge cake and arrange in a square mold or pan. Pour chocolate mixture over cake. Cover and refrigerate several hours.

Serve cold, with a fresh fruit sauce, if desired.

~

Stir melted chocolate into whipped cream. Stir in dissolved gelatin and egg whites.

2 Dice sponge cake and arrange in square mold.

3 Pour chocolate mixture over cake.

	1 SERVING	
724 CALORIES	77g CARBOHYDRATE	14g PROTEIN
40g FAT	1.7g FIBER	302mg CHOLESTEROL

CARAMEL PUDDING CAKE

4 SERVINGS

SAUCE

I cup	corn syrup	250 mL
I cup	water	250 mL
I tsp	vanilla extract	5 mL
I tbsp	butter or margarine	15 mL

CAKE

1/3 cup	softened butter or margarine	75 mL
3/4 cup	sugar	175 mL
2	eggs	2
1 1/2 cups	all-purpose flour	375 mL
I tsp	baking powder	5 mL
1/2 tsp	salt	2 mL
3/4 cup	skim milk	175 mL
I tsp	vanilla extract	5 mL

Preheat oven to 350°F (180°C). Grease an 8 inch (20 cm) square cake pan.

To make the sauce: combine sauce ingredients in a saucepan and cook over medium heat until hot and smooth; do not let boil. Pour mixture into prepared pan.

Beat together butter, sugar and eggs with an electric beater or in food processor.

In a bowl, stir together dry ingredients. Pour into egg mixture and beat at slow speed until mixed. Beat in milk and vanilla until batter is smooth.

Pour batter over sauce in baking pan. Bake 25 to 30 minutes, or until a toothpick inserted in the center comes out clean. Serve warm or cold.

~

1 SERVING		
801 CALORIES	143g CARBOHYDRATE	10g PROTEIN
21g FAT	1.6g FIBER	186mg CHOLESTEROL

GRANDMA'S MOLDED
RICE PUDDING

6 SERVINGS

1¹/₂ cups	short grain rice	375 mL
4 cups	skim milk	1 liter
1	pinch salt	1
²/₃ cup	packed icing sugar	150 mL
4 tbsp	ground almonds	60 mL
1 tsp	vanilla extract	5 mL
1 cup	graham cracker crumbs	250 mL
	grated zest of 1 lemon	

Rinse the rice well. Fill large pot half full with water. Bring to a boil. Add rice and boil 2 minutes. Let cool in water, then drain and set aside.

Heat milk and salt in a saucepan until it comes to a boil. Add drained rice. Stir and heat until liquid starts to boil. Immediately stir in icing sugar, ground almonds, vanilla and lemon zest. Let simmer 45 minutes over low heat.

Meanwhile, grease an 8 inch (20 cm) mold with about 1 tbsp (15 mL) oil or margarine. Sprinkle mold with graham crumbs. Pour rice mixture into prepared mold. Chill thoroughly in refrigerator before serving, with fruit sauce or jam, if desired.

1 SERVING		
379 CALORIES	67g CARBOHYDRATE	12g PROTEIN
7g FAT	1.4g FIBER	3mg CHOLESTEROL

APRICOT CLAFOUTIS

6 SERVINGS

³/₄ cup	warm water	175 mL
I tsp	sugar	5 mL
2 tsp	dry yeast	10 mL
³/₄ cup	all-purpose flour	175 mL
¹/₃ cup	ground almonds	75 mL
¹/₃ cup	sugar	75 mL
I	pinch salt	I
3	eggs, beaten	3
I tsp	vanilla extract	5 mL
14 oz	can apricot halves, drained	398 mL
	icing sugar	

Place water in a medium bowl and add 1 tsp (5 mL) sugar and the yeast. Stir well to dissolve.

In a large bowl, stir together flour, almonds, sugar and salt. Add yeast mixture, stirring well. Stir in eggs and vanilla.

Cover bowl with a damp cloth and let stand on top of refrigerator or in a warm place until mixture is well risen.

Preheat oven to 400°F (200°C). Grease a deep 10 inch (25 cm) baking dish. Pour mixture in pan and arrange apricot halves over top.

Bake in middle of oven 30 to 40 minutes or until top is nicely browned. Let cool and sprinkle with icing sugar before serving.

1 SERVING

207 CALORIES	*29g CARBOHYDRATE*	*7g PROTEIN*
7g FAT	*2.5g FIBER*	*137mg CHOLESTEROL*

STEAMED BLUEBERRY PUDDING

6 SERVINGS

1 cup	wholewheat flour	250 mL
1¹/₂ tsp	baking powder	7 mL
¹/₂ tsp	salt	2 mL
¹/₂ cup	butter or margarine	125 mL
¹/₂ cup	graham cracker crumbs	125 mL
¹/₄ cup	sugar	50 mL
1	egg	1
³/₄ cup	2% milk	175 mL
1¹/₂ cups	fresh blueberries	375 mL

BLUEBERRY SAUCE

²/₃ cup	water	150 mL
¹/₄ cup	sugar	50 mL
1 cup	fresh blueberries	250 mL
2 tsp	orange juice	10 mL
1 tbsp	cornstarch, dissolved in a little water	15 mL
	grated zest of ¹/₂ lemon	
	grated zest of ¹/₂ orange	

Preheat oven to 400°F (200°C). Grease a large loaf pan.

Place flour, baking powder, salt and butter in food processor. Mix until grainy.

Add graham crumbs, sugar, egg and milk. Process to combine. Stir in blueberries and spoon mixture into prepared pan. Cover with foil.

Place loaf pan in a larger pan half filled with water. Bake about 2 hours.

To make the sauce: combine all ingredients, except cornstarch mixture, in a saucepan. Bring to a boil. Stir in dissolved cornstarch. Remove from heat as soon as mixture returns to boil. Serve warm sauce with warm pudding.

	1 SERVING	
391 CALORIES	49g CARBOHYDRATE	6g PROTEIN
19g FAT	4.7g FIBER	92mg CHOLESTEROL

APPLE AND DRIED FRUIT GRATIN

~

4 SERVINGS

1 cup	dried fruit	250 mL
	(dates, figs, raisins, etc.)	
1/2 cup	unsweetened apple juice	125 mL
3	apples	3
2 tbsp	chopped walnuts	30 mL
1/2 cup	dry breadcrumbs	125 mL
2 tbsp	ground almonds	30 mL
	lemon juice	
	ground cinnamon	

Preheat oven to 400°F (200°C). Grease a baking dish.

Chop dried fruit and soak in apple juice at least 1 hour.

Peel and grate fresh apples coarsely. Sprinkle with a little lemon juice to prevent browning. Combine apples with chopped dried fruit and apple juice. Stir in nuts and breadcrumbs.

Place in baking dish. Cover with ground almonds and dust with cinnamon. Bake 10 minutes, or until top is lightly browned.

1 SERVING		
322 CALORIES	62g CARBOHYDRATE	5g PROTEIN
6g FAT	6.4g FIBER	0mg CHOLESTEROL

FROZEN LEMON AND
CREAM CHEESE MOLDS

~

12 SERVINGS

12	round vanilla cookies	12
8 oz	light cream cheese	225 g
1/2 cup	liquid honey	125 mL
1	egg yolk	1
1/3 cup	fresh lemon juice	75 mL
1/4 cup	plain low-fat yogurt	50 mL
2 tbsp	ground almonds	30 mL
	grated lemon zest for garnish	

COOK'S TIP

*For an elegant touch,
serve molds on a bed of
custard sauce, with a
swirl of fresh raspberry
sauce for color contrast.*

Line 12 muffin molds with paper liners. Place a vanilla cookie in each.

With a food processor or electric beater, blend cream cheese, honey, egg yolk, lemon juice, yogurt and almonds until smooth.

Divide mixture among molds. Place in freezer 2 hours. Unmold and top with grated lemon zest to serve.

~

1 Line muffin molds with paper liners. Place a vanilla cookie in each.

2 Combine cream cheese, honey, egg yolk, lemon juice, yogurt and almonds.

3 Divide mixture among molds.

1 SERVING		
153 CALORIES	17g CARBOHYDRATE	1g PROTEIN
9g FAT	0.1g FIBER	48mg CHOLESTEROL

APRICOT MERINGUES

4 SERVINGS

3/4 lb	dried apricots	350 g
2 tbsp	butter or margarine	30 mL
2 cups	skim milk	500 mL
1/2 cup	sugar	125 mL
1 tsp	vanilla extract	5 mL
1/2 cup	converted rice	125 mL
2	eggs	2
3/4 cup	sugar	175 mL
1 tbsp	icing sugar	15 mL

Cover dried apricots with warm water and let soak at least 4 hours.

Place apricots with soaking water in a saucepan. Add butter, cover, and simmer over low heat about 1 hour, or until liquid is completely absorbed.

Place milk and ½ cup (125 mL) sugar in a second saucepan and bring to a boil. Stir in vanilla and rice. Simmer over very low heat 20 minutes or until liquid is absorbed.

Separate eggs. Reserve whites, and stir yolks vigorously into rice mixture.

Grease 4 ramekins and divide rice mixture among them, filling ½ full. Arrange a layer of apricots over rice. Set aside.

Preheat oven to 375°F (190°C).

Beat egg whites to stiff peaks. Beat in remaining sugar until stiff and glossy. Pipe or spoon egg whites over apricots. Sprinkle tops lightly with icing sugar. Bake 15 minutes or until tops are lightly browned. Serve hot or cold.

1 SERVING		
698 CALORIES	140g CARBOHYDRATE	12g PROTEIN
10g FAT	7.1g FIBER	155mg CHOLESTEROL

MAPLE SYRUP MOUSSE

~

4 SERVINGS

COOK'S TIP

*Crêpes make attractive
and unusual bowls.
Drape them over upside-
down ovenproof bowls
and heat in a medium
oven until crisp
and browned.*

2 cups	2% milk	500 mL
½ cup	maple syrup	125 mL
3 tbsp	cornstarch, dissolved in a little water	45 mL
4	egg whites	4
1	pinch salt	1

Heat milk and maple syrup in a saucepan over medium heat. Stir in dissolved cornstarch as soon as mixture starts to bubble.

Cook over low heat until thickened, stirring, then pour into a large bowl and let cool in refrigerator.

Beat egg whites and salt to form stiff peaks. Gently fold beaten whites into maple mixture. Chill until serving time.

~

1 SERVING		
231 CALORIES	43g CARBOHYDRATE	8g PROTEIN
3g FAT	0g FIBER	10mg CHOLESTEROL

MASCARPONE MOUSSE
WITH STAR ANISE

4 SERVINGS

2	egg yolks	2
1/4 cup	sugar	50 mL
1/2 tsp	ground star anise	2 mL
1 1/2 cups	mascarpone cheese	375 mL
2 tbsp	marsala wine	30 mL
2	egg whites	2
	fresh fruit to garnish	

Beat together egg yolks and sugar until pale and frothy. Stir in star anise, mascarpone and marsala. Set aside.

Beat egg whites with clean beater until stiff peaks form. Fold egg whites gently into mascarpone mixture with a rubber spatula until well mixed.

Pour mixture into a serving dish or individual dessert bowls and refrigerate until serving time. Garnish with fresh fruit only when ready to serve, or fruit will stain the mousse.

COOK'S TIP

Raw eggs may pose a health hazard. Never use cracked or old eggs, and keep egg mixtures refrigerated.

1 SERVING		
448 CALORIES	14g CARBOHYDRATE	8g PROTEIN
40g FAT	0g FIBRE	235mg CHOLESTEROL

ICED DESSERT COFFEE

4 SERVINGS

COOK'S TIP

The perfect ending to a hearty summer meal; it's coffee and dessert in one!

3 tbsp	unsweetened cocoa powder	45 mL
3 cups	strong hot coffee	750 mL
1/2 tsp	ground cinnamon	2 mL
I tsp	grated orange zest	5 mL
2 cups	vanilla ice milk	500 mL
	shredded orange zest and cocoa powder to garnish	

Dissolve cocoa powder in hot coffee. Stir in cinnamon and grated orange zest. Refrigerate to cool.

Place coffee mixture together with ice milk in food processor or blender. Process until smooth and creamy. Pour at once into chilled cups or tall glasses, and sprinkle with cocoa and shredded orange zest to serve.

1 SERVING		
120 CALORIES	18g CARBOHYDRATE	3g PROTEIN
4g FAT	1.7g FIBER	10 mg CHOLESTEROL

HONEY BLUEBERRY MOUSSE

4 SERVINGS

2	egg yolks	2
1/4 cup	liquid honey	50 mL
2	egg whites	2
I cup	whipping cream	250 mL
1/2 cup	fresh blueberries	125 mL
	fresh mint leaves for garnish	

Beat egg yolks together with honey until pale and frothy. Set aside.

Using a clean beater, beat egg whites to form stiff peaks. Fold beaten egg whites gently into yolk mixture with a rubber spatula.

Beat cream until stiff. Fold into egg mixture. Layer mixture with fresh blueberries in tall glasses and garnish with fresh mint.

~

COOK'S TIP

Raw eggs may pose a health hazard. Never use cracked or old eggs.

1 SERVING		
317 CALORIES	19g CARBOHYDRATE	4g PROTEIN
25g FAT	0.5g FIBER	218mg CHOLESTEROL

CRANBERRY PARFAIT

6 TO 8 SERVINGS

3 cups	cranberries	750 mL
3 tbsp	water	45 mL
1½ cups	sugar	375 mL
3	egg yolks	3
2 tbsp	orange liqueur (optional)	30 mL
2 cups	whipping cream	500 mL

Place cranberries, water and ½ cup (125 mL) sugar in a saucepan. Cook 5 minutes over high heat, until cranberries burst. Set aside.

In a bowl, beat together egg yolks with remaining sugar until pale and frothy. Set aside.

Purée cooked cranberries in blender. Stir purée into egg yolk mixture. Add liqueur, if desired. Mix well and keep mixture cool.

Beat whipping cream to form stiff peaks. Fold gently into cranberry mixture until smooth. Pour mixture into a mold and freeze 8 to 10 hours. Remove from freezer ½ hour before serving time.

COOK'S TIP

If desired, serve with a sauce made from commercial cranberry juice. Heat 1 cup (250 mL) juice over medium heat and stir in 1 tsp (5 mL) cornstarch dissolved in a little water until thickened. Chill before serving.

1 SERVING		
420 CALORIES	48g CARBOHYDRATE	3g PROTEIN
24g FAT	2.4g FIBER	161mg CHOLESTEROL

ICED MANGO YOGURT

4 SERVINGS

I	ripe mango, peeled and pitted	I
¹/₄ cup	liquid honey	50 mL
3 cups	plain low-fat yogurt	750 mL

Purée mango in food processor or blender. Add honey and yogurt and mix well.

Pour mixture into a shallow metal dish and place in freezer 1 hour.

Stir mixture well to break up ice crystals. Freeze 1 more hour before serving. Garnish with berries and fresh mint, if desired.

~

COOK'S TIP

Crêpes make attractive and unusual dessert bowls. Drape them over upside-down ovenproof bowls and heat in a medium oven until crisp and browned.

1 SERVING		
188 CALORIES	37g CARBOHYDRATE	10g PROTEIN
0g FAT	1.0g FIBER	4mg CHOLESTEROL

TROPICAL FRUIT PASTRIES WITH STRAWBERRY COULIS

~

4 SERVINGS

COOK'S TIP

To garnish the plate as shown, pipe small dots of plain yogurt on the coulis with a pastry tube. Drag the tip of a sharp knife from one dot to the next to make a heart pattern.

5 oz	fresh or frozen strawberries	150 g
3	limes	3
1/3 cup	sugar	75 mL
1	banana	1
1	mango	1
1/2 lb	fresh pineapple (about 1/4 of a whole pineapple)	225 g
4	vol-au-vent shells, baked	4
	icing sugar	

Place strawberries in a saucepan, sprinkle juice of 1 lime over, and add 1/3 of the sugar. Cover, bring to a boil, then remove from heat and reserve.

Squeeze juice of remaining limes in a bowl. Peel and cut up remaining fruit and add to bowl. Sprinkle with remaining sugar and toss lightly.

Strain strawberries and their liquid through a fine strainer. Discard seeds, and place strained coulis on 4 serving plates. Place a vol-au-vent shell on each plate. Drain fruit mixture and spoon into shells. Sprinkle with icing sugar and serve at once.

~

1 Cook strawberries with juice of 1 lime and 1/3 of sugar.

2 Squeeze remaining limes into a bowl. Add cut-up fruit and remaining sugar.

3 Strain strawberries through a fine strainer to make a coulis.

4 Divide coulis among 4 plates. Top with vol-au-vent shell filled with fruit.

1 SERVING		
434 CALORIES	71g CARBOHYDRATE	6g PROTEIN
14g FAT	4.1g FIBER	0mg CHOLESTEROL

STRAWBERRIES ROMANOFF

4 SERVINGS

NUTRITION TIP

*Substitute low-fat yogurt
for some or all of the
whipping cream.*

1½ lbs	fresh strawberries	750 g
4 tsp	orange liqueur (optional)	20 mL
2 tbsp	sour cream	30 mL
1¼ cups	whipping cream, whipped	300 mL
2 tbsp	icing sugar	30 mL
	grated zest of 1 orange	

Hull the strawberries and cut them in half,
reserving 4 whole for garnish. Toss cut
strawberries with liqueur and grated
orange zest. Let stand 15 minutes.

In a second bowl, stir together sour cream
and whipped cream. Sprinkle in icing sugar
and stir gently to combine. Set aside.

Place a big spoonful of strawberries in
the bottom of 4 dessert bowls. Crush
remaining berries and stir them into
cream mixture. Spoon mixture over
berries in bowls.

Refrigerate until serving time. Decorate
each with a whole strawberry cut in a
fan shape.

1 SERVING		
340 CALORIES	19g CARBOHYDRATE	3g PROTEIN
28g FAT	4.3g FIBER	99mg CHOLESTEROL

PEACH MELBA

4 SERVINGS

¼ cup	sugar	50 mL
I cup	boiling water	250 mL
I tbsp	cognac	15 mL
8	canned peach halves in light syrup, drained	8
½ cup	frozen unsweetened raspberries, drained	125 mL
2 cups	vanilla ice milk	500 mL
3 tbsp	slivered almonds	45 mL

In a saucepan, dissolve ½ the sugar in boiling water. Add cognac. Place peach halves in liquid and simmer over low heat 3 minutes. Remove from heat and let cool in liquid. Drain peaches.

Purée raspberries in a food processor or blender. Add remaining sugar. Cook raspberry mixture in a saucepan 3 minutes over low heat. Let cool.

Divide ice milk among 4 dessert bowls. Place 2 peach halves in each, and add raspberry sauce. Garnish with almonds.

1 SERVING		
226 CALORIES	38g CARBOHYDRATE	5g PROTEIN
6g FAT	2.8g FIBER	10mg CHOLESTEROL

FRESH STRAWBERRY-STUFFED CRÊPES

4 SERVINGS

COOK'S TIP

These taste best if the crêpes are still slightly warm to contrast with the cool cheese and strawberry mixture.

2	eggs	2
1½ cups	all-purpose flour	375 mL
2 cups	2% milk	500 mL
4 tbsp	sugar	60 mL
2 tbsp	butter or margarine	30 mL
1 cup	low-fat ricotta cheese	250 mL
1 tsp	vanilla extract	5 mL
2 cups	fresh strawberries, hulled and sliced	500 mL
2 tbsp	icing sugar	30 mL

In a bowl, beat eggs until pale and foamy. Beat in flour, milk, and 1 tbsp (15 mL) sugar.

Grease a nonstick skillet and pour in about 3 tbsp (45 mL) batter. Swirl pan to spread batter thinly over surface. Cook until lightly browned on each side. Repeat with remaining batter. Layer cooked crêpes between waxed paper until ready to fill.

Beat together ricotta with remaining sugar and vanilla. Stir in sliced strawberries.

Spread 2 tbsp (30 mL) of this mixture down middle of each crêpe. Roll each crêpe and dust with icing sugar to serve.

1 SERVING		
509 CALORIES	69g CARBOHYDRATE	20g PROTEIN
17g FAT	3.3g FIBER	182mg CHOLESTEROL

SCANDINAVIAN HONEYED FRUIT SOUP

~

4 SERVINGS

I cup	fresh strawberries, quartered	250 mL
I cup	fresh raspberries	250 mL
I cup	fresh pitted cherries, halved	250 mL
2 cups	cranberry juice	500 mL
1/4 cup	liquid honey	50 mL
1/2 tsp	ground cinnamon	2 mL
I tbsp	chopped fresh mint	15 mL
	fresh mint for garnish	

Combine strawberries, raspberries and cherries in a bowl.

In a second bowl, stir together cranberry juice, honey, cinnamon and chopped mint. Pour over fruit and let soak 1 hour in refrigerator.

Serve fruit soup in dessert bowls decorated with mint sprigs, and with a piece of real honeycomb honey, if desired.

~

COOK'S TIP

Fresh berries are extremely delicate, and should be washed only at the very last moment, before preparing them.

1 SERVING		
201 CALORIES	47g CARBOHYDRATE	1g PROTEIN
1g FAT	2.9g FIBER	0mg CHOLESTEROL

STRAWBERRY KIWI SHORTCAKE

6 SERVINGS

½ cup	butter or margarine	125 mL
½ cup	sugar	125 mL
2	eggs, beaten	2
1 cup	all-purpose flour	250 mL
¼ cup	skim milk	50 mL
2 cups	whipped cream	500 mL
	sliced fresh strawberries	
	sliced kiwis	

Preheat oven to 350°F (180°C). Grease 2 round 8 inch (20 cm) cake pans.

In a bowl, beat together butter and sugar until creamy and light. Beat in eggs one by one.

Beat in flour. Texture should be light but stiff. Stir in milk until smooth. Pour mixture into prepared pans. Bake 20 to 25 minutes, until a toothpick inserted in the center of cake comes out clean.

Let cakes cool and unmold. Spread half the whipped cream over one cake. Cover with half the sliced fruit. Repeat layers. Serve at once.

1 Beat together butter and sugar. Beat in eggs one at a time.

2 Stir in flour and milk until smooth. Pour into prepared pans and bake.

3 Spread half of whipped cream over one cake. Cover with half the sliced fruit.

4 Repeat layers.

1 SERVING		
493 CALORIES	43g CARBOHYDRATE	6g PROTEIN
33g FAT	2.7g FIBER	190mg CHOLESTEROL

BLACKBERRY BAVARIAN

6 SERVINGS

COOK'S TIP

Use a clean beater to beat egg whites; the least drop of fat, as contained in whipped cream, will prevent them from beating up stiff.

2 cups	blackberries	500 mL
1/2 cup	apple juice	125 mL
1/3 cup	sugar	75 mL
2	envelopes plain gelatin	2
1 cup	whipping cream	250 mL
2	egg whites, stiffly beaten	2
	fresh fruit for garnish	

Place blackberries with apple juice and sugar in a saucepan. Simmer 5 minutes. Remove from heat and stir in gelatin. Let cool slightly.

Purée mixture in food processor or blender. Refrigerate until purée starts to set.

In a second bowl, beat cream until stiff. Fold in stiffly beaten egg whites and fruit purée. Pour into a lightly oiled mold and refrigerate several hours until set.

Unmold onto a serving dish and decorate with fruit before serving.

1 SERVING		
235 CALORIES	23g CARBOHYDRATE	2g PROTEIN
15g FAT	2.2g FIBER	54mg CHOLESTEROL

FRESH FRUIT PUFFS

6 SERVINGS

14 oz	frozen puff pastry, thawed	400 g
1	egg or egg yolk, beaten	1
6 tbsp	apricot jelly	90 mL
2 tbsp	lemon juice	30 mL
1 1/2 lbs	fresh fruit of your choice	675 g
1/2 cup	plain or flavored yogurt	125 mL
	icing sugar	

Roll out pastry to make a rectangle 8 x 12 inches (20 x 30 cm). Cut into 6 equal rectangles. Place rectangles on a baking sheet and refrigerate 10 minutes.

Preheat oven to 425°F (220°C).

Brush tops of pastry rectangles with beaten egg. Bake 20 minutes, or until tops are golden. Let cool.

Heat apricot jelly in a saucepan with the lemon juice until jelly is melted.

Cut pastry rectangles in half. Brush lower halves with apricot mixture. Arrange fruit on top. Brush fruit with more of apricot mixture and top with yogurt. Replace pastry tops and sprinkle with icing sugar before serving.

~

1 SERVING		
478 CALORIES	55g CARBOHYDRATE	6g PROTEIN
26g FAT	3.0g FIBER	48mg CHOLESTEROL

APPLE FILO ROLLS

4 SERVINGS

COOK'S TIP

Rewrap unused filo at once and refreeze. It will keep several months if wrapped in several layers of freezer wrap.

I cup	skim milk	250 mL
¹/₂ cup	coarsely chopped hazelnuts	125 mL
¹/₄ cup	sugar	50 mL
2 tbsp	cornstarch	30 mL
¹/₂ tsp	almond extract	2 mL
6 tbsp	water	90 mL
3	apples, peeled, cored, coarsely chopped	3
2 tbsp	sugar	30 mL
4 oz	frozen filo pastry, thawed	110 g
	icing sugar	

Preheat oven to 350°F (180°C).

In a saucepan, heat milk, hazelnuts and ¼ cup (50 mL) sugar over medium heat.

Dissolve cornstarch in almond extract and 2 tbsp (30 mL) water. Pour into milk mixture, and stir constantly until mixture thickens. Remove from heat and let cool.

In another saucepan, place apples, remaining sugar and 4 tbsp (60 mL) water. Cook over low heat about 15 minutes to make a thick sauce. Pour into a bowl and let cool.

Stir milk mixture into apple mixture.

Lay out 3 filo sheets on top of each other. Cut into 4 rectangles. Divide apple mixture among rectangles. Roll up filo pastry firmly. Place seam side down on a baking pan.

Bake 10 minutes, or until golden brown. Sprinkle with icing sugar. Serve hot or cold.

	1 SERVING	
343 CALORIES	55g CARBOHYDRATE	6g PROTEIN
11g FAT	3.1g FIBER	1mg CHOLESTEROL

SPICED FIGS IN CHAMPAGNE

4 SERVINGS

1/4 cup	sugar	50 mL
2 tbsp	corn syrup	30 mL
1/2 tsp	ground cinnamon	2 mL
1/4 tsp	ground cloves	1 mL
1/4 tsp	ground cardamom	1 mL
2 tbsp	15% cream	30 mL
8	fresh figs, sliced in wedges	8
1/4 cup	champagne or sparkling white wine	50 mL
	vanilla ice milk or ice cream	

In a saucepan, combine sugar, corn syrup and spices. Cook over medium heat until syrup begins to turn golden.

Stir in cream and add fig slices. Cook over low heat 3 to 4 minutes in the syrup to caramelize. Stir in champagne.

Remove from heat at once and serve with ice milk.

~

COOK'S TIP

Figs are delicate fruit and do not need to be peeled before eating. A ripe fig should yield slightly when pressed.

	1 SERVING	
199 CALORIES	38g CARBOHYDRATE	1g PROTEIN
1g FAT	3.2g FIBER	4mg CHOLESTEROL

TREASURE-STUFFED CRÊPE PURSES

4 SERVINGS

CRÊPE BATTER

1/2 cup	all-purpose flour	125 mL
3	eggs	2
1/3 cup	skim milk	75 mL
1	pinch salt	1
1 tsp	sugar	5 mL
1 tsp	vanilla extract	5 mL
1 tbsp	vegetable oil	15 mL

FRUIT FILLING

4	canned peach halves, drained and sliced	4
1/4 cup	toasted slivered almonds	50 mL
1/2 cup	cream-style cottage cheese	125 mL
1/2 tsp	ground cinnamon	2 mL
3 tbsp	liquid honey	45 mL
4	long strips of orange zest, blanched in boiling water until pliable	4
	plain yogurt	
	thinned blackberry jam	

Preheat oven to 350°F (180°C).

To make crêpes: beat together all batter ingredients in a large bowl. Let stand 20 minutes.

Ladle ¼ of batter into a heated, oiled nonstick pan, swirling pan to spread batter thinly. Cook over medium heat until golden on both sides. Set crêpes aside.

In a bowl, stir together sliced peaches, almonds, cottage cheese, cinnamon and honey. Divide mixture among crêpes. Tie crêpes closed with orange zest strips.

Place crêpes on a baking sheet and cook 5 to 8 minutes, until hot through. Serve hot crêpe packages on yogurt, garnished with thinned jam, if desired.

1 Prepare crêpe batter and let stand 20 minutes before cooking. Prepare 4 crêpes.

2 Stir together sliced peaches, almonds, cottage cheese, cinnamon and honey.

3 Divide mixture among crêpes. Fold up edges to make purses.

4 Tie closed with blanched orange peel. Cook in oven until heated through.

1 SERVING		
305 CALORIES	35g CARBOHYDRATE	12g PROTEIN
13g FAT	1.8g FIBER	210mg CHOLESTEROL

FRESH FRUIT WITH
WHITE CHOCOLATE DIP

4 SERVINGS

COOK'S TIP

*For an interesting
presentation, serve
white chocolate mixture
in hollowed-out
orange halves.*

4 oz	white chocolate	110 g
¹/₄ cup	whipping cream	50 mL
1 tbsp	liquid honey	15 mL
¹/₄ cup	ground hazelnuts	50 mL
2	egg whites	2
1	pinch salt	1
	assortment of fresh fruit, prepared for dipping	

Place white chocolate in the top of a
double boiler over hot water at medium
heat. Add cream and honey. Stir constantly
until chocolate is melted. Stir in hazelnuts
and let cool.

In a bowl, beat egg whites together
with salt until stiff peaks form. Stir
¼ of egg white mixture gently into
melted chocolate mixture.

Using a rubber spatula, fold remaining egg
white very gently into chocolate mixture
until no streaks of white are visible. Pour
mixture into dessert bowls or ramekins
and refrigerate at least 3 hours.

At serving time, surround each bowl
with freshly prepared fruit.

~

1 SERVING		
287 CALORIES	24g CARBOHYDRATE	5g PROTEIN
19g FAT	1.7g FIBER	16mg CHOLESTEROL

PEARS POACHED IN RED WINE

4 SERVINGS

4	firm ripe pears	4
1/2 cup	water	125 mL
1 cup	red wine (preferably Burgundy)	250 mL
1/3 cup	sugar	75 mL
1	cinnamon stick	1
1/2 tsp	crushed coriander seeds	5 mL
5	chopped almonds	5
	juice of 2 lemons	

Peel pears and cut out cores (using an apple corer if available) leaving stems in place. Dip cut surfaces in the lemon juice to prevent browning. Set aside.

Heat all remaining ingredients including remaining lemon juice in a saucepan. Place pears in this syrup. Bring to a boil, reduce heat and let simmer about 30 minutes, turning pears from time to time so that they take on color evenly.

Remove saucepan from heat and let pears cool in liquid. Refrigerate pears in the liquid overnight.

When ready to serve, strain the syrup and pour it onto plates. Slice the pears and arrange in a fan shape on top of syrup, garnished with a sprig of fresh mint, if desired.

1 SERVING		
185 CALORIES	43g CARBOHYDRATE	1g PROTEIN
1g FAT	5.2g FIBER	0mg CHOLESTEROL

WATERMELON GRANITA WITH LAVENDER

4 SERVINGS

COOK'S TIP

Flower extracts such as lavender water and rose water are available in specialty stores. They are highly concentrated, so only a few drops are needed to liven up a fruit salad.

5 cups	chopped watermelon flesh, seeded	1.25 liters
3 tbsp	fresh lemon juice	45 mL
2 tbsp	lavender water	30 mL
1 cup	icing sugar	250 mL
	fresh lavender flowers for garnish	

Place all ingredients except flower garnish in food processor. Process until puréed and smooth.

Pour mixture into a shallow metal dish and place in freezer at least 2 hours.

Break up the granita with a fork, then return to freezer for at least 1 hour. When ready to serve, break up ice crystals again with a fork.

Serve in small dessert cups garnished with lavender flowers or other edible flowers, or with fresh mint leaves.

1 SERVING		
189 CALORIES	44g CARBOHYDRATE	1g PROTEIN
1g FAT	0.9g FIBER	0mg CHOLESTEROL

CHOCOLATE FONDUE

4 SERVINGS

8 oz	semi-sweet chocolate, chopped	225 g
I cup	2% milk, heated	250 mL
I	banana, peeled and sliced	I
4	kiwis, peeled and sliced	4
2	pears, sliced	2
I	carambola, sliced	I
2	peaches, sliced	2
2	red apples, sliced	2
I cup	strawberries, hulled	250 mL
2	plums, sliced	2

Melt the chocolate with the milk in the top of a double boiler over simmering water. Stir well and pour into a fondue dish.

Serve with prepared fruit for dipping.

~

COOK'S TIP

This is an ideal opportunity to try some of the more exotic fruits now available, such as carambola, sometimes called starfruit, or Japanese pear. If you are unfamiliar with exotic fruit, ask the produce manager to help you identify those that are ripe.

1 SERVING		
570 CALORIES	95g CARBOHYDRATE	7g PROTEIN
18g FAT	12.0g FIBER	5 mg CHOLESTEROL

DELIGHTFUL DESSERTS

377

DESSERT PIZZA

4 TO 6 SERVINGS

¹/₂ cup	light cream cheese	125 mL
1 cup	cream-style cottage cheese	250 mL
1	plain pizza shell, baked	1
1 cup	strawberries, cut in half	250 mL
¹/₂ cup	blueberries	125 mL
¹/₂	cantaloupe, peeled and sliced	¹/₂
1	peach, sliced	1
1	apple, sliced	1
2	plums, sliced	2
2	oranges, peel, pith and membranes removed	2
¹/₂ cup	apple jelly, melted	125 mL
	fresh mint sprigs for garnish	

Combine cream cheese and cottage cheese in food processor or blender until smooth. Spread mixture over pizza shell.

Garnish top of pizza with fruit, using the larger pieces on the bottom. Pour or brush melted apple jelly evenly over top. The jelly will stop the fruit from browning and keep it looking fresh. Even so, do not leave this creation sitting too long before serving.

~

1 SERVING

| 367 CALORIES | 63g CARBOHYDRATE | 13g PROTEIN |
| 7g FAT | 4.9g FIBER | 17mg CHOLESTEROL |

INDEX

〜